# THE MILITARY IN GREEK POLITICS

THANOS VEREMIS

# The Military in Greek Politics

*From Independence to Democracy*

Montréal/New York/London

Black Rose Books No. AA255
Hardcover ISBN: 1-55164-104-6 (bound)
Paperback ISBN: 1-55164-105-4 (pbk.)
Library of Congress Catalog Card Number:

**Canadian Cataloguing in Publication Data**

Veremes, Thanos
The military in Greek politics : from independence to democracy

Includes bibliographical references and index.
ISBN 1-55164-105-4 (bound) -
ISBN 1-55164-104-6 (pbk.)

1. Greece—Politics and government—1821-
2. Greece—Armed Forces—Political activity. 3. Greece—History—182
4. Civil-military relations—Greece—History. I. Title..

DF902.V48 1997          949.507          C97-900702-X

Cover Design by Gyde Shepherd

**BLACK ROSE BOOKS**

| C.P. 1258 | 250 Sonwil Drive | 99 Wallis Road |
| Succ. Place du Parc | Buffalo, New York | London, E9 5LN |
| Montréal,Québec | 14225 USA | England |
| H2W 2R3 Canada | | |

To order books in North America: (phone) 1-800-565-9523  (fax) 1-800-221-9985
In Europe: (phone) 081-986-4854  (fax) 081-533-5821

Our Web Site address: http://www.web.net/blackrosebooks

A publication of the Institute of Policy Alternatives of Montréal (IPAM)
Printed in Canada

# CONTENTS

# PREFACE AND ACKNOWLEDGEMENTS

The military regime that took power on 21 April 1967 in Greece was the initial stimulus to my interest in civil/military relations. In the course of my research I discovered that the phenomenon of armed interventions in politics is in fact a latecomer in modern Greek history. Military coups acquired a disquieting frequency after the end of the irredentist wars (between 1912 and 1922) and coincided with the waning of parliamentarism elsewhere in Europe. Civilian supremacy was never really challenged, however, and *coups* that aspired to a lasting political impact merely sought to replace one civilian order with another, rather than permanently hand over the government to the army. In this sense interventions before 1967 were essentially restricted to a moderator pattern. Even the Metaxas dictatorship of 1936-41, which enjoyed the approval of a compliant army, was blessed by the King and run by civilians. The same regime, with its emphasis on nationalism and anti-communism, its concern for re-education, social discipline and a synthesis of ancient and Christian values, and its distaste for parliamentary and democratic procedures, also anticipated themes which were to be appropriated after 1967 by the Colonels, many of whom entered the Military Academy when General Metaxas was already firmly established in power.

Various factors prompted the military intervention in 1967: the conflict between the throne and the Prime Minister; the fear of liberalising measures to be initiated by the Centre Union party which would destroy the institutional framework of right-wing dominance within the state; and finally the professional grievances of the officers involved, accompanied by the usual rationalisations of an internal Communist threat and claims that the *coup* had secured the approval of Washington. However, in a country of old parliamentary institutions and entrenched civilian authority, the military felt the need to legitimise their intervention either by gradually handing over power to civilians or through a transformation that would make them acceptable political figures.

The subject of this book was suggested many years ago by Dr John Campbell of St Antony's College, Oxford, and I hope that some of the qualities of his thoughtful and succinct supervision passed on to this work. Professor P.J. Vatikiotis of the School of Oriental and African Studies in the University of London – an expert in, among other things, military interventions in the Arab world – was always a willing and stimulating conversationalist suggesting the most imaginative approaches. Professor John Koliopoulos of Thessaloniki University provided the encouragement given by true friendship. His *Brigands with a Cause* has been a constant source of inspiration for me.

The late Virginia Alexandrou Zanna became my mentor concerning the society of interwar personalities, both surviving and deceased. Thanks to her, several archives and private papers were revealed to me and our long discussions reconstructed an entire era of political and military turmoil.

The late Evgenia Hatzidaki, as curator of the historical archive of the Benaki Museum, alerted me to the Plastiras Papers donated by Fotini Tasiou. Yannis Mazarakis-Ainian, the energetic director of the Historical and Ethnological Museum, was always willing to help beyond the call of duty. My thanks also go to the Gennadios library, the National Archives and the Greek Literary and Historical Archive (ELIA).

Nicos Mouzelis, Charles Moskos, Paschalis Kitromilides, Nicos Alivizatos, Stephanos Papageorgiou, Nicos Economou and—last but not least—Youla Goulimi have at different times discussed parts of this book with me and offered valuable suggestions. I owe much to Anna Soulantika who cheerfully typed the whole work without flinching at my handwriting.

Finally, I am grateful for the fellowship offered by the Hellenic Foundation of London and the hospitality of St Antony's College, where most of the research was completed.

*Athens*                                                    THANOS VEREMIS
*Winter 1996*

# OUTLINE CHRONOLOGY OF GREEK
# HISTORY SINCE INDEPENDENCE

1821    The Greek War of Independence against Ottoman rule breaks out. Patriarch Grigorios V hanged by the Ottomans.

1822    The first constitution of independent Greece drafted.

1827    The joint Ottoman-Egyptian fleet at Navarino Bay destroyed by the combined fleets of Britain, France and Russia.

1828    Count Ioannis Kapodistrias arrives in Greece as its first President.

1830    France, Great Britain and Russia recognise the independence of Greece under the London Protocol of 3 February 1830.

1831    Kapodistrias assassinated by members of a powerful clan of Mani in the Peloponnese.

1833    Prince Otto (Wittelsbach) of Bavaria arrives in Greece as its first King. The Church of the Greek state declared 'autocephalous' (independent from the administrative but not doctrinal authority of the patriarchate in Constantinople).

1843    Troops of the Athens garrison and a popular demonstration in front of the royal palace force Otto to grant a constitution.

1844    The new constitution defines the regime as a 'constitutional monarchy'.

1854    The occupation and blockade of Piraeus by French and British troops imposes neutrality on Greece during the Crimean war.

1862    King Otto forced to abdicate after an uprising against his rule in Nafplion and Athens.

1863    Prince George (Glücksburg) of Denmark becomes 'King of the Hellenes'.

1864        The Ionian islands incorporated in the Greek state. The new constitution defines the Greek regime as a 'crowned democracy'.

1866-9      An uprising in Crete against Ottoman rule fails to liberate the island.

1871        The government of Alexandros Koumoundouros grants legal title-deeds to peasant squatters.

1875        King George accepts the principle that the leader of a party enjoying the support of the majority in parliament should be given the mandate to form a government.

1881        The province of Thessaly and the region of Arta incorporated into the Greek state.

1883-93     The heyday of the two-party system during which Harilaos Tricoupis and Theodoros Diliyannis alternate in power. Tricoupis puts reforms into effect.

1895        Tricoupis defeated in elections, and dies the following year.

1896        A further Cretan rebellion against Ottoman rule leads to Greece's involvement in the issue of Cretan liberation.

1897        Greek forces defeated within three weeks by the Ottoman army in the Thessaly campaign.

1898        Prince George (second son of King George) appointed governor of Crete after the granting of autonomy to the island.

1903        A 'Macedonian Committee' founded by Greek officers to counter Bulgarian claims in Macedonia.

1909        A display of force by the 'Military League' in Athens in August obliges the government to draft reforms in parliament. The Cretan politician Eleftherios Venizelos appointed by the officers of the 'League' as their political adviser.

1910        Eleftherios Venizelos wins an overwhelming popular mandate in general elections and launches his reforms.

1912        The Liberal party created by Venizelos wins by a landslide in the elections. Greece and its allies defeat the Ottoman empire in the First Balkan war.

1913        The Second Balkan war fought between former allies – Bulgaria against Greece and Serbia. Bulgaria defeated. King George assassinated in Thessaloniki. The Treaty of London (30 May) and the Peace of Bucharest (10 August) grant Greece significant territorial gains (Crete, Macedonia, Ioannina and islands in the Aegean).

1915    Venizelos and King Constantine clash over Greek foreign policy during the First World War. Venizelos proposes a Greek alliance with the Triple Entente, while the King prefers neutrality. Venizelos is twice forced to resign.

1916    Greece partitioned between north and south with the 'Revolutionary Government' under Venizelos, General Danglis and Admiral Koundouriotes in Thessaloniki and the official government in Athens appointed by the King.

1917    Constantine forced to abdicate. His second son Alexander becomes King and Venizelos re-establishes his government in Athens.

1918    Ten Greek divisions fight on the Macedonian front in the autumn campaign, breaking the back of German and Bulgarian defences.

1919    Greece takes its place among the victors of the First World War and expands its national territory at the Versailles Peace Conference.

1920    According to the Treaty of Sèvres (10 August), Greece acquires western and eastern Thrace and the rest of the Aegean islands, and is given a mandate to administer the larger Smyrna area pending a plebiscite about its future.

1920    King Alexander dies after a bite by a pet monkey, Venizelos is defeated in the ensuing elections, the royalists return to power and restore Constantine to the throne.

1922    Greek forces defeated in Asia Minor and the ethnic Greek population flees to Greece. Constantine abdicates in favour of his eldest son George and leaves the country.

1923    The Treaty of Lausanne draws the boundaries between Greece and Turkey and imposes an extensive exchange of populations. Close to 1.5 million destitute refugees arrive in a country of barely 5 million inhabitants.

1924    Greece becomes a republic following a referendum.

1924-6  Military coups follow one another during a period of military interventions in politics.

1926-8  An all-party government takes office.

1928-32 Venizelos' final four-year term in office.

1933    Tsaldaris, leader of the Populist (pro-royalist) party, wins the elections and Liberals fear the monarchy might be restored.

1935    An anti-royalist pre-emptive coup fails and speeds up the process of King George's restoration.

1936          A series of leading Greek politicians—Venizelos, Tsaldaris, Kondylis and Papanastasiou—die in quick succession. On 4 August, the King endorses a violation of the constitution enabling the caretaker Prime Minister Ioannis Metaxas to assume dictatorial powers.

1940          Greece resists Italian Fascist attack from Albania and wins the first Allied victories of the war.

1941          German armoured divisions overpower the Greek armed forces and occupy the country. British forces evacuate mainland Greece and Crete following a German airborne onslaught on the island. A Greek government-in-exile is established in London and Cairo while Greek armed forces regroup in Egypt.

1941-4        Greece occupied by German, Italian and Bulgarian forces. Thrace and eastern Macedonia are annexed by Bulgaria. Greek resistance obliges Germans to keep large forces in Greece and disrupts transports to the Middle East. Internal strife between left- and right-wing resistance groups called the 'first round' of the Civil War reduces their effectiveness.

1944          Athens liberated. The 'December events' mark the 'second round' of the Civil War.

1946-9        A fully fledged Civil War ('the third round') fought between the Communist-controlled 'Democratic Army' in northern Greece and the national army under a coalition government of Liberals and royalists.

1947          In accordance with the Treaty of Paris (10 February 1947), Greece acquires the Dodecanese islands. The Truman Doctrine leads to massive aid being granted to Greece.

1952          Greece becomes a member of NATO. Elections are won by the 'Greek Rally', a newly-created party led by the commander of the government forces in the Civil War, Marshal Alexandros Papagos. A reconstruction programme for war-ravaged Greece is launched with American aid.

1955          In September a mob in Istanbul demanding the annexation of Cyprus by Turkey wreaks havoc in the areas of the city inhabited by Greeks.

1956          Elections won by the newly-formed 'National Radical Union' (ERE) under Constantine Karamanlis, Minister of Public Works in the Papagos government. Archbishop Makarios of Cyprus deported to the Seychelles by the British. The Cypriots' struggle for union with Greece (*Enosis*) reaches a climax.

1958     In May elections, the ERE party under Karamanlis maintains its majority with 40 per cent of the popular vote.

1959     Greece applies to the EEC for associate membership. Greek and Turkish Cypriot leaders sign the London agreement on the independence of Cyprus.

1960     Cyprus becomes an independent republic with Archbishop Makarios as President and Dr Fazil Kütchük as Vice-President.

1961     ERE wins 51 per cent of the popular vote amid accusations of electoral fraud.

1963     Karamanlis loses the elections to George Papandreou, leader of the Centre Union, a party formed by the coalition of all the centre factions in Greek politics. Violence breaks out in Cyprus between Greek and Turkish Cypriot communities.

1964     In new elections the Centre Union turns its relative majority, achieved in the February elections, into an absolute one, winning 52.7 per cent of the vote.

1965     King Constantine II clashes with Prime Minister George Papandreou over the appointment of the Defence Minister. Papandreou resigns.

1966     The major parties agree in December to desist from attacks on the monarchy.

1967     A junta of colonels launch a *coup d'état* in April and establish a military dictatorship. The King flees the country after an abortive effort in December to oust the military regime.

1968     Close to 1,000 civil servants are dismissed by the junta.

1973     An abortive *coup* takes place in the navy against the regime. An attempt is made against Makarios's life by junta officers in Cyprus.

1974     The Turks invade Cyprus after a *coup* instigated by the junta in Athens ousts President Makarios and replaces him with a nationalist stooge. The junta collapses in July, democracy is restored in Greece, Karamanlis returns as Prime Minister from his Paris exile and wins the November elections by a landslide. Greece becomes a republic after the December referendum.

1975     A new constitution replaces that of 1952, briefly restored after the abrogation of the junta's 1973 constitution. A Turkish Federated State of Cyprus is proclaimed and recognised only by Turkey. There follows an influx of immigrants from mainland Turkey to northern Cyprus.

1976    Greek-Turkish relations go through a new crisis when a Turkish survey ship begins to carry out oil explorations in waters between the islands of Mytilini and Lemnos, claimed by Greece as part of its continental shelf.

1977    Karamanlis' New Democracy wins a comfortable majority in the November elections.
Law 660 of August 1977, reshaping the command structure of the armed forces, abolishes the junta law.

1979    Karamanlis signs a treaty of accession to the European Community with the nine EC members (28 May).

1980    Karamanlis becomes President of the Republic and George Rallis Prime Minister. Karamanlis visits Moscow.

1981    Greece joins the EC. The Panhellenic Socialist Movement (PASOK) under Andreas Papandreou wins the October elections.

1982    Papandreou visits Cyprus – the first such visit of a Greek Prime Minister.

1983    The Turkish Cypriot Assembly unilaterally declares an independent Turkish Republic of Northern Cyprus, which is recognised only by Turkey. A Defence and Economic Cooperation Agreement (DECA) is signed between US and Greece, replacing the 1953 one, together with other bilateral security arrangements.

1984    Constantinos Mitsotakis becomes leader of the New Democracy party.

1985    Karamanlis resigns and Christos Sartzetakis is elected President of the Republic. PASOK wins 45.82 per cent of the popular vote in the June elections.

1987    A new crisis breaks out in the relations between Greece and Turkey because of the Turkish intention to explore once again for oil in disputed Aegean waters. Greece and Albania formally put an end to the state of war which had technically existed between the two countries since 1940.

1988    Prime Ministers Papandreou and Turgut Özal meet in Davos, Switzerland, to the defuse problems between their two countries.

1989    A deadlocked June election leads to the formation of a government of 'limited duration' under the New Democracy deputy Tzannis Tzannetakis with the support of the Communist party. New elections in November 1989 also prove inconclusive. An all-party government is formed under Xenophon Zolotas, a non-party banker and economist.

1990    New Democracy under Mitsotakis wins the elections and Karamanlis once more becomes President of the Republic.

1992    The government imposes an austerity programme. The Balkan imbroglio with the FYROM issue dominates Greek foreign policy. There is an influx of refugees for economic reasons from the former Soviet Union, Albania and Bulgaria.

1993    Former Foreign Minister Andonis Samaras leaves New Democracy and in September instigates the defection of two deputies, causing the government to fall. PASOK is voted back into power at the elections of October.

1995    End of Karamanlis' last presidential term. Constantine Stephanopoulos elected President by Parliament.
        Law determining the sharing of responsibilities between civil and military authorities is passed by a vote in Parliament. The law favours centralisation of authority and enhances the government's control over the military.

1996    After a long illness Papandreou is replaced as Prime Minister by Constantine Simitis, and dies in June.

# INTRODUCTION

The most revolutionary outcome of the 'Greek Revolution' (1821-8) was the new state itself and its Western institutions. After nearly 400 years of foreign domination, the Greeks secured not only their own governance but governance fashioned after a model that rejected the decentralised oriental despotism of Ottoman rule.

Despite the vast devastation generated by the struggle for independence, the lifestyle of the average peasant did not change significantly. After independence, the farmers who had not fled their homes were still sharecropper tenants aspiring to an autarkic existence. However, independence altered the structure of land ownership and consequently the nature of production. Whereas in the pre-revolutionary period large Ottoman estates produced wheat and cereals, ownership of the land by the Greek state[1] and the cultivation of small plots by sharecropper families eventually made currants the chief export item. Estates in the plains were more productive than the smallholdings in the rugged highlands, but most of the countryside had been abandoned to grazing.

The elusive promise of land distribution, and eventual formation of small landholdings through squatting and usurpation of public property, attracted the mountain populations to the plain. This trend was encouraged by the state as bringing its least accessible subjects within reach of the law. Mountain villages served as the sanctuary of brigands, for whom dislocation destroyed a natural habitat. A casualty of the depopulation of the mountains was the once flourishing activity of animal husbandry.[2]

---

[1] Most of the Ottoman-held lands were either expropriated or bought by the Greek state so that by 1833, 70 per cent of all arable land was state-owned. Chrysos Evelpides, *Economiki istoria tis Ellados*, Athens: 1939, pp. 56-72.

[2] The most comprehensive work on land tenure is by William W. McGrew, *Land and Revolution in Modern Greece 1850-1881*, Kent, OH: Kent State University Press, 1986.

1

In the traditional communities that inhabited a land fragmented by geography and Ottoman administration, patriotism, as Campbell puts it, 'was an organic growth, both emotional and pragmatic, a relationship with a place which supported life and with which the life of the family was intimately connected'.[3] Since the family unit was the object of primary obligations and a seedbed of all values, an armed band, the threatened community and even the nation in arms were 'in some sense an enlargement of the family or a projection of its values'.[4]

Ideas about nationality were not the product of peasant society. The Greek merchants of the diaspora in the Habsburg, Ottoman and Russian empires and their offspring who managed family interests in Amsterdam or studied in Paris and Padua were the middlemen through whom Western enlightenment and revolutionary ideas trickled into the Greek mainland. There was also the Greek language, established by the Great Church and its institutions of learning as a medium of communication among the educated Orthodox people. This Balkan *lingua franca* facilitated the circulation of Western radicalism before it was made redundant in the non-Greek states, by budding nationalisms and their linguistic particularism. Nationalism was therefore an imported product which, along with other Western institutions, was adopted and systematically disseminated by the Greek nation state.

The formation of a Greek regular army with a professional officer corps was associated with the attempt of the newly established kingdom to emulate its Western prototypes and acquire modern institutions. This attempt of course was impeded by traditional practices and values which prevented modernisation from taking firm root in Greek reality. The hybrid that emerged from the forced marriage of Western institutions and indigenous mores resembled its local mother more than its foreign father. Heroic principles of courage and manliness among the military took precedence over discipline and respect for hierarchy.

When King Otto's regents imposed their military reforms in 1833, there were 5,000 irregulars and about 700 Greek regulars living off the land. The 5,000 Bavarian troops that replaced the demobilised irregulars managed, though not without opposition,

---

[3] John Campbell and Philip Sherrard, *Modern Greece*, London: Ernest Benn, 1968, p. 47.
[4] *Ibid.*

to consolidate the central authority of the Ottonian state. As J.A. Petropulos put it, 'Bavarians and disbanded regulars ... and Anatolian heterochthonous Greeks with absolutely no influence, were more dependable than irregulars, precisely because they owed everything to the Crown and nothing to the local patron. It is no exaggeration to say that, in dissolving the irregulars, the regency was attempting to deprive the parties of their military strength'.[5] Thus, the centralising process begun by Ioannis Kapodistrias, the first President of Greece, was completed by Otto – at the price of condemning a warrior class to a state of deprivation or a life outside the law.[6]

Although the German mercenaries left Greece in 1837, and the army was thereafter based on conscription, it did not become a credible force till the last quarter of the century. Thus the regular army was created in a vacuum. It possessed no aristocratic tradition and was cut off from the heroic exploits of the War for Independence. The officer corps did include elements of those families that had launched the revolution of 1821, but the vast majority were products of the anonymous peasant strata. Between 1844 and 1870 the regular army, on average barely 10,000 strong, maintained internal order and suppressed local uprisings, but was in no position to support the irredentist dreams of the state.

In its democratic constitution of 1864 that secured universal male suffrage, and its legal, administrative and political institutions, nineteenth-century Greece could be compared to the more developed states of Western Europe. It possessed a parliamentary system that functioned without interruption from 1844 to the First World War, but the social and economic condition of the country was not up to the standards of its institutions. The centre-periphery conflict was a clash between the old world of semi-autonomous communities and the new world of administrative centralism. This war between local notables and warlords on one side and the state on the other was resolved by mid-century. The central state emerged triumphant and the periphery settled

---

[5] John A. Petropulos, *Politics and Statecraft in the Kingdom of Greece, 1833-43*, Princeton University Press, 1968, p. 172. The work of Stephanos Papageorgiou, *I Stratiotiki Politiki tou Kapodistria*, Athens: Kollaros, 1984, is definitive on the Kapodistrian military reforms.

[6] John Koliopoulos, *Brigands with a Cause*, Oxford: Clarendon Press, 1987, pp. 76-84. On the Ottonian military reforms see unpublished dissertation of Dimitris A. Malessis, 'O ellinikos stratos stin proti othoniki dekaetia (1833-43)', Pantion University, Athens, 1992.

into permanent decline. The countryside, in spite of improving its output after two decades of inertia, was still in a state of underdevelopment that encouraged extreme familial and kinship loyalties and patron-client relationships. By 1871 what public land had not been already taken over by squatters was parcelled out to landless cultivators.[7] In a country of small landowners, as Legg points out, 'the independence of the peasantry minimised and discouraged collective activity outside the family'.[8] Individual clientelist arrangements with the socially and politically influential were therefore not replaced by collective action. Patronage continued to reign supreme as the most effective way to placate and indeed befriend the powerful. At the same time, patronage opposed change and was therefore a formidable obstacle to modernisation.

The only credible challenge to patronage did not come from Harilaos Tricoupis, the most important Greek politician of the nineteenth century, an exponent of development and growth who increased Greek's dependence on its foreign creditors, but from the populist traditionalist Theodoros Diliyannis. This formidable political opponent of Tricoupis believed that Greece could escape foreign dependence by concentrating on agricultural development that would make it self-sufficient in foodstuffs. Through his populism he recruited mass support and undermined one-to-one clientelistic relationships. This isolationism, however, was contradicted by his irredentism which required foreign help and ultimately led Greece to the disastrous campaign of 1897 against the Ottoman forces. Defeat brought the country's economy firmly under the control of the International Financial Commission which prevented, among other expenditures, any new procurement of armaments. However, despite public mismanagement the state never ceased to be the dominant power in Greek society and the large government sector in the economy made public employment the quickest route out of social misery.

By the end of the 1860s, internal unrest had been suppressed throughout Europe and national armies were once more free to engage in European conflicts. The Franco-Prussian war of 1870

---

[7] According to the distribution laws of 1871, the government recognised squatting and granted legal titles to nearly 50,000 peasant families.

[8] Keith R. Legg, 'The Nature of the Modern Greek State' in John Koumoulides (ed.), *Greece in Transition. Essays in the History of Modern Greece, 1821-1974*, London: Zeno, 1977, p. 289.

heralded an era of wide conscription and large standing forces. The Greek army began to change significantly after the Bulgarian schism of 1870. The creation of a Bulgarian national church deprived the Patriarchate of Constantinople of yet another Orthodox flock, but Bulgarian proselytism among the parishes of Ottoman Macedonia was directly antagonistic to Greek irredentism. Greece was thus confronted with Balkan competition over the much coveted territorial legacy of the Turks. It thus became clear that even if the great powers were prepared to put pressure on the Ottomans for territorial concessions, the Balkan seekers after such a prize would ultimately confront each other.

The view that the unification of Hellenism ought to be delegated to local uprisings and irregular troops with no official involvement of the Greek state was challenged by Miltiades Seizanis in 1878, who criticised the condition of the military as follows: 'In the Greek army one finds only individuals of mediocre intelligence ... with the exception of a very small number of noble young men from old military families or volunteers from abroad, who however lack the military education that befits the high ranks they are destined to occupy.'[9] While Seizanis spoke of the 'new struggle against the Turks',[10] the Greek forces were merely 25,028 strong[11] compared to the 700,000 that the Ottomans put in the field during the 1877 Russo-Turkish war.[12]

The military reforms of the Koumoundouros and Deliyiorgis governments gained momentum during the Tricoupis administration. Between 1882 and 1886 the Military Academy was reformed, the Naval Academy and the School for Non-Commissioned Officers were founded, officers were sent abroad (mainly to France) for training, and there were large purchases of military equipment.[13] These investments yielded results in the long run – the Venizelos period of 1910-20. In the mean time the poor state of public finances caused the military budget to be reduced from 58,800,000 drachmas in 1885 to 19,700,000 in 1893.[14]

---

[9] Miltiades Seizanis, *I politiki tis Ellados kai i epanastasis tou 1878 en Macedonia, Epiro kai Thessalia*, Athens: 1879, p. 28.

[10] *Ibid.*, p. 27.

[11] *Ibid.*, p. 29.

[12] K. Kallaris, *Genike tines pliroforie peri tou tourkikou stratou*, Corfu: 1886, p. 10.

[13] E. Stasinopoulos, *O stratos tis protis Ekatontaetias*, Athens 1935, pp. 113-16.

[14] Yannis Pikros, 'Pros ton Polemo tou 1897', *Istoria tou ellinikou ethnous*, vol. 14, Athens:

The war of 1897 and the unrest it generated in the officer corps, the secret war of terrorism, armed bands and sabotage in Macedonia, and the impotence of politicians to rise to the Balkan challenge caused the first autonomous Greek military intervention in politics in 1909. The subsequent advent of Eleftherios Venizelos to power owed much to the officers of 1909 who called on him as their political mentor and introduced him to the Greek political scene.

The officer corps began to deviate from its role as the servant of the state only after the occurrence of certain social and political changes in Greece. The 'subjective'[15] control of civilians over the military speeded up the politicisation of the latter – a phenomenon greatly enhanced by the crisis between crown and parliament in 1915-17. Officers were unprecedentedly susceptible to political enticement because the social structure of the corps was altered by changes between 1912 and 1923. An increase of the numbers admitted to the Military Academy and the introduction of free tuition in 1917 opened the military career to the less well-to-do. However, while the officer corps had been enlarged to meet war needs, it contracted in peacetime, threatening the professionally insecure with early retirement.

At the same time the social transformation caused by the enlargement of Greece, the inflow of diaspora Greeks and capital, and the arrival of 1,300,000 refugees in 1922-3 broadened and pluralised politics. The massive entry of new participants in the political game posed a new challenge to parliamentary institutions. The process of incorporating the newcomers into what had been a fairly homogeneous system affected the military.

Mouzelis characterises the first era of Greek parliamentary democracy – up to the second decade of the twentienth century – as 'oligarchic rule in the parliamentary semi-periphery'.[16] He observes:

> One of the results of the army's modernization in the parliamentary semi-periphery, combined as it was with quantitative growth and the officers being recruited from nonoligarchic strata, was that it weakened the nineteenth century fusion of

---

Ekdotiki Athinon, 1977, p. 95.

[15] Samuel Huntington, *The Soldiers and the State*, Cambridge MA: Harvard University Press, 1957, pp. 80-4.

[16] Nicos Mouzelis, *Politics in the Semi-Periphery*, London: Macmillan, 1986, p. 98.

civilian and military elites that had been based on a shared aristocratic background and orientation. This in turn meant that officers in the nineteenth century had tended to intervene in politics as individuals (that is, without strong feelings of corporate identity); during the first few decades of the twentieth century they did so as a relatively cohesive interest group with specific professional demands and with a predominantly middle-class anti-oligarchic outlook.[17]

The scope of most interwar *coups* was limited to redressing personal grievances, promoting professional interests or replacing one civilian government with another. Officers became arbiters in the struggle between the Liberal and Conservative (Populist) parties although they were ultimately controlled by them. Patronage networks were dominated by politicians, and with the exception of the 1935 *coup* all other military interventions conformed to the pattern set by patron-client relationships.

The 1935 *coup* was the watershed of an era in military politics. It was the first and last interwar *coup* to defy political networks, and its dismal failure proved that the odds against military corporatism were overwhelming. The strange assortment of the 1935 conspirators ultimately neutralised their own operation and turned an attempt against a moderate conservative government into the abject defeat of liberal republicanism in the armed forces.[18] After the wholesale purge of republican elements in the officer corps, the military once more became a homogeneous ideological body serving King and country. With the exception of the wartime upheavals in the Middle East forces of the Greek government in exile (1943-4), the officers of the Greek regular army remained till 1967 dedicated to conservative values, to anti-Communism and to the political authorities.

To understand the twist and turns of military behaviour during that last half-century, it is necessary to review the dramatic economic and social transformation at that time. The multitude of refugees that flocked into urban centres or were established in small plots in northern Greece caused severe political and social dislocation.

---

[17] *Ibid.* The term 'aristocratic' is somewhat exaggerated. 'Upper-middle-class' is probably more appropriate in a country with a commercial rather than an aristocratic upper class.

[18] T. Veremis, *I epemvasis tou stratou stin elliniki politiki, 1916-1936*, Athens: Odysseas, 1983, pp. 231-3.

Athens alone, a capital city with 453,000 inhabitants already,[19]
received 350,000 refugees who occupied public buildings, theatres
and parks, or built their makeshift settlements around the city.
Yet these destitute people, who were well endowed with commercial know-how and agricultural skills, diversified the Greek
economy and provided cheap industrial labour. Furthermore, lack-
ing family connections and patronage networks in their new locale,
they became a truly radicalised social force in Greek political life.
They soon occupied a leading position in labour union movements
and left-wing parties and altered the nature of political discourse.

From 1923 to 1927 the economy faltered under the pressure
of overwhelming odds as governments strove to halt the plunge
of the drachma and alleviate the plight of the refugees. Between
1927 and 1932 the drachma was at last stabilised and growth was
resumed, but international recession took its toll on recovery. In
1932 the Venizelos government suspended interest and amortised
its foreign debts. The years up till the outbreak of war on 28
October 1940 were given up to managing the crisis caused by
default. War in Europe had already compelled the Metaxas dictatorship to allocate additional funds for military appropriations.
The financial burden of Greece's war with Italy was met by
increased taxation, a war lottery and British loans without specific
terms of repayment.[20] Occupation dealt the economy its death
blow and destroyed the very basis of the country's productive
capacity for many years to come.[21]

Greece in the post-war and Civil War period was a state in
ruins and a nation in disarray. The Americans who took on the
task of financing this pit of the Danaids had good reason for
wondering in 1950 whether the country would ever be able to
stand on its own feet. Since 1945 it had received in foreign

[19] The number was given by the 1920 census. Quoted in William Hardy McNeill, *The
Metamorphosis of Greece since World War II*, Oxford: Basil Blackwell, 1978, p. 230.

[20] Naval Intelligence Division, *Greece*, vol. 2, Geographical Handbook Series, Norwich:
HMSO., October 1944, p. 146. For more information on the internal economy see A.F.
Freris, *The Greek Economy in the Twentieth Century*, London: Croom Helm, 1986, pp.
77-99.

[21] The occupation forces used 'the Greek area as a source of nonreproducible resources,
a form of plunder as it were, rather than maintain its organized forms and integrate them
into the global system of the Axis production'. Stavros Thomadakis, 'Black Markets,
Inflation and Force in the Economy of Occupied Greece' in John Iatrides (ed.), *Greece
in the 1940s*, Hanover, HN: University Press of New England, 1981, p. 63.

assistance over $2,500 million, more than three times the entire foreign debt Greece accumulated between 1821 and 1939, and was mostly used up arming government forces in the 1946-9 Civil War.[22]

The fratricidal struggle that raged for four years took a heavy toll on the Greek population. To the 550,000 (8 per cent of the total) who died during the war in 1940-4 were added a further 158,000 killed in 1946-9.[23] The operations of the Greek army were coordinated and supervised by the Joint United States Military Advisory and Planning Group (JUSMAPG). By 1949 the US mission exerted virtual control over the Greek armed forces and often expressed its impatience with politicians and parliamentary politics. Given the anomalous circumstances of the Civil War, the JUSMAPG advised that the military should be isolated from the rest of society and protected from the ideological influences that might destroy their cohesion. Many Greek officers subscribed to such views, and furthermore believed that for the sake of operational effectiveness the army should become an autonomous body answerable only to its foreign advisers. Such ideas were not abandoned when the war ended. American influence in the Greek army persisted through Military Assistance Programs (MAPs) even after involvement in Greek politics had ceased.[24]

The Civil War bequeathed a persistent legacy to Greek society. It polarised politics, ideology and institutions in a way that profoundly affected the life of the average citizen. This influence was not due to dictatorial rule; it existed, rather, in a state where, in spite of various constitutional irregularities and extraordinary measures, the essential rules of parliamentary democracy were observed. Ideological polarisation left little margin for middle-class politicians and the intelligentsia to deal with issues other than those of Greece's national identity and its place in Western Europe. The leftists (the Communist party) were outlawed or fled the country after their defeat. Consequently, Greece missed out on the constructive dialogue between liberals and socialists which occurred after the war all over Western Europe. High

---

[22] Bickham Sweet-Escott, *Greece: a Political and Economic Survey*, London: Royal Institute for International Affairs, 1954, pp. 145-63.

[23] T. Couloumbis, J. Petropulos and H.J. Psomiades, *Foreign Interference in Greek Politics*, New York: Pella, 1976, p. 117.

[24] T. Couloumbis, 'The Greek Junta Phenomenon', *Polity*, VI, 3 (spring 1974), p. 353.

unemployment and a wrecked private sector turned the state into the chief employer, and it remained a formidable patron even after the completion of reconstruction and the subsequent boom of the 1960s.

State ideology, though nominally pluralistic, presented an image of Greece as an integral nation fighting enemies – of the socialist or Communist variety – who threatened it with destruction and did not invoke principled liberal arguments. There emerged in this way a nationalism which, unlike nineteenth-century irredentism, was defensive, exclusive and parochial. Within the state apparatus a cluster of agencies developed, filled with functionaries (policemen, military personnel and other professional guarantors of public order and the state's creed) who enjoyed relative immunity from parliamentary control. Liberal attempts during 1964-5 to dislodge these functionaries from power provoked the wrath of the crown. Yet the state's scrupulous attachment to legalism often served to protect individual rights of citizens.[25]

The November 1962 treaty of Greece's association with the European Community (EEC) promised to remove tariffs and restrictions on trade between the two entities within a period of twenty-two years. This trade arrangement was heralded as a new alliance that would eventually replace the waning support of the United States. 'Dependence on one country was to be exchanged for association with a powerful and extensive economic alliance which in the popular imagination had brought immense prosperity and prestige to its members.'[26] The decision to become a full member of the Community was probably Greece's post-war decision with the most far-reaching implications for its future. And indeed it proved in the long run a relationship which altered the Greek mentality more than any other outside influence in the history of the modern Greek state. The decision also meant that in future Greece would rely heavily on foreign capital and technological know-how. Thus the occasional pipe-dreams of glorious isolation and self-sufficiency, expounded by Theodoros Diliyannis among others, were forever excluded from Greek foreign and economic policy options.

---

[25] Constantine Tsoucalas, 'The Ideological Impact of the Civil War' in Iatrides, pp. 329-31.
[26] Campbell and Sherrard, p. 319.

The 1960s witnessed yet another break with the past. The internal immigration throughout the post-war period renewed the population of the urban centres and, according to McNeill, solved the old conflict between the mountains and the plain. The traditional market orientation of peasant life facilitated the transplantation of the peasant family unit into the large marketplace of the capital. 'Greek rural society was and is organised into tight-knit, nuclear family units, accustomed to looking upon all outsiders as "them" rather than "us". Such families can move the geographical base of their operation from village to city with very little internal adjustment of family behavior.'[27] Although McNeill was correct about the magnitude of the metastasis from rural to urban life, his certainty about the preservation of traditional values in the urban environment may yet prove to be somewhat premature.

[27] McNeill, p. 208.

# 1

## THE FORMATION OF THE REGULAR ARMY

The complexity of the Greek political configuration between 1821 and 1833 defies any attempt to make a clear-cut distinction between civilian and military factions. Although the chieftains and their irregulars possessed a separate military identity which was enhanced by their vital role in the Greek War of Independence, they never formed a horizontal coalition transcending regional rivalries or personal conflicts. Civil wars were fought between groups that would be temporarily allied and then divided again by divergent regional aims. Hence the warlords of Rumeli in central Greece never considered joining forces with the Peloponnesian chieftains to challenge Peloponnesian primates, island notables and Phanariot[*] bureaucrats.

The formation of a regular army in the last years of the War of Independence and the first few of the kingdom was part of a state-building process conceived and implemented by Westernised Greek élites and European professionals.[1] The effort to replace the politicised and rebellious veterans of the war with troops loyal to the central government was inextricably connected with the fratricidal struggles of the various pretenders to power, as well as with the designs on Greece of European powers.

The wholesale demobilisation of the Greek forces which was finally carried out by the Bavarian regents in 1833 caused serious social problems as the unemployed troops swelled the ranks of the brigand bands. The memoirs of outraged chieftains[2] leave their reader with the impression that the military legislation of

---

[1] See John A. Petropulos, *Politics and Statecraft in the Kingdom of Greece, 1823-1843*, Princeton University Press, 1968. For the most detailed analysis of political and social forces in Greece before 1833, see pp. 19-144.

[2] I. Makriyannis, *Apomnimonevmata*, Athens, 1907, pp. 296-308.

[*] From the Phanar district of Constantinople.

12

the Bavarians was the naive improvisation of foreign blunderers. However, the formation of a regular army had preoccupied Greek governments ever since 1825, when the French-trained Egyptian regulars under Ibrahim, with their long bayonets and firing formations, overwhelmed the scimitar-wielding Greek irregulars.[3]

More than consideration of military performance had attracted Count Ioannis Kapodistrias to the idea of a state-controlled regular army. When he took the presidential office in 1828, the war against the Ottomans was still being waged with 20-30,000 irregulars in the army and 15-20,000 part-time sailors, commanded by a disproportionately high number of officers.[4] Most of the latter had earned their rank during periods of civil strife when, anxious to secure their loyalty and support, political parties had showered commissions on the leaders of armed bands.

If Kapodistrias' unitary state was to survive at all, the impediment posed by the irregulars had to be removed. He considered two alternative options for dealing with the future of the army – the wholesale replacement of irregular bands by foreign-led regulars, or a gradual taming of the irregulars by making them financially dependent on the state – and chose the latter. Apart from the likely consequences of changing horses in midstream (the war was still in progress) and the reaction of unemployed irregulars, Kapodistrias also feared that a strong standing army under French tutelage would either forfeit its national autonomy or be swayed into serving his political opponents.

The assortment of professional soldiers who formed the small Greek regular corps had failed to leave their mark on the war and suffered from low morale and neglect. The French government expressed keen interest in using the French troops already in the Peloponnese to help develop this corps into a full-scale army. The French troops were the 14,000 men under General Nicolas Joseph Maison, who had come to Greece in 1828 to ensure the evacuation of the southern Greek territories[5] by the Egyptian

---

[3] A. Vacalopoulos, *Ta ellinika stratevmata tou 1821*, Thessaloniki: Vanias, 1991, p. 190.

[4] A. Despotopoulos, *O Kyvernitis Kapodistrias kai i apeleftherosis tis Ellados*, Athens, 1954, p. 110 n. 6.

[5] Maison had distinguished himself in the Napoleonic wars and continued to serve the Bourbon regime faithfully. On embarking from Toulon, he reminded his men of the noble cause they were about to serve in Greece: 'We have been summoned to put an end to the trials of a great people. [...] It is the first time since the fifteenth century that the liberating flags of France will appear on the shores of Greece.' Quoted in P. Perrotis,

forces summoned by the Ottomans to quell the revolution. While this expedition had been invited by Kapodistrias and was approved jointly by Russia, Britain and France through the London Protocol of 19 July 1828, it acquired a broader significance given the antagonism between the great powers themselves. In the same year the Russians defeated the Ottomans and enhanced their own influence in the Balkans.

The position of Britain *vis-à-vis* the French military presence in Greece is illustrated by the Anglo-Egyptian pact to guarantee the departure of Ibrahim's troops, which was hurriedly concluded a few days before Maison landed in the Peloponnese in August 1828.[6] It appears that although the British welcomed France providing a counterbalance to the growing Russian power in the Balkans, they were less happy at the prospect of a wider French involvement in the Greek war, which could have turned the new state into a French protectorate.[7] By ensuring a voluntary Egyptian withdrawal, the British deprived Maison of much of the glory of driving out the occupying forces. Suspecting that Kapodistrias had come to an understanding with France, the British government increased its pressure against the French military presence in the Peloponnese, as the English press reported in February 1829.[8]

There is little doubt that the French officers in Greece served their country's long-term investment in the Greek army with considerable zeal. Kapodistrias, though welcoming French and Bavarian (but not British) military experts,[9] sought to confine the French influence to strictly technical matters and prevent political contacts between the French and the 'constitutionalist' opposition to his government.

As the head of the 'Russian party'[10] that had summoned him

---

'The Expedition of Maison in the Peloponnese' (in Greek), *Ellinika*, 9 (Athens, 1936), p. 38. For more secret information concerning Maison's expedition deposited in the archives of the French army (Château de Vincennes), see V. Dorovinis, 'The Archives of the French Army,' *Kathimerini*, 24, 28 November 1979.

[6] V. Kremmydas, 'O gallikos stratos stin Peloponniso', *Peloponnisiaka*, 12, Athens, 1976, pp. 77-9.

[7] Perrotis, p. 41.

[8] *Ibid.*, p. 42.

[9] D. Kokkinos, *I elliniki epanastasis*, vol. 12, Athens, 1968, pp. 60-74.

[10] Greek party factions sought patrons among the great power guarantors of Greece, and assumed names such as the 'French', 'English' or 'Russian' party. See Petropulos, pp. 96-106.

to Greece, and with no parliament to hamper his decisions, Kapodistrias used the authority of the state to establish his influence among regional power groups and local factions. By recruiting certain influential contingents into his party, however, he automatically alienated their local rivals. Although his 'governmentalist' party included formidable networks of followers, the various political opponents who rallied around the 'constitutionalists' represented a force that was by no means negligible.[11] Kapodistrias' policy for charting the future of the Greek army was seriously affected by his fear of the opposition and its relations with the French officers who were organising the Greek regulars and irregulars.

By far the most celebrated French officer in the Greek army was Charles Fabvier, a colonel who had distinguished himself in the Napoleonic wars and was cashiered after the fall of Bonaparte. He came to Greece by way of London in 1823 with the British philhellenes, and in 1825 the Greek government assigned him to the command of the small force of regulars which, until his resignation, he led with varying degrees of success. There is little doubt that the impulsive Bonapartist was a friend of Kapodistrias' constitutionalist opponents and made no secret of his criticism of the President's despotic regime.[12] His persistent dream was the formation of a large Greek regular army that, under his own command, would liberate all traditional Greek territories from Ottoman rule. Kapodistrias predictably resisted the fiery officer's plans and condemned him to forced idleness.

Fabvier's position became untenable after March 1828 when he returned to Methana having failed to capture the island of Chios from the Turks. Accusations were levied against him by the Chiotes, and the newspaper *L'Abeille Grecque* openly called him a French agent.[13] Although there is nothing in his correspondence with Kapodistrias that betrays the gulf that divided them,[14] the President of Greece was quick to accept Fabvier's resignation

---

[11] *Ibid.*, pp. 111-19. For a first-hand though totally negative account of the Kapodistrias regime, see the view of his contemporary German philhellene Frédéric Thiersch, *De l'état actuel de la Grèce*, 1, Leipzig, 1833.

[12] A. Debidour (Fabvier's biographer), *Le Général Fabvier. Sa vie militaire et politique*, Paris, 1904, p. 371.

[13] *L'Abeille Grecque*, no. 47, 29 March 1828, and no. 57, 7 May 1830, quoted in S. Loucatos, 'Ioannis Kapodistrias and Karolos Favieros', *Mnimosyni*, 2, 1968-9, p. 242.

[14] Loucatos, pp. 249-77.

in the spring of 1828. Christos Vyzantios, an officer who served under Fabvier, insists in his history of the Greek regular army that his commanding officer resigned for two reasons: Kapodistrias' lack of confidence in him and his fear that his own men would be left without provisions or pay as a result of his fall from grace with the government.[15]

A document in an envelope inscribed *'Mission du colonel Fabvier'*, which found its way into the private papers of General Maison,[16] has been cited as evidence of Fabvier's activities as a French agent from 1825 onwards.[17] Given that his name is mentioned in the third person and that the *'vers'* (about) on the envelope indicates uncertainty over the exact period covered by the text, it seems reasonable to assume that the title is not of Fabvier's making. In the eighteenth and nineteenth centuries the word 'mission' was freely used to describe all kinds of ventures in foreign lands, including private archaeological and botanical expeditions. The document may have been an account of his exploits written for a friend, or notes made for his own use.

After returning to France in the summer of 1828, Fabvier established contact with members of the French government in order to stage his comeback in Greece with official backing. Although the French Ministers of War and Foreign Affairs welcomed a collaboration with the Bonapartist officer, the ideological predisposition of the Bourbon regime precluded much sympathy for his democratic aspirations. His unrelenting effort to combine his own choice of a constitutionalist regime in Greece, probably under the anglophile Alexander Mavrocordatos, with the consolidation of French influence via the control of a large regular army, was doomed to failure.[18]

When Fabvier returned to Greece in late December 1828, he was unaware that on 16 November the London Protocol had sealed the fate of his mission, and this ignorance of the forces that militated against his plans made his brief stay in the Peloponnese even more pathetic. Maison was given orders to keep his hopes

---

[15] Christos Vyzantios, *I istoria tis organoseos tou taktikou sratou en Elladi (1821-1832)*, Athens, 1837, p. 156.

[16] The papers of Maison, deposited in the Archives Nationales de France (156 AP Maison 12, 13, 14, 15), were used by V. Kremmydas, 'O Gallikos Stratos'.

[17] *Ibid.*, p. 93.

[18] Debidour, pp. 383-9.

alive without providing him with the necessary muscle to impose his demands on Kapodistrias. Although Fabvier carried King Charles X's promise of a monthly allowance for the Greek regulars, this was never made an effective instrument of French policy.[19] In a confidential letter of instruction to General Maison (21 November 1828), the French Minister of War insisted that Fabvier should not be mistaken for a French agent, and that his return to Greece had not been ordered but merely approved by Charles X.[20] The letter concluded: 'We desire for him [Fabvier] no activity in the regular army which could be associated with French or Russian financial assistance. We are not pursuing a position of exclusive influence in Greece. [...] We should try to avoid any action that may upset our allies.'[21]

There were considerable limitations on any attempt by France to pursue a dynamic foreign policy in 1828. Maintaining a low profile in international affairs, it could satisfy the zeal for adventure of its officers only with expeditions of limited objectives, such as the one in Greece. In another letter of the same date, the French minister outlined the policy to be adopted on the matter of the regular Greek army. He believed that the best service that French officers could render to Greece while they were still in the Peloponnese was to help organise a 'national', i.e. regular force of 8-10,000 as a guarantee of order and security. He stressed that a lump sum of 1 million francs and a monthly endowment of 200,000 francs were to be used solely for the reorganisation of the Greek regular forces and for no other purpose.[22] The keen French interest in the formation of a regular Greek army also included a desire to make use of Fabvier, who by now was a well-liked figure in Greece. He was always willing to return to his old post provided that Kapodistrias accepted his terms concerning the role of the regulars and systematic recruitment to enlarge their ranks. Unlike the other letter, this one reflects an official French willingness to secure Fabvier's reappointment as

---

[19] *Ibid.,* pp. 390-9.

[20] Maison 13, dr 2, Paris, 21 November 1828, in Kremmydas, 'O gallikos stratos', pp. 83-4.

[21] *Ibid.*

[22] Also dated 21 November, and addressed to Maison. See Kremmydas, 'O gallikos stratos', pp. 81-3. Kapodistrias did not honour this condition. According to Kasomoulis, he confided to the irregulars in 1829 that he had used French financial aid to pay them. N. Kasomoulis, *Enthymimata Stratiotika,* Athens: Vartsos, 1941, vol. 3, pp. 267-8.

commander of the regulars, as well as the acceptance of another French officer by the Greek government to act as liaison between Fabvier, Kapodistrias and Maison. This officer would also keep the ministry informed of the progress of the regular forces – a task that would normally have been assigned to Fabvier had he really been a trusted agent of the French state.

Kapodistrias and the French government arrived at the same conclusion on the fate of the Greek regulars, though from different points of departure. After the London Conference of 16 November 1828, it became obvious that the English would not accept either French assistance to the Greeks north of the isthmus or an expansion of Greek operations against the Ottoman forces in central Greece. Compelled to remove their troops from the Peloponnese, the French abandoned any hope of the Greeks being able to pursue their irredentist goals alone and thus concluded that a large Greek army of regulars was no longer necessary. Instead they opted for a small force of a few thousand to police the countryside and maintain order.

Kapodistrias, who had been afraid of having a French-dominated regular army, was prepared to agree to the new plan but refused to abandon his irredentist operations. In a letter of 3 December 1828 to Count N. Loverdo,[23] an influential French general, Kapodistrias stated his preference for an army of 9-12,000 men, one-third of whom would be foreign regulars, one-third Rumeliot irregulars and one-third Greek regulars. He went on to express his apprehension about the turbulent Rumeliots and about the loyalty of a large conscripted force. He argued that an army of conscripts would deprive the Rumeliot irregulars of their employment and turn them into a social menace. His own plan was to integrate them with the regulars by controlling their pay and rations.[24] He considered the contingent of French troops essential for training the regulars.

By the time Fabvier arrived in Aigina to resume his old post, he had already become redundant: Edward J. Dawkins, the wily British diplomat in Greece, reported to the Foreign Office (5/17 January 1829) that he was on bad terms with Greek and philhellene

---

[23] *I allilographia tou Ioanni Kapodistria*, Athens 1841, pp. 324-33. C. Loukos, and V. Vartholomaiou, *Evretirio stin allilographia tou Kapodistria*, Athens, 1977, p. 172.
[24] *Allilographia*, pp. 325-6.

officers, and that the only reason why Kapodistrias had not dismissed him was concern for French sensitivity over the matter.[25] Fabvier, who had been under the impression that his recruitment plans had found approval, clashed with Kapodistrias on discovering that the latter had persuaded the French to leave 2-3,000 men behind as a temporary police force, with the task of training the Greek regulars. Finally, his dreams of heading a strong force of regulars against the Turks in Rumeli shattered, he left Greece for good in February 1829.[26] Thus the fate of the 1,000 regulars[27] was sealed and Kapodistrias could give his full attention to the organisation of the troublesome irregulars.

His understanding of 1/13 April 1829 with General Maison concerning French assistance and training for the regulars was of little benefit to the subsequent development of that corps.[28] In August 1831, in the course of quelling the anti-Kapodistrias rebellion in Poros, the regulars, acting as the government's police force, performed so badly that even their staunchest supporters were shocked.[29]

When Kapodistrias appointed Dimitrios Ypsilantis – an officer of the Russian army who had joined the Greek forces in 1821 – Commander-in-Chief of eastern Rumeli and assigned him the task of drafting a new organisational scheme for the Greek army, he was seeking to tame the warriors of Rumeli (*armatoloi* and *klephtes*) and the bands of Souliots from Epirus who had provided the military backbone of the Greek War of Independence. Since most of the Peloponnesian farmer and shepherd soldiers had returned home once the war moved north of the Isthmus of Corinth, there was litle reaction when Kapodistrias demobilised them.[30] However, the Rumeliots depended for their livelihood

---

[25] E. Prevelakis and F. Glytsis, *Summaries of Foreign Office Correspondence: Greece*, vol. 1, 1927-32, Athens, 1975, Dawkins to Aberdeen no. 7, 5/17 January 1829, summary no. 229.

[26] Prevelakis and Glytsis, *Summaries*, Dawkins to Aberdeen no. 12, 28 January-2 February 1829, summary no. 4/12. The Marquis de Valmy, Maison's representative with the Greek government, implies in his report to Maison that Fabvier was involved with the opposition against Kapodistrias. Maison 13, dr. 4, Valmy to Maison, Aegina, 22 January 1829, in Kremmydas, 'O gallikos stratos', p. 92 n. 2.

[27] Despotopoulos, p. 117.

[28] Maison 13, dr 3, Modon 1/13 April 1829, in Kremmydas, 'O gallikos stratos', p. 87.

[29] George Finlay, *History of the Greek Revolution* (Greek trans.) 2, Athens, 1963, pp. 220-33.

[30] The *klephts* or brigand-rebels of the Peloponnese were decimated by the Ottoman

exlusively on their weapons and were thus an entirely different matter. Backed in their claims by influential patron-politicians such as the francophile Ioannis Kolettis[31] and the anglophile Alexandros Mavrocordatos, they clamoured for the back-pay owed them by the government. The notion of an integrated national army was remote from the reality of the multitude of independent bands, each recognising only the authority of their own chieftains who paid and fed them and distributed the spoils of war.

The chronic difficulty experienced by Greek governments in controlling irregulars was due largely to the inadequacy of public funds for their regular payment and logistical support. As a contemporary notable put it, 'Regular wages would solve all difficulties.'[32] Yet securing the necessary funds was no simple matter. Kapodistrias' alternative was to create an institutional framework that would make the soldiers dependent on the state and gradually dissipate the influence of their chieftains or political patrons. His plans included a *'Genikon Frontistirion'* which would at first deal with logistics and then gradually develop into a kind of general headquarters for the army and navy, as well as the creation of units of uniform size: the pay allocations for these would be independent of the arbitrary claims of leaders of armed bands who usually exaggerated the number of men under their command.[33]

Although the goverment's ability to satisfy the financial claims of its soldiers did not substantially improve, its control over the irregulars tightened. After the battle of Petra in the autumn of 1829, which ended the War of Independence, Kapodistrias promoted a new army organisation that reduced the power of the chieftains further[34] and brought the Greek forces more in line with their Western prototypes. The new battalions separated men from their old leaders and forced new bands to coexist

---

authorities in 1805, while those in Rumeli continued to operate unchallenged. For the destruction of the Peloponnesian *klepht* warriors, see M.B. Sakellariou, *I Peloponnisos kata tin deuteran Tourkokratian*, Athens, 1939, pp. 241-3.

[31] Encouraged by the French who wished to maintain good relations with Kapodistrias, Kolettis used his influence with the Rumeliots to help implement the military reforms.

[32] See Vacalopoulos.

[33] Small bands were joined to form larger units, the *'Chiliarchies'*, of 1,125 men each. See also Stephanos Papadopoulos, 'I Organosis tou Stratou is tin Dytikin Rumelin kata tin Epochin tou Kapodistria', *Ellinika*, vol. 18 (1964), Thessaloniki, pp. 144-68.

[34] According to Maurer (King Otto's regent), Kapodistrias 'attempted to take military power away from the chieftains'. G. Maurer, *O ellinikos laos*, Athens: Tolidis, 1976, p. 338.

under new commanders.[35] As older officers were being eased out of the service and the ratio of soldiers to officers increased, so did the insecurity of the latter, and their growing dependence on the state prevented uprisings more serious than those that actually occurred. When Kapodistrias called on Rumeliots who wished to join his reformed army in 1828, about 8,000 men responded, a quarter of them officers. In the autumn of 1829, after the end of the war, only 5,000 men answered the call from the president to serve in the newly organised army.[36]

Kapodistrias' attempt to curtail the power-base of all-important actors (individuals and collective) of the 1821-7 period and neutralise his political opponents met with partial success. His paternalistic regime, inspired by the principles of Western enlightened despotism, tolerated no dissent. The centralising process he imposed on the Greeks involved a levelling of elements and institutions that had flourished during the revolutionary period and had now become nuclei of opposition to his government. He suppressed local autonomy, and the rugged individualism of the warriors was turned into permanent rebelliousness against the state. In his effort to control the irregulars as a force, Kapodistrias paved the way for the eventual *coup de grâce* of the Ottonian administration, when most of the ties between the Greek forces and the traditions of the War of Independence were cut. The phenomenon of the irregular soldiers turned brigands reached its peak during the Ottonian regency (1833-5). It had been endemic throughout the Greek revolution, but acquired disquieting dimensions after the Kapodistrian reforms.

With the establishment of fourteen battalions in western Rumeli, about 4,000 men were left without employment – those from territories still under Ottoman rule (Thessaly, Epirus, Crete, Macedonia etc.) who had no homes to return to.[37] Many turned to their old defiant ways which had been cherished by their countrymen during Ottoman rule but merited imprisonment and even execution under the government of Kapodistrias. Although the popular image of the outlaw did not change abruptly after

[35] Kasomoulis, *Enthymimata stratiotika,* p. 243.
[36] Finlay, p. 198.
[37] Kasomoulis, p. 310.

independence, the heroic *klepht* gradually gave way to the vicious brigand.

It appears from the letter Kapodistrias wrote to his Swiss banker friend Jean-Gabriel Eynard (3/15 February 1830) that the Greek President was fully aware of the dire social consequences of disbanding the armed Rumeliots. 'We shall send them home when we are in a position to compensate them with a few acres of land and can provide them with the means to cultivate it. Only by owning some property will they respect the property of others.'[38]

The year 1830 was a turning-point in Kapodistrias' administration, as well as in his relations with France. The London Protocol of February proclaimed Greece an independent state, and the throne was offered by the great powers to Prince Leopold of Saxe-Coburg. Distressed at the prospect of losing his position to a king, Kapodistrias did all he could to convince his potential rival that being King of the Hellenes was not a desirable prize. Yet his position was further undermined by the July 1830 revolution in France which toppled the conservative and philhellene Charles X and installed the liberal Louis-Philippe as King in his place. The constitutionalist opposition in Greece was greatly encouraged by this development, and the French government soon began to change its favorable attitude *vis-à-vis* the regime of Kapodistrias.

Throughout the five-year reign of Charles X (1825-30), as well as during the first few years of his Orléanist successor, French foreign policy was governed by fear of isolation and by the search for some agreement with other powers. The common goal of both Bourbon and Orléans monarchs was to restore France to its pre-1815 position in international affairs – an ideal that commanded a broad consensus among French politicians of all persuasions. The only difference between the republican and radical position and that of the extreme right lay in the means to be employed to achieve this regeneration of French power and influence. In their common pursuit of a revision of the 1815 treaties, the liberals advocated a war of liberation against the reactionary monarchies of the east, whereas the conservatives favoured an alliance with Russia.[39] Although Charles's nationalist policy was

---

[38] Kapodistrias to Eynard, 3/15 February 1830, *Correspondance du Comte Capodistrias*, 3, Geneva, 1839, pp. 472-3.

[39] Roger Bullen, 'France and the Problem of Intervention in Spain, 1834-1836', *Historical Journal*, 20, June 1977, pp. 336-64.

popular, his outdated conservatism militated against the continuation of his regime. While the conquest of Algiers was being completed in 1830, the French liberals rose against the absolutism of the last Bourbon monarch and installed a 'bourgeois King' in his place.

The obvious partner of post-1830 France was Britain. The two constitutional monarchies combined their joint sympathy for liberal movements and their dislike for authoritarian regimes with a resolve to maintain the *status quo* in the Near East and to block Russian expansionism in the eastern Mediterranean.[40] After the 1830 revolutionary upheavals in Europe, the ideological cleavage between the reactionary Eastern powers – Russia, Austria and Prussia – and liberal Britain and France illustrated the wide conflict of interests which divided the two ideological blocs.[41]

Kapodistrias' position at the end of 1830 was not an enviable one. Besides the ideological kinship between France and the Greek constitutional opposition, French fears of Russian influence through Kapodistrias may explain an apparent deterioration of the Greek President's relations with French officers. Furthermore, the Polish insurrection was absorbing Russia's attention and diverting it from the Balkans, thereby increasing Kapodistrias' insecurity and forcing him to rely on his own inexperienced brothers to run the Greek state. Augustinos, who managed army affairs with the single-minded determination of the ignorant, became a major target for the discontented and irritated irregulars. From the autumn of 1830 onwards, the government became even more rigid in the face of mounting opposition. Even the russophile Peloponnesians, who attributed the departure of the Egyptian troops from their lands to Kapodistrias' own intervention, complained that local clients of the regime had acquired freedom to engage in arbitrary activities that were causing anarchy in the Morea. At the same time the new French regime discontinued the economic aid allocated for the improvement of the regular forces and, according to Vyzantios, 'along with the English, encouraged opposition against the President'.[42]

[40] *Ibid.*, p. 365; David Thompson, *Europe since Napoleon*, London: Pelican, 1978, pp. 145-51.

[41] F. B. Artz, *Reaction and Revolution, 1814-1832*, New York, 1963, pp. 286-92.

[42] C. Vyzantios, *I istoria tou rolou tou taktikou stratou is tis ekstraties kai polemous apo to 1821-1833*, Athens, 1956, p. 259. Tricoupis claims that the allowance was terminated

Infantry Colonel Gérard became inspector of the Greek forces in November 1829 and continued to serve France after the 1830 revolution by accepting various posts in the Greek regular and irregular forces. On his first assignment following the reforms of the irregulars in 1829, he was faced with vociferous opposition from the Rumeliot troops.[43] In August 1830 Gérard replaced General G. Trezel in the command of the regulars and organised a 'model corps' (*Typikon*), with the function of training officers from the irregulars to instil orderly behaviour in their troops. The 'model corps' failed because too few irregulars joined its ranks, which were made up mostly of volunteers. The *Typikon* therefore became an ordinary regular corps (though with a mere 150 men) and brought about no improvement in the irregulars.[44]

We will not deal here with the events that led up to Kapodistrias' assassination or attempt to trace Franco-Greek relations after 1830 to illustrate French discontent with the Greek President. Instead, we shall look at some indications of French implication in the assassination plot as they emerged in the investigation by the Greek authorities after the event. The conventional wisdom of Greek historiography attributes the assassination of the first Greek President in September 1831 to a vendetta between him and the Mavromichali family from Mani. Accusing fingers have also been pointed at the British, but concrete evidence has failed to support the allegation of direct complicity. More recent findings, however, provide considerable evidence of French implication.[45]

As mentioned above, the presence of French military forces in the Peloponnese and their involvement in the organisation of Greek regulars and irregulars had given them an important foothold in Greek affairs. The tacit understanding between the authoritarian Charles X, the Russians and Kapodistrias obliged the 'French party' in Greece under Kolettis to cooperate with the President. The post-1830 change in French policy towards Russia had an immediate effect on the Greek regime. Kapodistrias became *persona non grata* and the Greek opposition received encouragement from

---

because Kapodistrias insisted on developing the regulars, cf. S. Tricoupis, *Istoria tis ellinikis epanastaseos,* Athens, 1879, pp. 269-70.

[43] Kasomoulis, pp. 302-4; and Pellion, *La Gréce et les Capodistrias pendant l'occupation française de 1828 à 1834,* Paris, 1855, p. 196.

[44] The private papers of Gérard were traced by the late Iphigenia Anastasiadou.

[45] V. Kremmydas, 'I Dolophonia tou Kapodistria', *Eranistis,* Athens, 1977, pp. 245-50, 262-70.

France. The Mavromichalis family maintained long-standing ties with the French and kept in contact with them throughout the plot. Evidence from the Greek authorities' investigations indicates a larger conspiracy whereby French troops, backed by naval contingents, would occupy the Greek capital (Nafplion) after Kapodistrias' assassination.[46]

Although one of the assassins, George Mavromichalis, sought sanctuary in the home of the French Minister, there is no other evidence that the minister, Achille Rouen, was implicated. However, there is incriminating evidence against Gérard, the commander of the Greek regular forces. His contemporary, Gennaios Kolokotronis, does not mince words over Gérard's complicity,[47] but more convincing than the blunt opinions of the russophile chieftain are facts that emerged from the official interrogations.[48] It appears that Gérard had planned in advance to keep the regulars in a state of alert on the Sunday after the assassination and, more important, to settle the problems of their arrears of pay before that date as a gesture to win their confidence. The regulars nevertheless refused to see or talk to either Gérard or his deputy Pellion on the day after the deed, which appears to have been a tacit accusation against the two French officers.[49] The Greek authorities subsequently asked Gérard to resign from his post.[50]

If personal motives are excluded from Gérard's actions, we are left with only one plausible explanation of his anti-Kapodistrian stance after 1830: namely, a change in the orders he received from Paris. Like most of his colleagues, Gérard faithfully served both the Bourbon and the Orléans monarchies without ever questioning the policy that inspired their instructions. During the Bourbon restoration the French officer corps, consisting of returned nobles and veterans of the Napoleonic wars, remained detached from political involvement. Discipline and obedience were the most respected qualities of the French officer, whose loyalty to the legitimate monarch remained unquestioned until the public verdict dethroned him in 1830. One regiment, which discarded

[46] *Ibid.*, pp. 264-5, and notes 85-8.
[47] G. Kolokotronis, *Apomnimoneumata*, Athens, 1955, p. 212.
[48] Kremmydas, 'I Dolophonia...', pp. 245-50.
[49] *Ibid.*, p. 247 n. 34.
[50] *Ibid.*, p. 248, n. 40.

equipment bearing the Bourbon insignia, was advised by its commanding officer, who had not been particularly enthusiastic about the previous regime, to restore the equipment until official orders were issued by the Minister of War.[51]

The breakdown of central authority after the death of Kapodistrias had a direct impact on the Greek military. Civil strife raged throughout 1832, destroying the feeble bonds that held the irregulars together. Once the institutional edifice built by Kapodistrias had collapsed and with it the state's ability to provide its soldiers with a livelihood, these same soldiers degenerated into bands of brigands looting villages and towns. It was the huge cost of anarchy which ultimately cowed politicians and chieftains alike into unqualified acceptance of the Bavarian regime of King Otto. When King Ludwig of Bavaria, Otto's father, agreed with Greece's guarantor powers that his son should become the first King of Greece, he made sure that the irregulars that posed problems to the central authorities would be cashiered and replaced with 3,500 mercenaries recruited from the German states.[52] The Bavarian regency that managed public affairs until Otto came of age issued royal decrees in March 1833 disbanding 5,000 irregulars and allowing only veterans of the War of Independence to enter the 'Akrovolistes-Kinigi' battalions. By doing this the Bavarians killed two birds with one stone: they endowed the state with a loyal army dissociated from the wild tradition of the irregulars and deprived political parties of their military clientele. In 1835 the regency founded the *'Phalanx'* – a retirement scheme for veteran warriors designed to win their loyalties over to the state.[53] The irregulars who had been excluded from state employment swelled the ranks of brigands and plagued the countryside. This phenomenon was endemic throughout the century until the state succeeded in extending its authority to all parts of the realm. Meanwhile, brigands were periodically pardoned and recruited for irredentist operations in Thessaly, Epirus and Crete.

---

[51] G. Girardet, *La société militaire dans la France contemporaine, 1815-1839*, Paris, 1953, pp. 129-30.

[52] Petropulos, pp. 165-72.

[53] The basic work on the Greek regular forces is by Christos Vyzantios, *Istoria tou taktikou stratou tis Ellados*, Athens, 1837. Also see Vacalopoulos, pp. 286-87, and George Maurer, *O Ellinikos Laos*, Athens, 1943, p. 24. John Koliopoulos' brilliant work on brigandage also deals with institutions of the regular army: *Brigands with a Cause: Brigandage and Irredentism in Modern Greece, 1821-1912*, Oxford: Clarendon Press, 1987, pp. 80-1.

# 2

# THE SELECTION AND EDUCATION
# OF OFFICERS

From its turbulent birth in the aftermath of the War of Independence to the Tricoupis reforms of the 1880s, the Greek regular army was limited to buttressing the authority of the new state. The very formation of state-controlled troops was based on the principle of restraining the internecine strife among the irregulars and their defiant claims on the central government. By the last quarter of the nineteenth century, the state had eliminated rival sources of power and proceeded to transform the diminutive forces that had policed the countryside into a massive institution that would serve the irredentist cause in the field.

Throughout the last century of the Ottoman presence in Greece, the two dominant social groups were landed notables functioning as a component of the Ottoman tax system and the armed chieftains entrusted with the protection of communications from brigands that obstructed the traffic of goods and people on the mainland. The War of Independence reconciled the two only temporarily. When the prospect of a new central authority began to materialise, politicians and military men competed for control of the emerging state. The traditional élites failed to realise that the state could make use of their services only if it secured their exclusive loyalty and ultimately their subordination to its will. In other words, political power could no longer remain fragmented on the periphery of the state, nor would the central state share its authority with the old order on a partnership basis.[1]

The defiant chieftains were eased out of the state service with decorations and land and replaced in 1833 by a state army made

---

[1] A definitive account of brigandage can be found in John Koliopoulos, *Brigands with a Cause*, Oxford: Clarendon Press, 1987.

up mostly of Bavarian professionals. From the outset the regular army was faced with the task of quelling rebellions by forces that resisted the centralising process as well as the hostility of the idle warriors and brigands who dominated the countryside. The new military was therefore divorced from the warrior tradition of challenging political authority.

Although rebel forces were outlawed, brigands were periodically employed by the state to support irredentist uprisings in Ottoman-held territories. Thus the revolutionary tradition was preserved and at the same time military employees were kept free of the virus of rebellion.[2]

Officer selection and training during the initial forty-five years of the Greek kingdom were subservient to the overriding priority of nation-building. The Military Academy was established at Nafplion, the first capital of liberated Greece, to provide the regular army with a professional officer corps. The intention of its founder, the Bavarian philhellene Colonel von Eydeck, was to encourage notables and warriors of the War of Independence to bring their sons into the service of the state. However, the local notables were slow to respond to this appeal, and it was the uprooted former volunteers of the diaspora and refugees from territories in which the revolution had failed who initially grasped the opportunity that promised professional security. Native warriors feared that free tuition and board would ensnare their offspring into the service of the government, whose disciplinary methods they abhorred. Of forty-three students who entered the institution in 1828, only eight graduated three years later. The output of graduates remained comparably low until the last quarter of the century.[3]

Ioannis Kapodistrias asked General Maison, who had cleared the Peloponnese of the Egyptian occupation forces, to release French officers and non-commissioned officers for service in the Greek military school, which was promptly restructured along the lines of the French École Polytechnique. The goal of imitating the French prototype proved too ambitious in view of the lack of educational background that would enable cadets to pursue intensive training in the sciences. The ages of the cadets, ranging

---

[2] T. Veremis, 'O taktikos stratos stin Ellada tou 19ou aiona' in D. Tsaousis (ed.), *Opseis tis ellinikis koinonias tou 19ou aiona*, Athens: Kollaros, 1984, pp. 165-76.

[3] E. Stasinopoulos, *I istoria tis Scholis Evelpidon*, Athens: Prodromou & Moussoulioti 1954, pp. 35-8.

from thirteen to seventeen years, and the varying degrees of literacy among first-year students were formidable obstacles. Furthermore, the prospect of three years of strict discipline and hard work discouraged the sons of influential families who could secure positions in the officer corps through the back door of patronage. Kapodistrias therefore established yet another category of future officers, the '*Akolouthi*', who acquired a brief acquaintance with principles of artillery and engineering and after passing examinations in these subjects became lieutenants.[4]

The continuing reluctance of prominent members of society to enter the Academy led Kapodistrias to seek recruits in other social strata. Thus in October 1829 he turned to the orphanage of Aigina, whose boarders were mostly children orphaned during the War of Independence. This source of recruitment did not last long but yielded a crop of officers dedicated to the service with an *esprit de corps* which they in turn passed on to their sons.[5]

The President's personal interest in the improvement of the Academy promised to make the institution an important centre for the dissemination of military as well as technical skills. However, his assassination took place only a month after he had attended the first graduation ceremony. King Otto and the Bavarian advisers who came with him to Greece in 1833 altered the charter of the Academy. According to the royal decree of 3 March 1834:

> Four junior and four senior classes are formed. The young men enter the lowest and pass a year in each, then, after undergoing an examination, are placed in the army ... where they are bound to serve for at least four years.[...] At the end of the initial four years the pupils undergo an examination; those who pass advance into the senior classes, the others must quit the Academy.[...] The studies of the four junior classes comprise ancient and modern languages, geometry, geography, calligraphy, algebra, history, drawing, dancing, gymnastics, swimming, fencing, surveying.[...] The instruction of the pupils in the four senior classes is suitably general and technical to fit them for the artillery and the engineers. Consequently, the higher branches and applications of mathematics, natural

[4] *Ibid.*, pp. 43-4, 50-1.
[5] *Ibid.*, pp. 52-3.

philosophy, chemistry, fortification, gunnery, the construction of roads and bridges, form the subjects of their studies.[6]

Full tuition was fixed at 1,000 drachmas a year (equivalent to the annual salary of an Academy instructor), but only 14 per cent of the enrolled cadets paid the entire sum. About 14 per cent paid 750 drachmas, about 20 per cent 500, and another 14 per cent 250. One-third of the places were reserved for the sons of civil and military employees who had given notable service and these were exempted from payment of tuition fees altogether. Between 1834 and 1840 the annual number of entrants varied from 140 to 60, but the average fee paid indicated that most cadets were recruited from the well-to-do sectors of society.[7]

The Academy operated in Aigina for three and a half years. Many of its graduates continued their education in the artillery and engineering school at Metz and the École Polytechnique in Paris. Others were given scholarships to study in Munich by King Otto's father, King Ludwig of Bavaria. Graduating cadets who had excelled in the more demanding courses were selected for the artillery and the engineering corps, while those of lesser aptitude entered the infantry. This method of selection for the three corps remained in force throughout the Academy's term in Piraeus between 1837 and 1894.[8]

During the initial twelve years of its operation, the Academy was run by foreign military instructors and directors. According to the Treaty of London, the King of Greece was empowered to raise a body of troops in Bavaria for the needs of the new kingdom, and between 1833 and 1835 close to 5,500 Germans were recruited into the Greek regular army; after their four-year engagement many began to return home.[9] The hellenisation of the army and its command coincided with the appointment of Lieutenant-Colonel Spyromilios, a hero of the War of Independence, as the first Greek director of the Academy in 1840. In the mean time, as Otto secured internal order and stabilised

---

[6] Frederick Strong, *Greece as a Kingdom*, London, 1842, pp. 272-3.

[7] *Ibid.*, pp. 272-4.

[8] D. Koromilas, an Academy graduate studying at the École Polytechnique in 1838, complained to the Ministry of Army Affairs that his monthly salary of 68 drachmas was hardly enough to pay for his tuition, books and board in Paris. Stasinopoulos, p. 72.

[9] Strong, pp. 280-1.

his regime, he began to feel that high expenditure on the military was no longer necessary. The military budget was accordingly cut from 9 million drachmas in 1833 to 4 million in 1833. The standing army was reduced from close to 10,000 in 1833 to 6,000 in 1838, although it later rose to 8,000.[10]

Although in theory all Greek males of conscription age were subjected to a selection process through lottery, in fact the well-to-do could pay off their military obligation or persuade less fortunate individuals to replace them at the draft boards. The anonymous author (who signed himself O.K.) of a tract addressed to his fellow-members of the 1844 parliament lamented the fact that conscripts were of the lowest social class and, instead of embracing the irredentist aspirations of their country, only wanted to rejoin their destitute peasant families or their orphaned herds. Those who could not stand the hardship of the four-year term of military service (although this fluctuated) simply deserted and disappeared into the landscape.[11] Forever changing its regulations, the Academy cut the length of the junior courses from four years to one and then increased it to two again when Spyromilios took command, while preserving the four-year duration of the senior classes. The overall six-year course lasted for the remainder of Otto's reign.

The 1843 political upheaval against Otto's absolute rule had a serious impact on the academy. Discipline among cadets declined, and teachers brought their political feuds into the institution or simply ceased to take an interest in its future. Between 1843 and 1846 the Academy, then under Lieutenant-Colonel G. Karatzas, reached its lowest point. The new Director, seeking to restore discipline, ignored the Academy's tradition of self-management and was ultimately faced with an armed rebellion. The government expelled nine cadets considered responsible for the rioting and closed the institution for a year. The incident illustrates both the free traffic of politics and civilian values in military institutions and the tolerant treatment of disciplinary infractions by the state. In his report on the condition of the Academy in 1851, Colonel E. Rainek, Inspector-General of the army, noted the freedom with which cadets could voice their criticism of the professional

---

[10] *Ibid.*, pp. 259-62.

[11] Anonymous, *Skepseis peri tou ethnikou stratou tis Ellados*, Athens, 1844, pp. 19-20.

shortcomings of the faculty. According to Rainek, too many cadets were being forced by their families to enter the military school either because it was seen as a proper choice of career or because it was hoped that studying there would reform their unruly characters. More than the cadets' social backgrounds and idiosyncrasies, it was probably the political anomalies that occurred in the latter part of Otto's reign that caused the decay of military education.[12]

During the long reign of King George I, which began in 1863, the education of officers was repeatedly altered both in form and in substance. In 1864 six years of studies were assigned to prospective officers of the artillery and the engineering corps, and four years to officers of the infantry and cavalry. The annual number of entrants, who were admitted between the ages of fifteen and eighteen, was not to exceed sixty. In 1866 the course was fixed at five years for all corps, and in 1868 the regulation of the Academy reverted to the charter of 1864, which remained in force till 1870. These frequent changes in regulations reflected the instability of the period and the inertia of an army whose peacetime strength remained at its Ottonian level of 8,000.[13]

Throughout the first sixty years of its life the Greek state was entirely dependent on the Military Academy for the dissemination of sorely needed technical skills and education. The curriculum included arithmetic, algebra, geometry, stereometry, trigonometry, methods of construction, topography, building and engine design. From 1870 theoretical subjects such as physics and mathematics were given during an initial five-year course, and applied military education was concentrated in the last two years of study. The cadets with the highest grades in these subjects were selected for the technical corps, but there were always students who chose to conclude their studies after completing an initial programme of theoretical subjects and pursue a career in teaching or civil engineering. Thus the institution produced civilian architects, engineers and teachers of theoretical sciences until the Greek Polytechnic Institute was founded in 1887. Officers of the engineering

---

[12] Stasinopoulos, *I istoria*, 1933 edn, pp. 78-9.

[13] A. Haralambis and K. Nider, *Istorikon ypomnima peri tou organismou tou taktikou stratou*, Athens: Ministry of Army Affairs, 1907, pp. 129-31. See also the somewhat incoherent set of grievances against interference by the Ministry of Army Affairs in the Academy examinations, expressed by a member of the teaching staff: S. Komnou, *Peri tis stratiotikis scholis skepseis*, Athens: Nikolaides Philadelpheus, 1867, pp. 10-13.

corps were often used by the Ministry of the Interior for the supervision of public works such as the construction of bridges, roads and government buildings, and their services were sometimes called in by the private sector also.[14]

The Bavarian captain of the engineering corps, Friedrich Tsetner, established a centre of technical education that included a collection of tools and engines for the use of students and artisans. This centre, offering technical information and literature as well as equipment, was inaugurated with government support in 1836. The military origin of technical education in Greece was obvious during the first decades of the Polytechnic Institute's operation while many of its professors were army officers.[15]

Between 1877 and 1897 a series of crises made the dismemberment of the Ottoman empire appear imminent, a prospect which heightened the antagonisms between Balkan nations over the future distribution of the territorial spoils. The evolution and development of regular armies in other Balkan states was instrumental in reviving the Greek army from its inertia. Greek governments finally abandoned the convenient policy of using irregulars to promote irredentist aspirations and realised that the final reckoning would take place on the field of battle.

A series of reforms which began in the 1870s and reached their peak during the term of Harilaos Tricoupis rejuvenated the Academy. The reformer statesman aimed at bringing the education of officers into line with a new policy that viewed the regular army as the future champion of irredentist struggles. Between 1879 and 1882 universal conscription was put into effect and the standing army was modernised and its strength increased to 30,000. However, the constant changes of governing regulations (in 1877, 1880, 1881, 1885 etc.) delayed the beneficial effects of reform.[16]

In 1882 the Academy entered one of its best periods since its foundation. It acquired a new set of regulations that lasted thirty years and cut the term of studies to five years, thus placing emphasis on military subjects rather than intermediate scientific education. Entrance required a high-school diploma and therefore saved the institution the loss of young men who, having entered the school

[14] Costas Biris, *Istoria tou Ethnikou Metsoviou Polytechniou*, Athens, 1957, pp. 13-16.

[15] *Ibid.*, pp. 265-6, 485-527.

[16] Alexander Mazarakis-Ainian, *Istoriki meleti 1821-1897 kai o polemos*, vol. 1, Athens, 1950, pp. 308-9.

at a tender age, often dropped out along the way: of 576 cadets enrolled from 1828 to 1882, 303 (barely 53 per cent) had gone on to become officers. The Academy remained closed to candidates below a certain financial level, since tuition, board and other expenses exceeded 2,500 drachmas a year, the average annual income of a civil servant. The institution concentrated on theoretical scientific subjects and failed to provide prospective officers of the technical corps with practical experience. It completely neglected the needs of the backbone of the army, also its largest branch, the infantry.[17]

The tuition-free School for Non-Commissioned Officers, founded in 1882, was designed to supply officers for the infantry and to a lesser extent the cavalry. An initial period of service as NCOs and three years of study gave candidates of moderate means the opportunity of entering the officer corps with seniority two months behind those who graduated from the Academy at the same time. Since the early years of the operation of regular troops, the overwhelming majority of officers had risen from the ranks, and although they possessed experience in ordinary military functions, they conspicuously lacked military education and acquaintance with modern methods. The disparity between Academy graduates and officers who had risen from the ranks was made plain by the almost exclusive presence of the former in the senior ranks. Most Academy graduates, however, chose to be placed in the two prestigious technical corps (see Table), which because of their small size were crowded, thus undermining their prospects of rapid promotion. Hence infantry officers often reached the middle ranks before their colleagues in the artillery but seldom rose above them.[18]

MILITARY ACADEMY GRADUATES
IN RELATION TO THE TOTAL OF OFFICERS
OF THE VARIOUS BRANCHES, 1891

|           | Officers | Academy graduates |
|-----------|----------|-------------------|
| Infantry  | 924      | 10                |
| Cavalry   | 110      | 5                 |
| Artillery | 152      | 147               |
| Engineers | 79       | 79                |
| *Total*   | 1,265    | 241               |

[17] *Ibid.*, pp. 309-10; Haralambis and Nider, pp. 240, 268-70.
[18] Haralambis and Nider, pp. 270-1.

The problem of improving the quality of infantry officers became a preoccupation of the Greek military after the ignominious defeat by the Turkish forces in 1897. Thus the entire Academy class of 1900 was obliged to enter the infantry. The long-term trend, however, was towards change in the entire structure and orientation of military education. In his influential tract on the reform of the officer corps written in 1909, M. Raktivan, an artillery lieutenant, insisted that the existence of two schools for officers and the lack of any schooling for the majority of them was responsible for the sorry state of the infantry and the lack of cohesion among officers. He proposed instead a single institution for the formation of future officers, free of tuition, so that no economic hindrance would inhibit able candidates from entering. Furthermore, he argued that theoretical subjects and the length of the course should be restricted and emphasis placed on training in applied military science.[19]

The Balkan wars of 1912-13 revolutionised military education and the recruitment of officers. After 1913 the Academy abandoned its École Polytechnique prototype and adopted Saint-Cyr as its model, concentrating mainly on preparing officers for the field. The emphasis shifted from mathematics and theoretical subjects to practical training, while the length of the course was reduced from five years to three. Non-commissioned officers were allowed to graduate from the Academy in two years, while civilians were obliged to pursue preparatory courses for a year before beginning a two-year programme. In 1914 the charter of the Evelpidon Academy was revised to supply a large officer corps ready for battle: 270 students entered the institution, almost equal to the number of its graduates throughout its initial fifty years of operation. Although admission quotas remained high until 1920, the proportion of Academy graduates in the officer corps diminished markedly between 1912 and 1922 (see Table overleaf) because of the influx of reserve officers who had been granted regular commissions.

Tuition fees were abolished in 1917, but the social origin of cadets at the Academy had been changing significantly since 1913. The large number of admissions made the institution readily accessible to those who could afford it, and the traditional preference for prominent members of society had therefore given way to

---

[19] M. Raktivan, *Mia meleti epi tou stratou mas*, Athens: Eleftheroudakis, 1909, pp. 17-48.

candidates who were socially less privileged. At the same time, prominent families became less eager to send their children to the Academy once the institution lost its exclusive character. Furthermore, the gradual growth and diversification of the economy increased the range of professional opportunities and therefore broadened the career options of young men. With its free tuition the Academy attracted mainly those who could not afford to finance their education.

MILITARY ACADEMY GRADUATES IN RELATION TO THE
TOTAL NUMBER OF OFFICERS, 1895-1925

| Army List | Officers | Academy (no.) | Graduates (%) |
|---|---|---|---|
| 1891 | 1,265 | 241 | 20.0 |
| 1895 | 1,230 | 344 | 28.0 |
| 1900 | 934 | 330 | 35.0 |
| 1904 | 1,396 | 373 | 27.0 |
| 1909 | 1,229 | 359 | 29.0 |
| 1912 | 1,301 | 372 | 28.5 |
| 1914 | 2,627 | 369 | 14.0 |
| 1919 | 4,705 | 872 | 18.5 |
| 1925 | 3,287 | 700 | 21.0 |

Source: T. Veremis, *I Epemvasis tou stratou stin elliniki politiki, 1916-1936*, Athens: Odysseas, 1983, p. 80.

The School for Non-Commissioned Officers was closed in 1915, and a new category of officers appeared during the wars in the Balkans. Reserve officers who had been granted regular commissions formed the largest group in the Army List of 1920. These were conscripts who at the end of their military service were offered the option of a permanent position in the army. Most of them had completed their secondary education and a few had attended university before being conscripted, and their decision to remain in the service was often dictated by lack of financial security. Their brief contact with military education and the circumstances under which they had entered the army determined the professional outlook of these officers. A measure of civilian behaviour that they inevitably introduced into the service accounts for their frequent involvement in politics and military societies. For this they earned the contempt of Academy graduates, who never accepted them as their equals either in character or in military education.[20]

The intense interest in military conspiracies shown by reserve officers who had been granted regular commissions can also be explained by their lack of professional security. The least stable group in the officer corps, they constituted a kind of thermostat of the corps: whenever the Army List was too crowded, they were the first to be retired; thus their dependence on military and political patrons had become a condition for professional survival. Since an unprecedented number of regular commissions were granted between 1913 and 1920, especially during the times when Eleftherios Venizelos was in power and at odds with King Constantine, there was a strong propensity among these officers to support the Liberal leader. When the 'great schism' (the *Dichasmos*—see more in later chapters) occurred between followers of the charismatic Venizelos and the no less popular Constantine, it was reserve officers rather than Academy graduates who supported Venizelos. The latter was obliged to resign twice because the King refused to endorse the entry of Greece into the war on the side of the Triple Entente. In the summer of 1916 Venizelos formed his own revolutionary government in Thessaloniki and summoned his followers to stand by him and his pro-Entente policy. Reserve officers holding regular commissions abandoned their posts in significant numbers and rushed to his side. Their vital role in the dispute between liberals and royalists eventually made these officers a source of radicalism in the army and the vanguard not only of Venizelism but also of antimonarchical currents.

From the last quarter of the nineteenth century onwards, the efforts of Greek governments to create a professional officer corps that would command and modernise an augmented regular army resulted in the development of a corporate identity among the more prominent of the military. The reformed Academy increasingly attracted an élite which by the first decade of the twentieth century had begun to voice both professional and national grievances. Between 1872 and 1895 the officer corps increased by over 240

---

[20] T. Veremis. 'The Officer Corps in Greece 1912-1936', *Byzantine and Modern Greek Studies*, 2, 1976, pp. 116-17.

per cent, from 700 to 1,800.[21] In the same period, officers constituted between 7 and 15 per cent of the deputies in parliament,
a significant overrepresentation, and among these Academy
graduates formed at large majority.[22]

Between 1897 and 1909 it was Academy graduates too who
became the most vociferous critics of royal interference in military
matters as well as the vanguard of military corporatism. The *pronunciamento* of 1909 against the monarchy and its political clients was
spearheaded by the Military League, an organisation that consisted
almost entirely of young Academy graduates.

The expansion of a peacetime force of 25,000 in 1900 into
an army of 150,000 at the outbreak of the first Balkan war in
1912 transformed the officer corps not only in size but in social
background. Between 1912 and 1920 the corps became more
representative of Greek society and less willing to accept the
supremacy of civilian rule. According to the revised constitution
of 1911, officers were prohibited from running for office, but
the propensity for them to become involved in politics by making
use of extra-parliamentary means increased dramatically throughout
the interwar period.

---

[21] Ibid.

[22] Christina Varda, 'Politevomenoi stratiotikoi stin Ellada sta teli tou 19ou aiona', *Mnimon*,
8, 1980-2, p. 53.

# 3

# THE MILITARY AND 'ETHNIC TRUTH'

The emergence of the Greek state and its institutions coincided with the gradual decline of the influence of Hellenic culture in south-eastern Europe. The very nature of the nationalist ideology that accompanied the state militated against the ecumenical spirit of a culture that was disseminated to the Christian Orthodox élites by the only source of higher education in the Balkans – the Church. Coopting Serbs, Vlachs, Albanians and Bulgars into the Hellenic linguistic tradition had not been resisted by the Balkan peoples so long as the education that served as a springboard to social mobility was not controlled by a single state.

The rise of different independence movements and the implicit tensions between the exclusivity of nationalism and the ecumenicity of the Church transformed the content of an identity that was prominent in south-eastern Europe. The new Greek state inherited a people homogenised by language and religion, but based its own ideology on the Western secular prototypes that had been ushered in by an enlightened merchant class. The identity that slowly took shape was a hybrid between an exclusive claim to antiquity and an all-inclusive religious tradition that had been colour-blind to race and ethnicity. The transformation elicited strong protest by the Ecumenical Patriarchate, but the single-minded efforts of the state resulted in ethnic parochialism engulfing the Church of Greece. There are few modern perceptions as anachronistic as the view that the Church was a vanguard of nationalism before the second half of the nineteenth century.[1]

The transition from ecumenicity to nationalism, heralding an entirely new development of Hellenic identity, was never registered

---

[1] Paschalis Kitromilides, ' "Imagined Communities" and Nationalism' in M. Blinkhorn and T. Veremis (eds), *Modern Greece: Nationalism and Nationality*, Athens: ELIAMEP, 1990, p. 33.

accurately in modern Greek perceptions. Mistaking two separate traditions as identical accounts for a serious malaise in the Greek psyche. Fear that an ever-contracting Hellenic culture in the Balkans threatens the very survival of the Greek nation is still responsible for a common misconception that Greece is diminishing when in fact it expanded continuously between independence and 1947.[2] The corollary of this fear was the birth of irredentism aspiring to a revival of a Greek empire that would bring Hellenism back to its true geographic dimensions. The purpose of the irredentist ideology that dominated Greek society in the nineteenth century was twofold. On the domestic front the 'grand idea' sought to extend the writ of central authority to a fragmented realm. On the external front Greece strove to liberate and reunite traditional Greek territories under Ottoman rule.

Up till the last quarter of the nineteenth century, the mission of the small force that formed the initial nucleus of the regular army was mostly to buttress the state and protect it from internal predators.[3] Furthermore the regular army, along with other improved institutions, constituted an attempt to emulate the West and attain the legitimacy bestowed by modernisation on every new state. Perceived truth and reality, or 'ethnic truth and truth',[4] were not easily reconcilable. The anonymous volunteer of the 1860s who left his comfortable existence in Constantinople to join the Greek army discovered that the condition of that institution and indeed of the entire Greek state fell short of his expectations.[5] However, perhaps without realising it, he became part of a process that incorporated individuals from all corners of the kingdom and even beyond it into the national community and, what was more

[2] The difference between pre-revolutionary ecumenical Hellenism and the ethnic nationalism of the state escaped even the keen eye of William Hardy McNeill, who deplored Greece's dwindling and 'beleaguered nationality' since independence. *The Metamorphosis of Greece since World War II*, Oxford: Basil Blackwell, 1978, p. 56.

[3] 'Neutralizing sectional interests and building a regular army formed one of the major components of the regency's statecraft.[...] It was in this context that it became imperative to develop a code of unifying national values that might provide the normative framework for bringing society under the control of the new state.' Kitromilides, p. 36.

[4] Romilly Jenkins, *The Dilessi Murders*, London: Longmans Green, 1961. Of course what Jenkins means is 'national' rather than 'ethnic' truth, but he tends to confuse the two. It was romantic nationalism that contributed to the acculturation of ethnic Albanians, Vlachs and Slavs into the Greek national community.

[5] Anonymous, *I stratiotiki zoe en Elladi*, Athens: Hermes, 1977, pp. 6-14.

important, into an imagined community.[6] The reader of his vivid account discovers the extraordinary appeal which the 'grand idea' exerted on Greeks of all walks of life. For the average citizen the adventurous prospect of liberating his unredeemed brethren elevated 'ethnic truth' above everyday reality and gave meaning to his otherwise mundane existence.[7]

Despite the concerted efforts of King Otto in the early 1850s, the progress of irredentism depended more on international conjuncture than on the raw will of the Greek people. During the Crimean war the cause suffered a major setback when the Anglo-French forces put a stop to Russian designs to dismember the Ottoman empire. An Allied blockade (1854-7) of the most vital Greek harbour obliged the King to withdraw his troops from Ottoman Thessaly and Epirus and prepared the way for his ultimate overthrow.[8]

Another decade passed before the coast was clear internationally for a sortie of Greek irregulars which led to yet another reversal. The suppression in 1869 of a major Cretan uprising against the Ottomans that raged for three whole years and, more significantly, the emerging Balkan nationalisms obliged the Greek state to review its priorities. Slavic nationalist movements, with their overlapping claims on the European provinces of the Ottoman empire, posed a new, formidable obstacle to Greek irredentism.

During the last quarter of the century Greek nationalism underwent a serious identity crisis. Faced with formidable external obstacles and financial problems, the official dedication to irredentism of the Ottonian period was overtaken by internal priorities. The most convincing reformer of his time, Harilaos Tricoupis, believed that national unification was unattainable without prior modernisation and economic development. His distaste for adventures abroad was shared by followers who viewed the obsessive adherents of irredentism as single-minded madmen obstructing progress at home.[9] There were others who disavowed the principle

---

[6] Benedict Anderson, *Imagined Communities: Reflections on the Origin and Spread of Nationalism*, London: Verso, 1983.

[7] The term 'grand idea' was first used in a 1844 parliament meeting by Ioannis Kolettis in support of the unredeemed Greeks. For the popular impact of the concept see the first-hand account of Charles Tuckerman, *The Greeks of Today*, London, 1872.

[8] The role of brigands in Otto's irredentist ventures is described by Spyridon Pilikas, *Apomnimonevmata*, Athens, 1893.

[9] Elli Skopetea, 'To Protypo Vasilio kai i Megali Idea (1830-1880)', unpubl. Ph.D. thesis, University of Thessaloniki, 1994, p. 332.

of the 'grand idea' altogether and felt that the state should pursue its own improvement as an end in itself.[10] The other side, however, castigated the state for its inertia in national issues and its self-seeking materialism. This criticism overlooked the bloodless incorporation of the Ionian islands in 1864 and the bread-basket of Thessaly in 1881, and glorified the unsuccessful and costly uprisings in Epirus, Thessaly and Crete. Anastasios Vyzantios, an influential journalist, deplored Greek inactivity: 'Behold our decline since 1821. [...] Where are the Greek dreams of fifty years ago? The descent in our ladder of expectations progresses with the passing years. The realm of the ideal Greece approaches the boundaries of the real one.'[11]

The thrust of the 'development' advocates was blunted by Tricoupis' ultimate failure. Throughout his terms in power he had given absolute priority to the modernisation of the state apparatus and to infrastructural works that would encourage the private sector to take the initiative. His costly undertakings led the state to bankruptcy and destroyed its credibility. When his cardinal opponent, Theodoros Diliyannis, took office, the state was briefly reconciled with the concept of its unredeemed nation, and irredentist passions were once more unleashed. In 1897 the Greek David confronted the Ottoman Goliath in the plain of Thessaly. However, the conclusion of the campaign bore no resemblance to the biblical outcome. The Greek forces were badly beaten and retreated in disarray. Only through foreign intervention was Greece saved from catastrophe, but the price of this service was the establishment of an international financial control agency to supervise the repayment of the country's debts to its foreign bondholders. By the end of the century the state had lost its credibility, both as the main representative of the nation and even as a reliable administrator of its own fortunes.

Between 1833 and 1897 the involvement of regular forces in political conspiracies and upheavals was minimal. Officers, whether ones who had risen from the ranks or graduates of the Academy, were imbued with a sense of professionalism that usually kept them away from political intrigues. The Acarnania rebellion of

---

[10] D. Bikelas, *Le rôle et les aspirations de la Grèce dans la Question d'Orient*, Paris, 1885, p. 23.

[11] Skopetea, p. 310.

1836 against the government was instigated by followers of the French and Russian parties and their local armed clients, and was put down by those rebels whom the government chose to employ in the '*Falanga*'—a venue of honorary retirement for veterans of the 1821 War of Independence.[12] Such local expressions of discontent against the state died out during the last decades of Ottonian rule.

The more conspicuous presence of officers in the September 1843 demonstration that forced King Otto to grant his subjects a constitution, and in his overthrow in 1862, was due to the fact that on both occasions wide public participation was mobilised. In neither instance did the military plan the event or take the initiative. In fact most military operations that caused embarassment to the state were the responsibility of politicians and public pressure.

Major irredentist upheavals in the second half of the century usually resulted in a spree of pillaging by the all too eager bands of 'volunteer' irregulars that exasperated their professional commanders. The 1854 expedition across the border, the 1867 misadventure in Crete, the 1878 single-day invasion of Thessaly and the costly general mobilisation of 1886 against Bulgaria that came to nothing were operations led by regular officers under official instructions and manned by lawless bands of mercenaries and brigands who discredited the state.[13] With the disaster of 1897[14] the credibility gap between 'ethnic truth' and truth became immense.

The sobering effect of 1897 on the officer corps slowly took the form of criticism of royalty and, in particular, of Prince Constantine, the Commander-in-Chief in that ill-conceived war. Much of the invective directed against the ineptitude of the heir-apparent to the Greek throne was published many years after the event by officers who, in the mean time, became attached to Constantine's later rival, Eleftherios Venizelos. However, there was considerable

---

[12] John Koliopoulos, *Listes*, Athens: Ermis, 1979, pp. 19-22.

[13] For the 1867 and 1886 incidents see Koliopoulos, *Brigands with a Cause*, pp. 184-6, 213-14. The 1878 events are rendered by an intelligent contemporary, Miltiades Seizanis, *I politiki tis Ellados kai i epanastasis tou 1878 en Makedonia, Ipiro kai Thessalia*, Athens, 1879.

[14] Officers were not without responsibility for the outbreak of the 1897 hostilities. '*Ethniki Etairia*', a secret organisation that inflamed public opinion and infiltrated the Ottoman territory with volunteers before the war, was founded in 1894 by junior officers. It was dissolved after the defeat. E. Stasinopoulos, *O Stratos tis protis ekatontaetias*, Athens, 1935, pp. 61-2; Al.-Mazarakis-Ainian, *Istoriki Meleti, 1821-1897, kai o polemos tou 1897*, vol. I, Athens, 1950, pp. 290-304. Yannis Pikros offers original evidence about the secret society: 'Pros ton polemo tou 1897', *Istoria tou ellinikou ethnous*, vol. XIV, Athens, 1977, p. 95.

contemporary criticism on 1897 which appears reliable. Nicolaos Dimitrakopoulos, who became a jurist of wide reputation, described in the darkest hues his own experience as a foot-soldier and placed much of the blame on Constantine and the crown.[15] However, two incidents convinced officers with qualms about royal favouritism that no politician could safely contradict the royal interest. They were connected with the bills of 1899 and 1902. In 1899 two drafts of a bill aimed at reforming the army were simultaneously introduced for discussion: the work, respectively, of the Army Affairs Minister, C. Koumoundouros, and the pro-royalist General Staff. Each treated Constantine's position in the army in a different way that threatened to spark a controversy between crown and parliament. Koumoundouros was promptly asked by Prime Minister Theotokis to withdraw his draft, and resigned. According to the new charter of the army that went through parliament in March 1900, Prince Constantine assumed two newly established posts: those of the 'General Commander' and the 'Inspector of the Army'. The Minister of Army Affairs was left with almost no authority, and this caused reactions among the military.[16] Disappointment with the Theotokis government drove many officers to place their hopes with Theodore Diliyannis who had promised during his 1902 campaign that he would revoke the unpopular law. In February 1903 Theodore Limbritis, Minister of Army Affairs in Diligiannis' government, introduced bills in parliament that reduced the powers conferred on Constantine. The reaction of the throne was immediate: like his predecessor, Limbritis was compelled to resign once Diliyannis yielded to royal pressure and withdrew the bill. This second disappointment convinced officers that politicians were unreliable and would never dare to oppose the royal authority. This realisation determined the subsequent behaviour of the officer corps in relation to the state and eventually led to their autonomous intervention in 1909.[17]

   Few corporate entities in Greek society were as attached to

---

[15] Nicolaos Dimitrakopoulos, *Polemika apomnemonevmata*, Athens, 1897, p. 140.

[16] Ministers of Army Affairs such as C. Koumoundouros were often officers who ran for office while on active duty. If they were elected to parliament their seniority would be frozen for the duration of their political term.

[17] E. Hourmouzi, 'I Ellada meta ton polemo tou 1897', *Istoria tou Ellinikou Ethnous*, vol. XIV, Athens, 1977, pp. 169-70. Aspreas differs from the opposition to Constantine over the 1900 controversy, but fails to offer a convincing argument in defence of the Prince: G. Aspreas, *Politiki istoria tis neoteras Ellados*, vol. III, Athens, 1924, p. 9.

the ideals propagated by state ideology as were the military. Education of officers in the Academy was supplemented with ancient Greek history[18] and an emotional acquaintance with a glorious heritage. The gloomy barracks resounded with references to an ancient past that would live again, and the anniversaries of independence or the deaths of philhellenes elicited orations in the spirit of Thucydides or even Pindar.[19] More than other Greeks, officers lived in the realm of 'ethnic truth' and deplored the state to which the nation had been condemned by adverse circumstances. The 'grand idea' treasured by all officers became the ideal vehicle of 'ethnic truth' and a promise of national renaissance.

The outcome of 1897 generated a wide discourse aimed at salvaging the imperilled nation from the blunders of an ineffectual state. Throughout the decade following the war, military exponents of irredentism came to the realisation that internal reforms were the necessary precondition for national rejuvenation. Some, such as Athanassios Souliotes-Nicolaides,[20] went as far as to disclaim the Greek state altogether and to look towards a multinational 'Eastern Empire' as the ideal stamping-ground of the modern Greeks.

The *pronunciamento* (display of force) of 1909 was the first autonomous political action ever taken by the Greek military. Yet so unaccustomed were they to pressing their demands on the state that the 250 conspirator officers who gathered in the barracks of the Goudi camp on the night of 14 August 1909 presented their grievances in the most timid language. The next morning, King and government were alerted to the disquieting fact that the army was protesting against political corruption, royal

---

[18] George Tertsetis left a vivid account of his experience in 1832 as a professor of Greek history in the Military Academy (Evelpidon). While lecturing on Plato's *Crito*, he discovered that the cadets (some as young as fourteen years old) were so engrossed in his lecture that they offered to light his reading with candles after the sun had gone down. 'As I left the room I felt like Socrates, blessing his students who were no more his progeny in spirit and blood than my own': Dinos Conomos (ed.), *George Tertsetis. Logoi kai dokimia*, vol. II, Athens, 1969, p. 350.

[19] See oration of K.A.R. Rangavis in memory of Charles Fabvier, *Logos Ekphonitheis en Akropoli*, Athens: Vilaras and Lioubis Press, 1855, pp. 1-14.

[20] Athanassios Souliotes, an officer in the Greek army, served as a volunteer in Macedonia during the struggle between Greeks and Bulgarians for the Ottoman legacy (1903-8). He assumed the name Nicolaides and was sent to Constantinople in 1908 to initiate secret contacts with the Ottoman authorities. In his *Organosis Constantinoupoleos*, Athens: Dodoni 1984, he propagated the idea of maintaining the Ottoman empire intact as a multinational hothouse of Hellenism.

patronage in the forces and mismanagement of public affairs in general. Without having to fire a single shot, the military reaped an unexpected triumph as, one after another, the institutions of the state surrendered to their demands. The King withdrew his princes from their military commands (one of the few 'heroes' of 1897, General C. Smolensky, took over Constantine's posts), the government of Ioannis Rallis resigned, and the leader of the third party in parliament, Kyriakoulis Mavromichalis, became Prime Minister with the blessing of the insurgents.[21]

The young officers (lieutenants and captains) who joined forces to form the 'Military League' which launched the *pronunciamento* were only conscious of their own exasperation with the political mishandling of national priorities, the exclusiveness of royal clientelism and their overall professional grievances. They could not possibly have foreseen that their cause would soon be heralded as the cause of an entire nation.

The first caucus to gather in Theodore Pangalos' home in October 1908 was made up entirely of lieutenants. In a subsequent meeting a protocol was drafted and signed by nine lieutenants and a single captain.[22] Although in 1909 one-third of officers in the artillery, engineers, infantry and cavalry were Academy graduates (the percentage declined in lower ranks), only one out of ten of the original gathering was not an Academy graduate and had risen from the ranks.

The 'Military League' had been formed in May 1909 when a group of captains who had seen action in the covert Macedonian war merged with the lieutenants. The revolutionary zeal of its members was in inverse proportion to their years of service and those who had risen from the ranks were on the whole more content with their professional status than the well-to-do from the Academy. The reasons that sparked off their common action had been hibernating for almost a decade before the rapid Balkan developments of 1908 and the subsequent affronts of the Young

[21] The literature on the 1909 events is vast. The memoirs of Colonel Zorbas, who was asked to lead the 'Military League', are coloured by the prejudices of their author but contain valuable first-hand information. Nicolaou Zorba, *Apomnimonevmata*, Athens, 1925. By far the best account by a contemporary is contained in a letter written by the Socialist poet, Costas Hatzopoulos, to a German neohellenist, Karl Dieterich, on 20 February 1910, published in the literary journal *O Noumas*, 1922, no. 32, issue 19, pp. 118-23.

[22] Theodoros Pangalos, *Ta Apomnimonevmata mou*, vol. A, Athens: Aetos, 1950 pp. 46-9.

Turks against Greece rallied the military around the endangered nation-state. The prospect of regional conflict caused peacetime ambiguities to be dispensed with, and the officers felt free to promote professional interests while serving a national cause.

The existence of the 'Military League' was disclosed to the government on 25 June 1909 by an agent who had been present at a meeting of the conspiracy. Once news of the meeting reached the authorities, the 'lieutenants' and 'captains' patched up their differences and elected a temporary governing body of fifteen to draft a new protocol. The government of Georgios Theotokis[23] resigned on 4 July 1909 and Dimitrios Rallis was sworn into office. Despite the critical position he had taken towards the crown in the past, Rallis once in power began to praise the performance of Crown Prince Constantine in military affairs. Furthermore, twelve of the more active members of the 'League' were sacked for insubordination and others were given prison sentences. This served as the spark that ignited the dry military haystack. After sounding out several candidates, the 'League' decided to ask a respected officer who had fallen out with the crown to become leader of the organisation. This was Colonel Nicolaos Zorbas. He had been made a scapegoat by the royal interest for the 1897 disaster, and although he was not promoted for years, his assignments as Inspector of War Material and as Director of the Military Academy won him the admiration of young officers for his outspoken criticism of the establishment that ruled the army. Following the success in Goudi, the military appealed for support to the people. A huge demonstration on 14 September proved that public sympathy for the officers was both unqualified and intense,[24] yet neither the members of the 'League'

---

[23] In 1906-7 Theotokis put into effect a programme of significant arms purchases, and his 1908 military manoeuvres proved that the Greek army was in good condition. Even such an avowed member of the 'League' as Pangalos testifies to this in his memoirs, pp. 43-4. For a general account of the Theotokis reforms see S. Victor Papacosma, *The Military in Greek Politics: The 1909 Coup d'Etat*, Kent, OH: Kent State University Press, 1977, pp. 24-6.

[24] The massive support for the 'Revolution of 1909' (as it was later called) was seen by various historians and social analysts as proof that the event was a veritable bourgeois revolution. Georgios Ventiris has been the strongest exponent of the 'middle-class revolution' theory: G. Ventiris, *I Ellas tou 1910-1920*, vol. A, Athens: Ikaros, 1970 (1st edn Pyrsos, 1931), Chapter I. George Dertilis has made an intelligent refutation of this theory in his *Kinonikos metaschimatismos kai stratiotiki epemvasi, 1880-1909*, Athens: Exantas, 1977, pp. 115-21. The first social analysis of the Goudi phenomenon was made by Georgios Skleros

nor the politicians had any programme of action or priorities in mind.

The Souliotes-Nicolaides correspondence conveys the prevailing confusion among members of the 'League'. Although Souliotes propagated the independence of the nation from the state, he felt that 'if the nation lends a hand to the state, we will win the war and then we will implement our programme quickly'.[25] An officer who made his name in the struggle for Macedonia, Spyros Spyromelios, made some perceptive observations about his colleagues in a letter to Nicolaos Zorbas: 'The army is not an autonomous body but an organised class which reflects the virtues and evils of the society that has produced it.'[26] He went on to point out, however, that 'this class which is the best organised body in society, is the only force that could support the hopes of the nation'.[27] Thus for a brief period the military attained wide social recognition and assumed the task of guiding the establishment, and indeed the nation, to vital reforms which all applauded but none could determine.

Most European powers greeted the *coup* at Goudi with hostility. The international financial control imposed on Greece as a consequence of the 1897 war tried to ensure that no political turbulence or large military expenditure would divert Greek resources from the prompt servicing of Greece's foreign loans.[28] The British King Edward VII asked that ships of the Mediterranean fleet remain moored off Faliron so that the King of Greece could rely on them for moral support. No great power wished to see the dynasty forced out by the younger and more militant members of the 'Military League' who executed the *coup*; this would have appeared to be the first step leading to unknown developments. The British would suffer the loss of a firm friend in King George, and Germany in the heir to the throne, Crown Prince Constantine. Throughout

---

in *To Koinonikon mas zitima*. See publication in *Erga*, Athens: Epikairotita, 1976, pp. 292-7.

[25] Letter to Ion dated March 1909, Correspondence of Souliotes-Nicolaides: Letters to Ion, Athens: Gennadios Library.

[26] See the Spyros Spyromelios papers at the Historical and Ethnological Society of Greece, file: 'Macedonian Struggle, 1897-Military League'. This copy of the original is dated January-February 1910.

[27] *Ibid.*

[28] Papacosma, pp. 101-2.

the period of his ordeal (the autumn of 1909 and the winter of 1910), George confided his worries to the British Minister in Athens, Sir Francis Elliot.[29]

Although the 'Military League' shrunk from overthrowing the civilian authorities, it nevertheless influenced the deliberations of parliament between August 1909 and January 1910 and encouraged the legislative body to pass no less than 169 bills during that time.[30] By the end of 1909, however, tensions between politicians and the military were rising, especially since the younger and more radical elements in the 'League' pressed for outright control of the state. At that particular juncture 'League' members decided to seek advice from a Cretan politician who had made his mark by opposing the appointment of Prince George (second son of King George) as high commissioner of Crete: Eleftherios Venizelos. He was greeted at Piraeus harbour on 10 January 1910 by eager officers, and advised his hosts to ease themselves out of power and supervise the transition to a parliamentary form of government that would be friendly to their cause. The military followed his advice. By the end of 1910 Venizelos was established in power with an overwhelming majority in parliament; in the assembly of January 1911, 300 out of 364 deputies were Venizelists. His subsequent performance in Greek politics removed most of the causes of the upheaval of 1909, and his sweeping reforms prepared the state for its irredentist thrust. The gap between 'ethnic truth' and truth was bridged at last and the military could claim some credit for this extraordinary feat.[31]

---

[29] *Ibid.*, pp. 83, 106, 123.

[30] T. Veremis, *I epemvaseis tou stratou stin elliniki politiki, 1916-1936*, Athens: Exantas, 1977, p. 24.

[31] T. Veremis, 'Martyries gia to Stratiotiko Kinima tou 1909 kai tis epemvaseis tou stin politiki zoe tis Ellados', *Deltion tis istorikis kai ethnologikis etaireias tis Ellados*, vol. 25, Athens, 1982, pp. 395-426.

# 4

# THE IMPACT OF THE FIRST WORLD WAR ON CIVIL-MILITARY RELATIONS

Greece's armed involvement on the side of the Triple Entente in the First World War was accomplished at the expense of internal peace and the orderly operation of parliamentary politics. The clash between the heads of state and government in 1915 over neutrality or Greece's alliance with England and France disrupted the consensual basis on which Greek politics had rested in the past. The break between King and Prime Minister had a direct impact on military institutions and unleashed forces that had been simmering since the turn of the century.

With a parliamentary system already seventy years old in 1914 and an orderly record surpassed by few European examples, the Greek state could claim the allegiance of its armed forces with only a brief interval in 1909. The involvement of the military in politics between 1911 and 1915 was minimal. Venizelos' forceful leadership as well as the priorities of the two Balkan wars (1912-13) left little room for military opposition. The grievances of the 1909 officers over their professional prospects were satisfied by war needs, and the expansion of the corps speeded up promotions to a degree unprecedented in Greek military history. It is not therefore surprising that the protagonists of 1909 did not react effectively against Venizelos' decisions to reinstate the royal presence in the armed forces by appointing Crown Prince Constantine as Inspector-General and to pardon royalist officers who had actively opposed the *pronunciamento*.[1]

---

[1] Douglas Dakin, *The Unification of Greece, 1770-1923*, London: Ernest Benn, 1972, pp. 188-9. For an appraisal of the parliamentary debate (14 June 1911) on the law that would make Constantine Inspector-General of the army and its consequences for the democratic polity, see N. Alivizatos, *I syntagmatiki thesi ton enoplon dynameon*, Athens: Sakkoulas, 1987, pp. 67-70.

A supporter of irredentism, Venizelos gave absolute priority to the creation of a strong army. Thus in his cabinet of 1911 he assumed the Ministries of both Army and Navy to ensure that his policy would be carried out. In October 1912 an army of 148,000 men was mobilised. By 1913, with the return of immigrants from the United States to enlist and the call-up of new classes, the number had grown to 200,000.[2]

In 1914 the morale of the officer corps was high because its performance in the Balkan wars had redeemed it from the 1897 defeat and so increased its popularity. As for promotions, officers had been satisfied beyond their wildest expectations. Between 1909 and 1914 sergeants became lieutenants, captains and colonels. Venizelos had completed his most important social and institutional reforms and Greece had increased its territory from 64,786 to 108,606 square kilometers and its population from 2,666,000 to 4,363,000.[3] The national division or schism (*dichasmos*) came like a bolt from the blue.

The issue which subsequently caused vehement division between the Greeks was basically centred on a choice of foreign policy. Either the nation would enter the war on the side of the Entente to protect territories won during the Balkan wars – a policy held by the anglophile Venizelos – or neutrality would be observed, as was advocated by the germanophile King Constantine. Not without justification the public attached great significance to this decision because Greece's future did indeed depend on how conflict among the great powers would be resolved.[4] The subsequent clash of personalities between Venizelos and Constantine made the controversy an acrimonious contest of personal loyalties.

Venizelos resigned for the first time in March 1914 as a result of the King's final decision to reject his plan of Greek participation

---

[2] 'The Success of the Greek Army in the Recent Balkan Wars', *Army Review*, January 1914, London, pp. 48-52.

[3] E. Prevelakis, 'Eleftherios Venizelos and the Balkan Wars', *Balkan Studies Journal*, Thessaloniki, 1966, p. 378. E. Driault, *Histoire diplomatique de la Grèce de 1821 à nos jours*, Paris: Presses Universitaires de France, 1926, vol. V, p. 136.

[4] N. Kaltchas, *Introduction to the Constitutional History of Modern Greece*, New York, 1940, p. 6. 'For a century the course of Greek politics was determined by the exigences of foreign policy rather than by the correlation and clash of forces within the nation. The fact that the anti-monarchy movement originated in a conflict over foreign policy and triumphed as a result of military defeat is a striking demonstration of the influence of international factors and the protecting powers – the third party to the constitutional development of modern Greece.' *Ibid.*, p. 137.

in the operation against the Dardanelles. At the general election of 13 June 1915, the Liberal party emerged victorious with 184 seats in a chamber of 310. On 4 October, the day of the Bulgarian attack on Serbia, Venizelos stated his government's intention to honour Greece's obligation to Serbia by entering the war against its aggressor. Constantine rejected his Prime Minister's proposition, thus forcing him to resign once more.[5]

The abstention of the Liberal party from the elections of December 1915 marked the start of a long struggle between the King and Venizelos, who accused Constantine of ignoring the constitution[6] and took the issue to his friends in the army and to officers with grievances against the crown. Some of the leading figures of 1909 were convinced by the argument of the Liberals that the King had no right to ignore the will of the electorate, but others had lost their old zeal for reform and did not wish to jeopardise their promising careers by opposing him. Most members of the 'League' of 1909 had been Academy graduates with high professional expectations and a strong drive for reform, and by 1915 they had been made content by promotions and thus become conservative in outlook.[7] We shall not examine here the question of whether Venizelos was justified in involving the military in the political disputes of 1916, but we shall try to prove in the following pages that he in fact did so.

The Venizelos revolt of 1916 in Thessaloniki had a lasting effect on the development of the Greek army. Those officers

---

[5] J. Campbell and P. Sherrard, *Modern Greece*, London: Ernest Bern, 1968, p. 120. For an excellent analysis of Venizelos and Constantine as the charismatic prototypes attracting the devotion of the two opposed camps, see George Th. Mavrogordatos, *Stillborn Republic: Social Coalitions and Party Strategies in Greece, 1922-1936*, Berkeley: University of California Press, 1983, pp. 55-64.

[6] 'Neither constitution nor laws made it clear whether the King in his exercise of his undeniable right to appoint and dismiss ministers had the power to dismiss a Prime Minister who had a majority in parliament and to compound the difficulty by doing the same thing twice in the same year and after the election had reaffirmed the majority' J. Carey and A. Carey, *The Web of Modern Greek Politics*, New York: Columbia University Press, 1968, p. 93.

[7] Out of the following members of the Military League of 1909 – Tombros, Hadjimihalis, Passaris, Psychas, Falireas, Sarros, Georgakopoulos, Couvelis, Liolios, Mimikos, Pappas, Lidorikis, Parnassidis, Tavoularis, Katsoulis, Pangalos, Katheniotis, Zymbrakakis, Hadjikyriakos, Havinis and Fikioris – the latter six joined the 'National Defence' of 1916, at least four became ardent royalists, and the rest remained at their posts serving the official government when the split occurred. T. Veremis, *I epemvasis tou stratou stin elliniki politiki*, Athens: Odysseas, 1983, p. 65.

who either by design or accident found themselves on the side of the insurgents became a cause of disruption in the military hierarchy for at least two decades. George Ventiris, the most articulate of Venizelist apologists, dismissed his mentor's involvement in the planning of the revolt.[8] The Venizelist line of argument – namely that the uprising had been a spontaneous act of the Macedonians along with the Greek military stationed in their province – is also promoted by Captain Neokosmos Grigoriadis, an early participant: 'Those who organised the revolt had no time to ask for advice or to improve their organisation.[...] Venizelos had not been consulted.'[9]

Grigoriadis' ignorance of Venizelos' plans is typical of the relationship between the latter and his military clients. By encouraging the impression among junior officers of the 'National Defence'[10] that he had played no part in their decision to rebel, he could make it appear that he was bowing to their will rather than they to his. As late as June 1916, Lieutenant Vakas was still ignorant of Venizelos' intentions:

> In June 1916 there were 70-80 officers in Eastern Macedonia in the Fourth and Fifth Army Corps wanting to help Venizelos prevail, convinced that his leadership alone could avert the catastrophe of our race...We had repeatedly sent emissaries to him, and more recently Captains Havinis and Kondylis, but Venizelos advised us to remain calm. We in Eastern Macedonia had no idea what the ethnarch had in mind.[11]

Periclis Argyropoulos, the former Venizelist Prefect of Thessaloniki, had been in contact with French officials in the city as well as with Venizelos. At the beginning of December 1915 he was informed by his friend Alexandros Zannas that the French command had given up hope that Constantine would enter the war on the side of the Entente, and had decided to allow the

---

[8] G. Ventiris, *I Ellas tou 1910-20*, vol. II, Athens: Ikaros 1971, p. 211.

[9] N. Grigoriadis, *Ethniki amyna tis Thessalonikis tou 1916*, Athens, 1960, p. 18.

[10] 'National Defence' (*Ethniki Amyna*): the organisation that launched the revolt of 1916 in Thessaloniki was directed against the policy of neutrality inspired by King Constantine. The only military member in the initial phase of the revolt was Colonel Pamikos Zymbrakakis, commander of the mounted police in Thessaloniki.

[11] D. Vakas, *O Venizelos, polemikos igetis*, Athens: Daremas, 1965, p. 75. The word 'ethnarch', meaning head of the nation, is here used by an adoring follower.

Serbian King-in-exile to establish his headquarters in Thessaloniki. This decision, according to Zannas, amounted to a deposition of the Greek authorities in Macedonia:

> We decided to act against the threat. After three days of discussions [4, 5 and 7 December 1915] Zannas and I along with other members of the Liberal Club signed a protocol with the intention of forming the 'National Defence'....[12]

Although by the end of 1915 Argyropoulos had been called up for military service, he continued to be in touch with Venizelos and the organisation in Thessaloniki.[13]

The date of the protocol of the 'National Defence' coincided with a letter from Venizelos to General Leonidas Paraskevopoulos, the influential commander of the 3rd Army Corps. Thanking the General for his good wishes on his nameday, Venizelos added:

> ...Is there, I wonder, still an army to support our participation [in the war on the side of the Entente] or has the destruction of military morale effected by the General Staff transformed our forces into a mere gathering of docile individuals unable to make any decisions?[14]

This letter gives an early hint by Venizelos of what the position of the military should be towards official policy.

In view of recent publications on Venizelos' foreign contacts in 1916, there is evidence that he was contemplating a coup with the help of the French and the English in May. His suggestion that he should go to Thessaloniki with General Danglis to form a provisional pro-Entente government found no support in London and was not pressed any further. However, Venizelos gave his approval to the recruitment of Greek volunteers by the French in Macedonia.[15] When the French Commander Sarrail proclaimed a state of siege in the city of Thessaloniki, the time seemed to

---

[12] P. Argyropoulos, *Apomnimonevmata*, Athens, 1970, p. 180. A. Zannas, article in the newspaper *To Vima* of 19 May 1959. Zannas had been in contact with Venizelos since November 1915.

[13] Argyropoulos, p. 182.

[14] Letter from the archives of Paraskevopoulos in the possession of Nikos Petsalis, dated 24 December 1915.

[15] D. Portolos, 'Greek Foreign Policy, September 1916 to October 1919', unpubl. Ph.D. thesis, Birkbeck College, University of London, 1974, p. 34.

be ripe for a separatist movement. Compton Mackenzie, Director of British Intelligence in Athens, commented on Venizelos' dilemma in his memoirs:

> The disinclination of Mr Venizelos to take the plunge at the beginning of June may have been increased by the unsatisfactory relations that now existed between the French and British Commands. [...] General Milne [the British commander]... had shown himself openly opposed to the proclamation of martial law in Salonica...[16]

While appearing to discourage revolutionary activities, Venizelos was biding his time. Argyropoulos may not have been aware of all the details of his leader's negotiations with the Entente, but certainly knew that he was planning to move against the government.[17]

> Venizelos, who since December 1915 had been preparing to intervene by revolutionary means, felt he could no longer remain a spectator of the unfolding treachery [this is a reference to the capitulation of Fort Rupel in eastern Macedonia to the Bulgarians; in his frantic efforts to keep Greece out of the war, Constantine agreed to give up the fort and its entire garrison]. He called me while I was on leave and told me that he had already communicated to the French and British ambassadors that in view of the Bulgarian invasion of Greece he had decided to abandon legality. He asked me to announce his decision to our organisation in Thessaloniki. I accepted with great joy.[18]

At the beginning of August 1916, a restless infantry captain, Nicolaos Plastiras, along with several future members of the 'National Defence' (Tertikas, Protosyngelos and others) asked Venizelos to advise them whether they should abandon their posts to join the French army in Thessaloniki. Venizelos, who was anxious to secure as much support as he could get for his intended *coup*, begged them to wait until he had made his final appeal to the King to enter the war. He assured them that if Constantine remained

---

[16] Compton Mackenzie, *Greek Memories*, London: Chatto & Windus, 1939, p. 179.

[17] Argyropoulos, p. 182.

[18] *Ibid.*, p. 183.

adamant he would organise a revolutionary army for the defence of the country, and referred them to his trusted Colonel Fikioris for further instruction. Fikioris asked them to seek out officers sympathetic to the Venizelist cause and organise them for possible action in Macedonia.[19]

Having failed once more to convince the King, Venizelos resumed his contact with the military commanders. On 17 August he wrote to General Leonidas Paraskevopoulos as follows, urging him to join the 'National Defence' movement:

Dear General,

Mr Diomidis[20] is coming to talk to you on my behalf. In view of Romania's entry in the war, any further hesitation on our part to enter the war is no longer a mere mistake of policy but rather a criminal act against the nation. Furthermore we are in danger of having Bulgaria sign a separate peace treaty with the Entente, annexing all Greek territory already in its possession and maybe more. [...] Only the army can still save us from such a predicament. The heaviest responsibility lies with the 3rd Army Corps under your command. If the 3rd Army Corps decides to throw in its lot with those who are trying to force Bulgarians out of Greek territory, the government might feel coerced into joining the war effort. But even if that fails to materialise, you would still have made the right decision.

General, do not hesitate to take the step. And if you feel that my career up to this point entitles me to speak with any authority, I assure you that I will bear all political responsibility for the act which I strongly recommend.[21]

The officers who joined the 'National Defence' between August 1916 and March 1917 were only a small percentage of the whole officer corps. Out of 4,500 officers in the Greek army, only 280-300 regular officers joined. The initial shortage of regular

---

[19] I. Peponis, *Nicolaos Plastiras (1890-1945)*, vol. 1, Athens, 1946, pp. 41-4.

[20] Alexandros Diomidis, a prominent economist and later governor of the National Bank, had acted as Venizelos' emissary to Paraskevopoulos, who was married to Diomidis' sister.

[21] Letter of Venizelos to Paraskevopoulos from the latter's archive held by Nicos Petsalis-Diomidis.

officers was more than compensated for by a large contingent of reserve officers who in time acquired regular commissions.

The decision of the Greek government to demobilise troops as a further guarantee of its neutrality caused great apprehension to Venizelos, who felt it would be futile to launch a *coup* in Thessaloniki without support from Greek forces. As it turned out, he had been over-optimistic in assuming that the military commanders in Macedonia could be persuaded to assist his cause. After the government had refused his plea to exclude the troops in Macedonia from the demobilisation plan, Venizelos decided to postpone action in Thessaloniki. The outbreak of the revolt in August 1916 took him by surprise, and Alexandros Zannas had to risk a trip through hostile government territory to pacify the angry Liberal leader in Athens.[22]

When the revolt began, demobilised troops had not yet been moved from Thessaloniki. Instead of aiding the 'National Defence', however, the 11th (demobilised) Division under General Tricoupis chose to remain loyal to the government and the King, and turned against the insurgents. Ignoring British protests, the Commander-in-Chief, General Sarrail, promptly intervened, forcing the 11th Division out of the city, and helped the members of the 'Defence' install their own provisional government.[23] Argyropoulos, who played an important part in the uprising, admitted the failure of his organisation to infiltrate the army. Only one officer defected from the entire 11th Division; a unit of lesser significance under Constantine Mazarakis supported the revolt.[24]

The fact that only a small number of regular officers joined the movement in Thessaloniki did not necessarily give a true picture of the feelings of the officer corps. Leonidas Spais mentions in his memoirs that only seven officers from his regiment – two of them Academy graduates – escaped to Thessaloniki; the rest were bound by family obligations and had to stay.[25] Many officers – especially after the surrender of Fort Rupel to the Bulgarians – agreed with the objectives of the 'Defence' but felt bound by their oath of allegiance to the King. Others were afraid of aban-

---

[22] Incident related to the author by Mrs A. Zannas.

[23] Argyropoulos, pp. 191-2.

[24] *Ibid.*, p. 210.

[25] L. Spais, *Peninta chronia stratiotis*, Athens, 1970, p. 89.

doning their families to the mercy of fanatical royalists and the marauding 'reservists'.[26] A letter by Major Kalogeras to General Panayotis Danglis in Thessaloniki[27] makes this clear. General Moschopoulos, who had been sounded by Kalogeras, refused to join the movement because he believed that extremist officers such as the Zymbrakakis brothers would eventually put pressure on Venizelos to abolish the monarchy.[28] Moschopoulos, who agreed in principle with the need to fight against the Bulgarian invasion, became Constantine's choice to replace Dousmanis and Metaxas in the General Staff. By seeming to soften his position, the King had managed to keep the British hopeful that he would finally enter the war on their side.[29]

Pangalos, who apparently felt that he had been cheated of his rightful position in the operation, attacked its leaders for their untimely decision to act. Throughout his memoirs he never ceases to attribute the problems that bedevilled the revolt of 1916 to its having been launched prematurely. He claims that if Argyropoulos and Zymbrakakis had waited for a signal from Venizelos instead of acting on their own initiative, the movement would have gained respectability and therefore have attracted wider support among the military. Although Pangalos' assertion is not unfounded, he presses it with such emotion that it is hard not to assume that his view is biased by his own aspirations. On page 125 of his memoirs he claims that of the sixty officers who had promised to support a pro-Entente coup, only fifteen appeared in Thessaloniki; only six pages later there are said to be seventy officers pledged to the cause, of whom thirty decided to appear when the *coup* took place. He accuses the Zymbrakakis-Mazarakis clique, as he calls it, of arbitrarily awarding regular commissions

---

[26] The paramilitary organisation of the 'League of Epistrati' or 'reservists' included civilians who had fought in the Balkan wars as reserve officers. They were presumably responding to a mock mobilisation against the enemies of the King. Although the organisation was not strictly legal, it was led by such a prominent royalist as Colonel Metaxas and members of the royal family. Soldiers disguised as civilians often took part in 'reservist' demonstrations against the Entente and in raids against the homes of Venizelists. Between August and December 1916 they caused considerable damage.

[27] In September 1916 Venizelos, Admiral Pavlos Koundouriotis and the former Chief of General Staff Panayotis Danglis landed in Thessaloniki to form a triumvirate that would manage the administration of Greek participation in the war. A provisional government in direct rivalry to that in Athens was established.

[28] P. Danglis, *Anamniseis, engrapha, allilographia*, vol. 2, Athens, 1965, p. 199-201.

[29] *Ibid.*, p. 201.

to its clients.[30] Officers of the Military Academy who joined the 'Defence' were mostly of junior rank. Along with the scores of reserve officers who were given regular commissions, they became the most consistent clients of Venizelos in the army between 1916 and 1923.

On 24 September 1916 a despatch from the British consul in Thessaloniki included the following information about troops who had joined the 'Defence':

> Christodoulou's soldiers, who appear to have been told that the whole of the Saloniki Division had adhered to the movement, were disappointed when they found out that this was not the case and there was much dissatisfaction among them. Some managed to desert to their homes and others caused a riot in their barracks. This was put down at once and half a dozen of them lost their lives. [...] Recruits have come in reluctantly from the country districts. This is particularly the case in Halkidiki where it was found necessary to send Captain Kondylis...with a press gang to bring them in. He met with a very unfavourable reception and at Galatista the peasantry offered armed resistance. Several of them were shot.[...] The general feeling seems to be that without Mr Venizelos' open patronage the Salonica revolution cannot be a success....[31]

According to British diplomats the movement had not quite succeeded until Venizelos, accompanied by Koundouriotis and Danglis, appeared in Thessaloniki.

> In continuation of my despatch No. 80 of the 24th ultimo, I have the honour to report that the departure of Mr Venizelos from Athens and the establishment by him of a provisional government in Crete came in the nick of time to save the movement here [Thessaloniki] which to all appearances was in a poor way.[...] Not only has Mr Venizelos' action put fresh spirit into its promoters here, but it has encouraged recruits to come forward from Macedonia where, as I have already

---

[30] Th. Pangalos, *Ta apomnimonevmata mou*, vol. 2, Athens 1959, pp. 125, 156, 157, 193, 194.

[31] Christodoulou was a colonel who had been active in 1909. FO 371/2625/203978/12 October. Despatch by Wratislow from Thessaloniki to Elliot in Athens. Sir Francis Elliot was the British Minister in Athens.

reported, very little enthusiasm had hitherto been manifested. The Committee of National Defence...assured him [Venizelos] of their readiness to obey his orders. The Committee must now have at its disposal nearly twenty thousand men but the majority are only raw material and need prolonged training to make them of any use as soldiers.[32]

Regardless of what position one chooses to take over the question of Greece's entry into the war on the side of the Entente, it would be necessary to suggest that Franco-British infringements of Greek national integrity throughout 1916 contributed greatly to the sense of offended *philotimo* (honour) in Athens. The germanophile Constantine's policy of neutrality found support in that segment of the population whose xenophobia was aggravated by high-handed Franco-British tactics. Drawing up lists of royalists and German nationals to be deported, effecting house searches independently of any legal authority and delivering ultimatums to the King, the legations of the two powers in Athens had indeed become veritable states within the state.[33] The outcry against blatant foreign intervention was heightened during the blockade of Piraeus and the landing of its colonial troops by France in December 1916. Armed civilians and reservists clashed with the foreign intruders and vowed to protect their King. But the Allies demanded simultaneously that the Greek government should withdraw its forces from Thessaly and move them to southern Greece. For Constantine to comply would have amounted to leaving territories still under his control exposed to foreign influence or to a Venizelist attack.[34]

Forced by a Venizelist ultimatum and French pressure, Constantine finally abdicated in favour of his second son, Alexander (the heir-apparent being politically tainted), and left Greece on

[32] FO 371/2625/210988/21 October 1916. Despatch from Wratislow in Thessaloniki to Elliot in Athens – Des. No. 235 to FO.

[33] Compton Mackenzie's *Greek Memories* provide en eye-witness account of foreign activities in Athens. A letter from British Minister at Athens Sir Francis Elliot to Sir Edward Grey, written on 20 April 1916, is quoted on page 131: 'It is necessary for us to act in close agreement with Mr Venizelos and to be ready to use a show of naval force when the proper time comes. Since we have already committed so many infractions of the rights of Greece as an independent and neutral State, we need not hesitate to take a further step.' See also pp. 206, 220, 222, 322 and 323.

[34] George Leon, *Greece and the Great Powers, 1914-17*, Thessaloniki: Institute for Balkan Studies, 1974, pp. 439-46.

2 July 1917. At about the same time French troops occupied Thessaly.[35] Ten days later Venizelos returned from Thessaloniki to assume the reins of government in Athens and on 2 July 1917 the armies of the two countries joined together on the Macedonian front, thus officially terminating Greek neutrality. The return of Venizelos was followed by a proclamation of martial law and a purge of Constantinists from the civil service and the army. Senior officers who were known germanophiles were removed from their commands and many royalist politicians were exiled.[36] The task of merging two parallel military hierarchies, embittered by political passion, was never properly accomplished. Officers of the 'National Defence' were viewed by their Athens colleagues as a band of adventurers who would not hesitate to promote their interests 'with French bayonets'. The mutual ties of dependence between the Venizelist politicians and the officers of the 'Defence' tightened with every royalist threat, and created the impression that a separate order in the army was being encouraged by the government.

In October 1916 the provisional government of Thessaloniki introduced an act whereby promotion would be granted for heroic deeds in the field of action. It was clear that only officers of the 'Defence' would benefit from such a measure. Pangalos, head of personnel in the Ministry of Army Affairs, devised his own methods of self-promotion. General Danglis, who failed to check the transgressions of this officer, wrote in his memoirs:

Pangalos, who was in complete control of Michalacopoulos [Minister of Army Affairs], ... wished to achieve his own promotion despite the fact that he had become lieutenant-colonel a mere ten months ago (May 1917). Not being able to take advantage of promotions 'on special request' he introduced a plan effecting mass promotions. [...] In December 1917, before Venizelos' return from Paris, Michalakopoulos promoted 1,500 officers from all ranks. [...] Pangalos was one of the 65 lieutenant-

---

[35] N. Petsalis-Diomidis, *I Ellada ton dyo kyverniseon*, Athens: Filippotis, 1988, p. 81. This publication contains a wealth of documentation on the diplomacy of Venizelos' government in Thessaloniki.

[36] S. Markezinis, *Politiki Istoria tis Neoteras Ellados*, vol. 4, Athens: Papyros, 1968, pp. 210, 222, 230.

colonels who became colonels without any substantial reason. Many had been promoted only a few months before.[37]

Arbitrary acts and favouritism reigned in matters concerning the Army List. In spite of a law clearly specifying that at least ten years of service were necessary before an officer could attain the rank of major, officers had done so between 1917 and 1919 after only four or five years' service. (Although this phenomenon is not unusual in wartime promotions, in this particular instance 'Defence' officers appeared to be the sole beneficiaries.) Venizelos, when warned by Danglis of what was happening, answered that there was no way of reversing accomplished facts.[38] Settling political scores by dismissal had become common practice in both army and navy.

> The new Minister of Marine [Koundouriotis] is actively engaged in changing the entire personnel of the navy... After the departure of Venizelist officers... many remaining royalist officers were promoted, now that the Venizelist officers are returning, numbers are too great. Difficulty is being met by arbitrary retiring of a number of royalist officers who are being retired for purely political reasons.[39]

The new government was not only faced with the task of dismissing officials guilty or suspect of royalism, but also with the problem of providing places for the officials of the provisional government. On 6 July 1917, 134 field officers were placed '*en disponibilité*' – without attachments. The list included Generals Sotilis, Gennadis, Kallaris, Dousmanis and Yannakitsas, a former Minister of Army Affairs. General Papoulas, a leading 'reservist', did not wait to be dismissed but fled to Acarnania and from there to the mountains of Aetolia. When a British diplomat complained to Venizelos about the widespread dismissals, the Cretan politician replied that he was endeavouring to be as moderate as possible by imprisoning only fifteen out of the 134 who had been dismissed. He had some justification for believing that these officers would cause discord within the forces.[40]

---

[37] Danglis, vol. 2, p. 254.

[38] *Ibid.*, pp. 254, 255.

[39] FO 371/2889/135959 Crackanthorpe tel. no. 14477, 9 July 1917.

[40] Danglis, vol. 2, pp. 252-6. F0 371 2887 14315'2 Des. no. 266, 29 July 1917, from

By 15 November 1917 the policy of removing and imprisoning adherents of the old regime had been carried too far:

> Venizelos declared that it was absolutely necessary to remove officials and officers who were known for their Constantinist opinions and who made propaganda against the new regime.
> There have been cases where recruits had joined the colours with enthusiasm and after a few days had become sulky and ill-affected solely as the result of insidious speeches made to them by their regimental officers.[41]

When mutinies occurred against the Venizelist leadership, former officers of the 'Defence' (*Amynites*) were ordered to suppress them. Major Neokosmos Grigoriadis, who was sent to put down the revolt in the 2nd Infantry Regiment at Lamia under Colonel Markou, barely survived an attempt on his life on 2 May 1918, and only quelled the uprising with great difficulty. He recounts in his memoirs how 'royalist' officers pretended to give orders and at the same time encouraged their soldiers to disobey them.[42] In February 1918 a mutiny instigated by NCOs in protest against the war took place in the regiment of Lamia and spread to Thebes, Levadia and Atalanti. The government suppressed the revolt with the aid of a Cretan regiment and set up courts-martial which summarily tried and executed several officers, NCOs and soldiers. The munity of the 3rd Division *en route* to Kozani attained serious dimensions: a regiment of Evzones under Lieut.-Colonel Zoiopoulos and members of the 12th Infantry Regiment under Colonel Yannetakis broke ranks and deserted, killing an officer who tried to stop them. Venizelos must be held responsible for allowing disorder to increase: instead of appointing moderate and professionally-minded officers in key positions, he gave a free hand to his more extreme political adherents.[43]

The officer corps between 1916 and 1920 may be roughly divided into the extremists of both camps and the neutralists in

---

Elliot to Balfour at the FO.

[41] FO 371/2888/218498/15 November 1917. Des. from Elliot to Balfour at the FO.

[42] N. Grigoriadis, *Apomnimonevmata*, Athens, 1966, p. 79.

[43] Danglis, vol. 2, pp. 289-90; Markezinis, vol. 4, pp. 231-3. The most complete account of the purges precipitated after Venizelos' return is given by W. Edgar, 'The Purges of 1917' in O. Demetrakopoulos and T. Veremis (eds), *Meletimata gyro apo ton E. Venizelo kai tin epochi tou*, Athens: Filippotis, 1980, pp. 519-50.

between. Royalist extremists ('*Apotakti* ') had been dismissed, imprisoned or exiled and therefore ceased to pose a threat to the Venizelist officers of the 'National Defence' (*Amynites*). As already mentioned, many who remained at their posts under the government of Athens had viewed the revolt of Thessaloniki as a necessity, and had not joined the movement partly because of their inability to abandon their posts and partly because they disapproved of some of their colleagues who went to Thessaloniki.

Officers who had failed to join the 'National Defence', however, were scornfully termed '*Paraminantes*' (those who remained), a term implying opportunism and cowardice, by the '*Amynites*'.[44] Venizelos had inevitably shown bias towards his revolutionary companions of the 'Defence' while alienating the more numerous and undecided '*Paraminantes*'. These voters have been rightly called the 'floating voters' of the army. In 1920 they voted against Venizelos, but royalist favouritism in the Ministry of Army Affairs in 1920-2 drove them back to sympathise with him.[45]

Venizelos' decision to hold elections at the end of 1920 caused great alarm among his committed followers. For those who had openly committed themselves to the opposition, a defeat at the polls would raise the spectre of royalist retribution. As early as 1919, a group of middle-ranking officers had planned to organise a movement with the object of intimidating anti-Venizelists during the elections. Vakas, one of the officers involved, regretted that the plan did not materialise.[46]

Accusations against high-ranking Venizelist officers for putting pressure on their troops to vote for the government abound. However, it is best to dismiss such biased evidence as that of M. Malainos, a royalist, who wrote that Venizelos himself gave instructions to General A. Mazarakis to ensure victory in the district where he happened to be stationed. Mazarakis' more reliable testimony has it that Pangalos, Chief of the General Staff, had offered him the Ministry of the Interior in a military government to be formed if Venizelos were defeated.[47]

---

[44] Whereas the '*Amynites*' are easy to identify, the dismissed royalists of 1916 often hide under the guise of the '*Paraminantes*'.

[45] M.L. Smith, 'The Greek Occupation of Western Asia Minor and the National Schism', D.Phil. thesis, St. Antony's College, Oxford University, 1970, p. 272.

[46] Vakas, p 428.

[47] M. Malainos, *Mikrasiatiki katastrophi*; Athens 1962, pp. 71-8; Mazarakis, p. 283.

The army vote did not after all change the result of the November 1920 elections (Venizelos acknowledged his defeat before the army vote had been counted), but it certainly worsened the existing division within the military. Officers such as Georgios Kondylis, who tried to influence soldiers voting in his Asia Minor regiment, had to flee to Constantinople when it became apparent that the anti-Venizelists were going to win. However, plans to remove the popular Colonel Plastiras from his command of the 13th Division were cancelled when his soldiers threatened to mutiny.[48]

The new regime's first concern was for those who had been victimised by Venizelism; 1,500 officers dismissed or forcibly put on the reserve list between 1916 and 1920 were reinstated by royal decree after Constantine was reinstated by plebiscite.[49] But there was a more complex matter arising from the readmission of the '*Apotakti*', namely to determine their rank in relation to the '*Amynites*' and the '*Paraminantes*'.[50] The latter two categories of officers had acquired three years' active service while the '*Apotakti*' had been absent. The notorious law 927 of 29 September–12 November 1917 had credited 'National Defence' officers ('*Amynites* ') with ten months of war service (September 1916–July 1917). This law, known as the '*Dekaminon*' (it was abolished in 1920 and revived in 1923 by a Venizelist government), became a major bone of contention between Venizelist and anti-Venizelist officers throughout the next fifteen years.

Concern for the Asia Minor campaign prevented the new government from carrying out a wholesale purge of Venizelists from the forces. To repeat what had already been done to the civil service would have deprived the army of any capacity for battle until the new officers could become familiar with their tasks.

Through a series of complicated measures, the '*Apotakti*' were granted ranks that they would normally have attained if they had not been dismissed. Officers who had remained on active duty between 1917 and 1920 and benefited from Law 927 reverted to the seniority they would have had if the law had never existed. Those who had been dismissed or retired, or had resigned between

---

[48] K. Athanatos, *To ethnikon kinima Chiou kai Mytilinis*, Athens, 1923, p. xi.

[49] *Government Gazette*, vol. III, 1920 (lists of appointments and dismissals).

[50] A. Korozis, *I polemi tou 1940-1941*, vol. 1, Athens 1957, p. 12 (on the '*Paraminantes*').

28 June 1917 and 14 November 1920 and did not wish to return, regained the ranks they had held before leaving the army for the purpose of fixing their pensions. The reinstatement of the '*Apotakti*' to ranks that the government thought appropriate caused resentment among the '*Amynites*' who were suspended on three-quarters pay until other officers caught up with them in rank. All other criteria affecting promotion besides seniority were abolished. The unfortunate practice of the Ministry of Army Affairs of promoting officers by royal decree over and above the fixed numbers of posts available had overstaffed the higher ranks.[51]

By the end of 1921 there were many more officers than commands, and constant pressure from the royalists to occupy vital positions had demoralised the service. The readmission of 1,500 '*Apotakti*' without a simultaneous purge of Venizelists created a chaotic state of affairs in the chain of command.[52]

The impact of the change of regime on the Asia Minor army, though not as dramatic as had been expected, still caused significant alterations in the command structure. General Paraskevopoulos, the Commander-in-Chief, resigned and was replaced by General Anastasios Papoulas, an opponent of Venizelos (he had been imprisoned in 1918 for deserting his post and organising guerrilla warfare against the Venizelos government). The appointment of Papoulas came at a time when royalists believed that their Venizelist colleagues were planning a coup to reverse the electoral results and Venizelists were expecting the royalists to avenge themselves for past injuries.[53] About 150 Venizelist officers, four of them generals, deserted their posts and revived the 'National Defence' movement in Constantinople. Others resigned finding it impossible to work with the new regime. Generals Othonaios, Hadjimihalis, Mazarakis and Nider all left the army. By the time[54] the spring operations of 1921 began, only two of the old Army Corps and

---

[51] Smith, pp. 302-4. Seniority was determined by the date of an officer's first commission in the service, but the seniority of Academy graduates was also determined by their overall performance as cadets. Promotion based on seniority alone would in fact constitute a guarantee of normality in an army whose hierarchy was constantly disrupted by patronage. Unfortunately, seniority criteria were usually superseded by laws that benefited one or the other group or promotions '*kat' eklogin*' (by preferment).

[52] The whole procedure was contained in the Decree of 15/28 December 1920.

[53] *I Mikrasiatiki Ekstrateia*, Athens, an army General Staff publication, 1963, vol. II, pp. 265-8.

[54] M. Malainos, *Istoria ton xenikon epemvaseon*, vol. 6, Athens, 1963, p. 22.

divisional commanders, Tricoupis and Leonardopoulos, remained. The Commander-in-Chief, all three Army Corps commanders and seven out of nine divisional commanders had been replaced. Those who left were few in number but they were the most politically active and had the highest reputation in the field.[55]

The majority of Venizelist middle-ranking officers remained at their posts and continued to serve under the new government. Not all fared as well as Plastiras, who retained his command and remained active till the end of the campaign. Captain S. Saraphis, a staff officer in General Othonaios' division (which had acted as the Athens garrison during the 1920 elections), was recalled to the capital and given a travel warrant for Kalamata, where he was held with thirty other Venizelist officers of the *'Amyna'* in enforced idleness and forbidden to leave the city.[56] Major Leonidas Spais, accused of inciting rebellion among the troops, was imprisoned but later the charges were dropped.[57] If to the highly speculative number of 400 Venizelists who resigned, were removed to unimportant commands or placed *'en disponibilité'* on two-thirds pay one adds those who fled to Constantinople to form a new version of the 'National Defence', the sum will be 600 officers, either removed from active service or kept in various forms of suspension.

Venizelist allegations that royalist officers were inexperienced and therefore performed poorly in Asia Minor do not have an altogether firm basis. Mutual mistrust between Venizelists who remained and royalists who had just arrived at first created more problems for the efficient conduct of the campaign than the relative inexperience of the newcomers, but by the end of 1921 the problem had changed. Despite his known anti-Venizelist position, General Papoulas proved a far less intransigent figure than the Venizelists expected; he did his best to ignore royalist pressures and to treat officers on equal terms regardless of their politics. Before his arrival in Smyrna, royalists had begun to take matters into their own hands. By 1922 'the tensions and disagreements between Venizelists and royalists in Asia Minor tended to be

[55] Generals Ioannou, P. and B. Zymbrakakis, Miliotis-Komninos, Constantine and Alexander Mazarakis, Ch. Tseroulis and L. Kalomenopoulos, and Colonels Pangalos, Kondylis, Zaphiriou, L. Sakellaropoulos and others (all members of the *'Amyna'*).

[56] S. Saraphis, *Istorikes anamniseis,* vol. 1, Athens, 1953, pp. 205-6.

[57] Spais, p. 136.

subsumed by a more general feeling of isolation, a (tentavive) solidarity of all those serving in Asia Minor as against the civilians in Old Greece and the officers (many of them "*Apotakti*") of the War Ministry and home front.'[58]

With the failure of the spring offensive against Ankara in 1921, criticism of the government transcended party lines. The mismanagement of the campaign became a common topic of discussion among officers of all political positions. Lack of coherence in military decisions and the poor quality of rations caused constant protests against the government and petitions for improvement. Much of the propaganda against Athens was directed from Constantinople by the group of runaway Venizelist officers who worked hand-in-glove with retired officials of the previous administration. The military aspect of the revived 'National Defence' was not clearly distinguished from the civilian aspect since the organisation's work was basically propaganda. Figures of the Thessaloniki '*Amyna*' such as Kondylis, the Zymbrakakis brothers, K. Mazarakis, Ioannou and A. Siotis were busy distributing literature inciting mutiny among the Greek troops in Asia Minor. According to P. Argyropoulos, a leading member of the '*Amyna*', Venizelos had been kept fully informed of the activities of the organisation.[59]

> However, he [Venizelos] did not see any necessity to assume the leadership of an organisation determined to overthrow Constantine. He rightly thought that if he were accused of trying to assume power by any means, that would turn our struggle into a conflict of personal ambitions.[60]

A subsequent rift between generals and junior officers under Kondylis made the 'National Defence' useless for the purpose of organising a *coup* against the royalist government.[61]

We will not examine the events that led to the military disaster in Asia Minor, but will note the temporary unity that prevailed among the majority of officers – irrespective of political affiliations – in turning against the royalist government. Only once before, in 1909, had officers acted with such unity against the political

---

[58] Smith, p. 314.
[59] Argyropoulos, pp. 308–10.
[60] *Ibid.*, p. 310.
[61] *Ibid.*, p. 316.

authorities, united by a defeat which challenged the honour of the entire army. However, the implications of the 1922 disaster were much more serious than those of 1897, a fact which made the military reaction all the more violent. The 'Revolution of 1922' began in the islands of Chios and Lesbos among officers who had maintained order in their retreating units and managed to bring them to safety. Although many royalists closed ranks with Venizelists to overthrow the government and force King Constantine to abdicate, the gulf between the two was never bridged. When the initial threat to national security subsided, corporate differences re-emerged. The Pandora's box that had been opened in 1916 had not been closed.

The period between 1916 and 1922 marks the beginning of systematic military involvement in Greek politics. Military clients became attached to such patrons as Venizelos and Constantine, and their professional grievances were no longer matters for the army to deal with but rather an important consideration in each party's policy. Politicians (including the King) manipulated officers in order to promote their own ends, regardless of the consequences. Spurred by a combination of professional insecurity and opportunism (since the personal benefits to be gained or protected by political involvement became obvious), the military and especially reserve officers who had been granted regular commissions became a major political anomaly throughout the interwar period. Thus the heritage of the 'national schism' continued to plague interwar politics and set a precedent of military involvement in civilian affairs that upset parliamentary practice for years to come.

# 5

## SELF-IMAGES, PROFESSIONALISM AND PATRONAGE IN THE OFFICER CORPS (1897-1936)

'The army embodies in itself its morality, its law and its mystique and this is not the mystique of the nation.'[1]

This statement, made with justice about the French army of the time, could not have been applied to the Greek army of 1922-35. The code of behaviour to which the military did adhere must be sought largely in the values and social structure of rural Greece and its urban centres in which, before the Second World War, traditional attitudes were still strongly entrenched. Whatever professionalism existed among officers of well-to-do origin was disrupted by the influx of reserve officers granted regular commissions between 1912 and 1919.[2]

The myth of the Greek army's professionalism, expounded in interviews many years later by most officers of the interwar period,[3] is derived wholly from its Western prototypes, the French, German and British armies. The military cultivated a self-concept inspired by contempt for officers who involved themselves in political activity and the conviction that the military were more virtuous and heroic than any civilian group. There was also a tendency among officers to exaggerate the splendid background of their colleagues before 1910, as well as the comfortable middle-class origin of post-1910 Academy cadets. It thus followed that young

---

[1] Michael Howard, 'Introduction' in Michael Howard (ed.), *Soldiers and Governments*, London: Eyre and Spottiswood, 1957, p. 16.

[2] Nur Yalman, 'Intervention and Extrication: The Officer Corps in the Turkish Crisis' in Henry Bienen (ed.) *The Military Intervenes*, New York: Russell Sage, 1968, pp. 128-33.

[3] In 1969-73 a questionnaire was distributed to 150 interwar officers, of whom fifty were interviewed.

men who decided to give up a prosperous future and embrace the hardships of military life would never be moved by selfish motives. Among those interviewed, not one admitted entering the service for lack of better alternatives. However, those Academy graduates who showed the greatest professional pride discouraged their sons from following the military vocation; hence there are few cases of second-generation officers in the post-1920 Greek army. Although officers took a highly idealistic view of their own calling, they became extremely practical when it came to choosing careers for their offspring.

General Michalis Antonopoulos, an Academy graduate of the class of 1916, made a typically idealised evaluation of his experience in the army:

> The military profession has lived up to my expectations fully. Choosing to become an officer does not entail furthering personal ambitions or finding a way of securing a comfortable livelihood. Rather, it requires high principles and moral character so that the future officer may understand the meaning of service to the nation.

Whether adherents of Venizelos or of the King, Academy graduates or reserve officers granted regular commissions, all agreed in their general attitudes towards the role of the military. They condemned interventions in principle but made exceptions of those particular *coups* of which they approved.[4] They all felt that military intervention should have limited objectives and occur only at times of national emergency.

Self-images involve much wishful thinking and therefore form normative aspects of professionalism (what it ought to be rather than what the actual case is). However, it would be simplistic to contend that the officers had exclusively self-interested motives

---

[4] They differentiate between intervention for personal gain and intervention in times of national crisis. Deciding when the nation is truly in danger is a highly speculative matter; even then, the purpose of the *coup* is presumably to restore order rather than to take over. According to S.E. Finer, the moment when a distinction is made between the nation and the government in power, the military begin to invent their own private notion of the national interest. Thus domestic opponents may easily be turned into enemies of the nation. 'This purported care for the national interest as defined by the military is indeed one of their main reasons for intervening. [...] The point here is that it flows inexorably from one particular facet of military professionalism.' S.E. Finer, *The Man on Horseback*, London: Pall Mall, 1962, p. 26.

such as may be found in patron-client relationships or desire for material improvement. Their efforts to emulate the professionalism of their Western prototypes and to live up to national ideals cannot be ignored. In wartime they would forget private attachments and differences arising from competitiveness and act according to the high principles they espoused. However, it is not our task to describe the wartime record of the Greek army but rather to concentrate on its social and political attitude.

The army's failure to attain the high standards of the Western military élites to which it aspired was largely due to that aspect of Greek society which discouraged, among groups and individuals, the development of a sense of responsibility towards the state. On the one hand, civic consciousness was impaired by the social consequences of the character of the Greek family to which the individual owes his most categorical obligations, and the social consequences that follow from that. But on the other hand, the state did not win the confidence of most Greeks because it failed to serve its citizens without the interference of the personal networks of political patronage. Experience had taught that attachment to a powerful patron was the best guarantee of success in achieving one's ends, rather than reliance on an unresponsive government mechanism or any corporate organisation.[5]

Professionalism and hierarchy were seriously impaired in the Greek army because of the corruption of its organisational patterns by clientelism. Antagonistic networks demanded exclusive loyalty of their members at times of strife and a lower-ranking officer would therefore obey only a superior of his own network. Since officers were linked to the authority structure through personal ties rather than a set of impersonal institutions and rules that were particular to their profession, there could hardly exist any notion of differentiation of roles as understood in a modern society. Because of the proximity of the military to civilian mentality, *coups d'état* had almost acquired during the interwar period an informal status as a means of political pressure. Since the social

---

[5] It was for this reason that political parties defending class interests as well as trade unionism failed to attract a significant following. The absence of autonomous political organisations among the Greek peasant population is treated by N. Mouzelis and M. Attalidis in their article, 'Greece' in Margaret S. Archer and S. Giner (eds), *Contemporary Europe: Class, Status and Power*, London: Weidenfeld and Nicolson, 1971, pp. 162-93.

fabric was never seriously threatened by the *coups,* civilian society had more or less adapted itself to such practices.

This casual view of military rebellion may best be shown by the fate of officers on the losing side of a conspiracy. In Greece, contrary to what one would expect in states where rebellion against civilian authorities is considered a deviation from the very nature of the military profession, participation in a failed *coup* did not necessarily bring disgrace and dishonour. Papagos, who was dismissed for his role in the *coup* of 1923, was readmitted, made Chief of Staff and later Commander-in-Chief.[6] Plastiras, who fled Greece after his abortive *coup* in 1933, was elected Prime Minister after the war.[7] Zervas, the commander of the praetorian 'Republican Battalions' under the dictator Pangalos, headed the largest non-Communist resistance group during the German occupation and held ministerial positions in post-war cabinets. Finally, Metaxas, who fled the country in 1923, became a dictator and the architect of the 'Third Hellenic Civilisation' in 1936.

Military interventions between 1909 and 1935 divide into two basic categories: first, those that acquired wider national significance and were endorsed by the public; and, secondly, those aimed merely at promoting the private interests of various influential military figures and their clienteles. The *coups* of 1909, 1916 and 1922 made the army the champion of middle-class aspirations, expansionist dreams or an instrument to punish erring politicians. Civilian participation and public interest were considerable in these *coups* whose main objective was to substitute one set of civilian rulers for another. With the exception of the *coup* of 1935, interventions between 1923 and 1935 were usually instigated by officers with personal grievances, leaving civilians uninvolved and uninterested.

The *coup* of 1935 represented many different tendencies at

---

[6] Alexandros Papagos was born in Athens into a prominent royalist family, studied in the Brussels Academy and joined the cavalry in 1906. He stood by the monarchy throughout its long dispute with Venizelos, and was dismissed from the army in 1917. In 1921 he was given a cavalry command in Asia Minor and in 1923 was dismissed again, this time for aiding a *coup* against the government. He was readmitted in 1927 by the government and worked for the King's restoration.

[7] Nicolaos Plastiras served in the Balkan wars and then joined the Venizelist movement in 1916, winning rapid promotion for distinguished service in Macedonia and Ukraine. As a colonel and regimental commander in Asia Minor, he remained at the front after November 1920, despite his known Venizelist loyalties. He led the revolution of September 1922 and thereafter pursued an active political career for the rest of his life.

once. Control of the *coup* by politicians was attempted but did not succeed. A group of officers promoting corporate military interests for the first time was at odds with civilian participants and the traditional military politicos who tried to assume the leadership. The group that formed the ESO (*Eliniki Stratiotiki Organosis* – Hellenic Military Organisation) sought to promote the interests of a generation of Military Academy officers and to repudiate the traditional client networks that fragmented the army during that period.

The very competitiveness that existed within the officer corps and the improvised character of military conspiracies account for the numerous abortive *coups* as well as for the limited objectives and the relatively short duration of the regimes that followed successful attempts.[8] *Coups* often became the means by which officers achieved trivial benefits or found a solution for their uneventful life in the provinces. The most significant difference between civilians and the military in Greece was simply the military's control over the means of mass violence – a fact which would indeed have added greatly to their bargaining power in politics had they been able to resolve their internal conflicts. The inability of the military to prevail or even to promote their professional interests effectively was due to their fragmentation into competing clientelistic groups.

Despite the tendency of the various individuals or groupings in the army to react to every alteration of the Army List, failure to organise effectively in secret associations has been the most significant reason for the limited impact of military *coups* on national policy. Interest groups such as reserve officers who had been granted regular commissions, Military Academy graduates, or junior officers with grievances over the system of promotion rarely formed homogeneous organisations in which all members were activated by the same interest. Instead the military retained the civilian practice of forming patron-client relationships which brought together officers of diverse origin, rank and aims. The isolated nature of the relationship between patron and client discouraged group activity and fragmented attemps at horizontal organisation. Since such a relationship is based on a contract between people

---

[8] According to Janowitz, 'Lack of cohesion leads to unstable and fragmented involvement and the likelihood of countercoups'. Morris Janowitz, *The Military in Political Development of New Nations*, University of Chicago Press, 1965, p. 68.

of unequal status, it follows that it will cease as soon as their interests no longer complement each other. The fewer their common interests, the more superficial is their relationship. Pangalos, who established his dictatorship in 1925 after his military clients had prepared the way, fell from power mainly because he could not appeal to new followers without alienating his old ones. His former friends were the first to turn against him when he tried to broaden his base. Similarly Plastiras, during the 1928 controversy over the readmission of dismissed officers, defied his clients who were opposed to the measure because he felt that his own future lay in a political career. He therefore sided with the politicians and prevented his friends' plan to overthrow the government.

However, the most dramatic example of the failure of patronage to promote a military *coup* can be found in the forces that organised the insurrection of 1935. Despite the effort of Venizelos to unite all the client networks under his influence, conflicting interests, personality clashes and traditional mistrust between different patrons and clients undermined the uprising from its very inception.

The ESO was perhaps the only exception to the rule governing military organisations in the interwar period. Its founding members, all of whom were in the same class at the Academy, tried to emphasise the homogeneous aspect of its membership. The initial qualifications were to have graduated from the Academy, to be of junior rank and to subscibe to republican ideology, making the organisation the only one formed on common interests and equality of status. Had the ESO kept its initial character it might have had a lasting impact on Greek politics, but the force of patronage, based on the conviction that only by depending on individuals of higher status could one achieve one's ends, destroyed its potential.

Military organisations such as the 'National Defence of 1916', the 'Revolution of 1922', the 'Military League', the 'Republican Battalions' (an official unit that occasionally turned against the government), as well as less important ones such as the 'Organisation of Majors', 'Kondylis', 'Kynigi', the 'League of Recalcitrant Officers' and paramilitary organisations like the '*Epistrati*' and the 'Republican Defence', all consisted of a diverse assortment of followers held together by a weak bond of ideology and vulnerable to dissolution at every change in the terms of patronage. Membership was by no means a levelling element among members of unequal status while all the implications of vertical recruitment were maintained.[9]

Given the need for ambitious Academy graduates to attach themselves to influential figures in the army, friendship bestowed by Constantine (as Crown Prince and later as King) and his principal military adherents was a guarantee of good fortune during the first two decades of the century. Officers who found their way to royal patronage were automatically exposed to an atmosphere of germanophile sentiment, and such royalists as Stratigos, Ex-adaktylos, Metaxas and Papavasiliou were all sent to Germany for post-graduate military studies at the request of their patron. Among them Ioannis Metaxas, a scion of impoverished Cephalonian gentry, saw himself as allied to the King by bonds of tradition. The anti-royalist prejudice of such officers as Mazarakis, Danglis, Paraskevopoulos and Pangalos are explicable by the particular events that led each to become a client of Venizelos and his pro-Entente policy during the First World War. Some of their contemporaries alleged that these officers had acquired a liberal outlook precisely because they had been trained in republican France, whereas those who had studied in Germany had been favourably predisposed towards a strong monarchy. However, since the dedication of the French army to liberal ideology was debatable before 1914,[10] we would venture to suggest that it was not so much a question of French-style liberalism determining the affinity of some officers to Venizelos' policy but *vice versa*. Metaxas' complaints against the politically disruptive influence of the French diplomatic mission in Athens are hardly justified by the small number of officers who took part in the pro-Entente *coup* by Venizelos in 1916. Since we are dealing with a sample of officers who formed the vanguard of both camps, Venizelist and royalist, it should be noted that similarities in their social origin and economic position make it hard to relate each group to specific class allegiances. Danglis, a Venizelist, and Dousmanis, a royalist, came from prominent families in the same sense that Metaxas, a royalist, and Mazarakis, a Venizelist, belonged to a kind of traditional gentry.

---

[9] For an excellent analysis of clientelism in Greek Macedonia, see Vasilis Gounaris, 'Vouleftes kai kapetanioi. Pelatiakes scheseis stin Mesopolemiki Makedonia', *Ellinika*, vol. 41, Thessaloniki, 1990, pp. 313-35.

[10] A. Vagts, *A History of Militarism*, London: Hollis and Carter, 1959, p. 318.

Paraskevopoulos, Stratigos, Pangalos and Exadaktylos shared a middle-class background. All were graduates of the Academy.

The general inability of the military to defend their interests by forming legal associations was usually compensated for either by a traditional code of behaviour that enabled them to withstand professional hardships, or by the formation of secret associations leading to military interventions. The usual radicalism of reserve officers granted regular commissions, although it contained no coherent ideology, was indicative of their relative powerlessness to protect their weak position. The Populist government of 1933 made concerted efforts to increase the numbers of officers with the greatest sense of professional security, namely Academy graduates, at the expense of other categories. Realising that Academy graduates were the most law-abiding officers, the Minister of Army Affairs Kondylis demanded a doubling of the number of such officers in the army, while the Liberals vehemently opposed the measure.[11]

The memoirs of General Alexander Mazarakis–Ainian provide a rare insight into the life of an Academy graduate who held the highest ranks and posts between 1922 and 1935. Given that his older brother Constantine had already entered the army, the ambition of the younger Alexander to follow in his footsteps was contrary to the usual practice of large families where each son was urged to enter a different profession, thus increasing the versatility of the family unit. Fascinated by the predominant irredentist ideology of 1890 and the romance of military life, Alexander Mazarakis abandoned his law studies to enter the Evelpidon Academy. However, the conditions there fell short of the young cadet's expectations: 'There is no real comradeship among cadets, which is why later in life the brittle bonds of friendship among graduates are easily destroyed by the slightest rivalry.'[12]

There is nothing in his recollections to indicate that family influences were ever transcended by a strictly military outlook.

---

[11] *Official Parliamentary Minutes*, period D, sessions 1-28, 27 March-11 September 1933, vol. A, Athens, 1934, pp. 311-12, 314, 335.

[12] Mazarakis' testimony concerning relationships among Academy cadets is confirmed by General Thrasyvoulos Tsakalotos, an anti-Venizelist: 'I don't know whether it is a spirit of competition or simply a selfish concern for personal promotion that is responsible for the loosening of the bonds of friendship forged among fellow-students at the Military Academy.' A. Mazarakis-Ainian, *Apomnimonevmata*, Athens: Ikaros, 1948, p. 7; T. Tsakalotos, *Saranta chronia stratiotis tis Ellados*, Athens, 1960, p. 36.

He testifies that the Evelpidon Academy of 1893 was an exclusive social club where favouritism was rife. He regretted, however, that after the Balkan wars prominent families preferred to make their children 'brokers and dealers' rather than officers.

> I do not believe that the military profession should belong to one social class. [...] I believe, nevertheless, that a measure of tradition is necessary so that young officers can survive the material temptations of civilian life and persevere in a love for their profession in spite of the hardships it offers.[13]

Mazarakis explains why the sons of good families had ceased to enter the army: first, the hardships of the wars between 1912 and 1922, and secondly the enlargement of Greece, which created posts away from urban centres. Up till 1910 most units were stationed in Athens or nearby, allowing officers to indulge in social activities in their ample spare time.[14] He felt that the idealism of the ruling class had been overlaid by materialism and egotism. His declared opposition to materialistic bourgeois values typifies the attitude of most officers of the interwar period.[15]

Unlike Venizelist 'patricians' such as Mazarakis, Haralambos Papathanasopoulos, also a Venizelist, belonged in the military sense to the wrong side of the tracks. He was born in 1890 of poor parents and was conscripted in 1911. He became a reserve officer in 1912 and was granted a regular commission under Law 328 of 1911. In 1917 he became a first lieutenant, in 1919 a captain, and in 1923 a major. During the Asia Minor campaign he befriended Plastiras and was made his *aide-de-camp*.[16] His attachment to Plastiras in the patron-client sense continued throughout the interwar period, a time when he felt that his duty was to keep his patron informed on everything, including his personal problems. In April 1924 he wrote to Plastiras:

> It is difficult for an officer to live in the army with his honour intact if he has not graduated from the Military Academy. I have often thought of retiring...but I was restrained by the

---

[13] Mazarakis, p. 7.

[14] In 1903 three-quarters of the 1,876 officers on active service were stationed in Athens. W. Miller, *Greek Life in Town and Country*, London, 1905, p. 245.

[15] A. Mazarakis completed his memoirs in 1943.

[16] N. Deas, *Mesouranima kai syntrimia*, Athens, 1976, pp. 55-6.

fear that it would be generally supposed that I had left in pursuit of utilitarian concerns....[17]

Papathanasopoulos' bitter complaints are directed against the preferential treatment of Academy graduates refusing to accept him as an equal. Since honour required a certain amount of independence and integrity, his inferior position in the army had been a constant danger to his *philotimo* (sense of honour). The paradox about honour is that the more one tries to safeguard it, the more liable it is to be slighted. The search for patrons to improve a client's position entailed obligations which imposed further limitations on one's independence. This partly explains how, despite concern for his honour, Papathanasopoulos most often managed to be on the winning side – the republicans in 1924 or the Pangalists in 1926.

Papathanasopoulos was in many ways a typical product of the competitive spirit prevailing in the army. His basic distrust of others and his cynical view of human nature justified his authoritarian inclinations. On 2 February 1924 he wrote to Plastiras: 'Greece does not need an Assembly or a Democracy, it needs an enlightened tyrant.'[18] In another letter on 23 February 1924 he expressed approval of the military putting pressure on the government in order to promote the republican cause, thus making a lucid appraisal of politics in interwar Greece:

> Here in Greece the public is always divided into three categories: the two or three factions who make up the minority of the voting population, and the moderates or *attentistes* [those unwilling to take sides] who form the majority. This latter category always accepts power as an accomplished fact and hence joins the ranks of the most powerful faction. The great electoral victories are due to this phenomenon. That is why we [the army] ought to present the public once more with an accomplished fact and win them to our side during the plebiscite. The attitude of Kaphandaris [the Prime Minister] had given the impression that he was weak, whereas ours convinced the people that we are strong.[19]

---

[17] Plastiras papers, in the Benaki Museum, Athens.

[18] *Ibid.*

[19] *Ibid.* cf. J.K. Campbell, *Honour, Family and Patronage*, Oxford: Clarendon Press, 1970, p. 197: 'Strength and not justice appears to be the basis of honour in a traditional society of the mountains'.

Papathanasopoulos had no compunction about asking for occasional favours, which he considered normal in the context of their relationship. In return he informed Plastiras of every single turn of events. The role of Plastiras as a patron was not limited to material favours, but extended also to moral guidance. In 1925 Papathanasopoulos made Plastiras his confessor by admitting that because of his pitiful financial state he had been driven to appropriate funds from a regimental treasury. His father-in-law had not only failed to deliver the dowry that had been promised but had also abandoned his own wife, leaving her to the care of his son-in-law. To Plastiras he wrote that he expected no sympathy from him, and that it was only from a need to abase himself before a 'higher individual' that he had decided to make this confession. On this occasion Plastiras must have shown a patron's magnanimity because the flow of correspondence did not cease. During the Pangalos dictatorship, Papathanasopoulos deplored the waning prestige of the officer corps, and claimed that had he completed the years of service required for an adequate pension (letter of 18 April 1926), he would already have given in his resignation.[20]

The need to rely on personal contacts for professional advancement, although this varied according to an officer's position in the army, drove junior officers to search frantically for military patrons. The nature of military patronage was flexible (except in periods of political division), which gave a client the chance to change patrons if his present one was not in a position to help him. The client then became in turn the patron of lower-ranking officers, and so on. In this way client networks were formed which included NCOs and both junior and senior officers. Although such networks often followed the hierarchical pattern of the army, as in the case of the 'Military League' of 1923, a client was only responsible to his own patron. Each patron could offer his client's services to his own superior, but then it was only through his personal intervention that this transfer of loyalty could be effected. However, any similarity that may appear to exist between client networks and formal hierarchies – where each subordinate is obliged to obey all his superiors in rank – is superficial. Since client networks were often mutually antagonistic, a general

[20] Plastiras papers.

might be denied obedience by junior officers under his command if they belonged to a hostile network.

Antagonisms among officers of the same political camp but of different client networks were frequent. Pangalos in his memoirs reserves a paragraph of abuse in each chapter for Mazarakis who, he reminds the reader, was a spiteful fanatic and a plagiarist of historical facts. By the very rancour of these attacks the reader is led to think that Pangalos himself was not without similar flaws of character. On the other hand, General Paraskevopoulos, who was the patron of Pangalos, is given generous praise.[21]

The table below indicates the basic changes in the character of military patron–client relationships between 1897 and 1935:

*1897-1909*
Exclusive character of royal patronage was opposed by the majority of the officer corps. Demands that the princes be removed from the army and navy were combined with aspirations for modernisation.

*1909-16*
Period of contentment due to Liberal reforms and the prospects of professional improvement opened by the Balkan wars. Exclusive royal patronage was replaced by a flexible and open patronage.

*1916-23*
The breakdown of flexible patronage with the coming of *dichasmos* (national schism over the issue of joining the Triple Entente during the First World War) affected the army as much as it did civilian society. The ability to change patrons from one political camp to another was no longer possible. Patrons on the other hand could recruit clients from the opposite camp as they were in a position of strength.

*1923-33*
With the removal of the King and the eclipse of his political following, flexible patronage was restored in an army dominated by antagonistic patrons of Venizelist origin.

*1933-5*
The advent of the Populist party revived the old *dichasmos*. The failure of the Venizelist *coup* of 1935 removed the republicans from the army and heralded a period of royalist influence in the armed forces.

Flexible and open patronage that regulated military relationships before 1895 was transformed into a relatively exclusive and static one as soon as members of the royal family assumed command

---

[21] Th. Pangalos, *Ta apomnimonevmata mou*, vol. 2, Athens: Kedros, 1959, pp. 9, 14.

of the army. Prince Constantine's clients had all reached prominence thanks to their protector, but none constitutes a better example of the working of royal patronage than Metaxas. As a young officer he had often been critical of the royal family. In his diary he noted on 24 September 1896: 'It is time for corruption to cease; and the King is not uninvolved in this dirty business of extending favours, though he will regret it.'[22]

Later, in the course of the war of 1897, Metaxas met Dousmanis who introduced him, along with Papavasiliou and Stratigos, to Prince Constantine. His new relationship with the palace was heralded by a serious reconsideration of his past views. He discovered that the Prince (Constantine) was the only important figure of his time, and that only people of aristocratic descent like himself could harbour a deep loyalty for the monarchy:[23] 'A struggle has begun between the Crown Prince and parliamentary government. It is only a phase of the great conflict that will follow. I hope to find a chance to drink the blood of some parliamentarian.'[24]

In 1898 Constantine promised Metaxas that he would be sent to Germany for military studies on state funds. Metaxas' hopes were momentarily jeopardised by a government act proclaiming open competition for the scholarships; he feared that if forced to submit to examinations he might fail. Dousmanis came to his rescue by persuading Constantine to reverse the official decision over the examinations. The Prince in turn asked the Prime Minister to introduce an amendment to the bill, narrowing the qualifications of eligible candidates to fit a description of Metaxas, who thus left for Germany full of praise for the wisdom of his patron. Although accustomed to scrutinising the Prince's actions, nowhere in his diary does he betray signs of a guilty conscience at having secured his scholarship by such means.[25] George Seferis quotes a client of Metaxas justifying his patron's germanophile stand during the First World War: 'You see, at the time Metaxas had been in debt to King Constantine who had been his benefactor and had educated him....'[26]

[22] I. Metaxas, *To prosopikon tou imerologion*, vol. I, Athens: Ikaros, 1951, p. 94.

[23] *Ibid.*, p. 507.

[24] *Ibid.*, p. 461.

[25] *Ibid.*, pp. 382-3.

It had apparently been expected that Metaxas should share his patron's political views in times of crisis, even at the expense of other priorities. However, loyalty to all patrons was not equally forthcoming. The exclusive and therefore more gratifying patronage of the King demanded and indeed secured a lasting obligation. Whereas Metaxas was consistently loyal to Constantine till the King's death, he disavowed his other patron, Dousmanis, when he ceased to be of any use.

Despite the noble pronouncements of the 'Military League' of 1909 that it would abolish favouritism, what it did achieve was to substitute a flexible open patronage system for static royal patronage, thus increasing the number of patrons in the field. Complaints against biased entrance examinations in military schools had been widespread before 1909. The notorious *'bilietaki'* – the visiting card of some patron with the name of his client on it, slipped into the pocket of the examiner – would largely determine success. Infantry Sergeant Nicolaos Plastiras attributed his failure to enter the school for NCOs in 1908 to this kind of practice. His conviction that he had been a victim of favouritism became a primary motive in his subsequent activities. In October 1908 he collaborated with colleagues of his regiment to organise a chapter of the 'Military League' there.

When the *pronunciamento* of 1909 was made, Plastiras was among its most active supporters. After failing once more to enter the school for NCOs, he took issue with the head of the movement, Colonel Zorbas himself. He had previously threatened the members of the examining committee that he would not tolerate such treatment since he was a dedicated member of the 'League' who had fought to abolish favouritism. Whether or not he was correct in assuming that it was a lack of connections rather than a lack of ability that had denied him entrance, Plastiras was finally granted admission at the end of 1909.[27]

Mazarakis mentions a similar instance after 1909, indicating that favouritism had merely changed its character as well as patrons and clientele: 'In Athens we took examinations at the War College [a postgraduate institution for staff officers]. Three out of the seven candidates had failed to secure entrance, but one of them

---

[26] G. Seferis, *Chirographo, Sept. 1941*, Athens: Ikaros, 1972, pp. 44.

[27] I. Peponis, *Nikolaos Plastiras, 1909-1945*, vol. I, Athens, 1948, pp. 23-6.

happened to be the brother-in-law of Zorbas, then Minister of the Army, and the results of the examination were annulled.'[28]

The case of General Leonardopoulos and Lieutenant Tsakalotos is one where patronage crossed political lines despite the national schism (*dichasmos*) period. This was possible because at a time of Venizelist supremacy Leordanopoulos, although a Liberal, could afford to be magnanimous and extend his favours to a repenting member of the royalist camp. Tsakalotos had been among the many royalists accused of sedition and imprisoned by the courts in 1918. Leonardopoulos, who met Tsakalotos while inspecting his prison cell, offered him the option of fighting under his command in a dangerous mission. Tsakalotos accepted the offer with enthusiasm and became Leonardopoulos' devoted client. He followed his patron in the Asia Minor expedition, in Thrace, and finally in launching the abortive coup of 1923 against Plastiras and Gonatas. After the failure of the *coup* and Leonardopoulos' downfall, Tsakalotos managed to escape arrest and dismissal by attaching himself to another influential Venizelist officer, General Klados. The latter, as Chief of the General Staff in 1925, transferred him to an important position in the general headquarters. But the fact that he had fared so well under his Venizelist patrons did not prevent him from applauding the restoration of the monarchy in 1935 and the Metaxas dictatorship in 1936. His case is atypical only because he managed to change camp during the period of the schism, a feat which required considerable agility.[29] However, the flexibility of his ideological position and of his attachments to personalities from whom he could derive benefits, regardless of what they stood for, epitomised the way clients behaved in military politics.

Personal relations were often resistant to ideological cleavages. Leonidas Spais mentions his friendly relations with Captain Gavalias before 1915 and notes with surprise that Gavalias refused to talk to him after he, Spais, had joined the Venizelist revolt of 1916 in Thessaloniki: 'It was a strange thing indeed that this cultured man and brave patriot should become the victim of such a strong passion that he could change into an enemy of his friends.'[30]

---

[28] Mazarakis, p. 101.

[29] Tsakalotos, I, pp. 52, 66-8. Despite the usual pattern of inflexible relations caused by the *dichasmos*, such is the nature of patronage that it must always leave margin for manoeuvre.

[30] L. Spais, *Peninta chronia stratiotis*, Athens, 1970, p. 59.

Spais clearly did not regard the national schism as a serious reason for disrupting personal relations, but qualifies his doubts about Gavalias' capacity to maintain personal loyalties by adding: 'Before the Balkan wars, Queen Sophia [wife of Constantine] had sent him to Switzerland for medical treatment and ever since then he had become her blind instrument out of gratitude.'[31]

In a proud display of the extent of his personal influence, Papathanasopoulos boasted to Plastiras that royalist officers had voted for the republic during the plebiscite of 1924 'for his own sake'.[32] Besides being an issue of social criticism, the favour of a powerful patron was considered a sign of personal worth. Little else carried as much weight as the use of a prominent patron's name in case of emergency or as a means to gain social prestige. Dousmanis in his memoirs insists on informimg the reader that it was through Constantine's personal intervention that he achieved his various positions of influence in the army.[33] What typified the system was that the more a favour was contrary to ordinary procedure, the more its recipient provoked envy for his good fortune and respect for his ability to associate with important people. In the same sense, the more complex the irregularity a patron had to commit in order to assist his client, the more reason this gave him to boast in public about his influence and power. However, this practice was not without its dangers. Besides earning the criticism of the more educated and Westernised elements of society for what they would consider provincial behaviour, an officer would provoke the jealousy and dislike of his peers precisely because of his good fortune. There was a delicate balance to be drawn somewhere between acquiring status as a potential patron and provoking criticism.

In his analysis of civil-military relations in Western societies, Huntington points out the tendency of civilians to maximise their control of political power. The two types of civilian control available, i.e. subjective and objective, also define the nature of the society in which they operate. Whereas in subjective control emphasis is put on subjecting the army to political concerns, objective control focuses on maximising military professionalism by granting

---

[31] *Ibid.*, p. 59.

[32] Plastiras papers.

[33] V. Dousmanis, *Apomnimonevmata*, Athens, 1946, p. 28.

the army a sphere of professional autonomy. Thus subjective control will civilianise the military while objective control aims at militarising them further. Demand for the latter type of control has, according to Huntington, traditionally come from the military, while demand for the former has come from the multifarious civilian groups anxious to maximise their power by manipulating the army.[34] Subjective control introduces officers into political life by giving them extra-military roles to play: 'The taming effect of political power makes officers good liberals, good fascists or good communists (depending on the prevailing civilian ideology) but poor professionals.'[35]

Obviously there is incompatibility between the ways that a political soldier and a professional perceive themselves. The military profession experiences tension between its inherent professional aspirations and the extraneous politics in which it may become involved. Because of the profession's crucial significance to society —and the vast power it is able to wield when the state is threatened —it exhibits this tension more than most other professional bodies.'[36] The Greek military did not achieve significant autonomy either in the sense of objective control where the army is not obstructed in its function by political considerations – or, as may occur in new nations, where political life is dominated by the military. The interpenetration of army and politics produced a relationship in which influential political figures took the initiative in applying subjective control on the military.

Greek society in the nineteenth century possessed a distinct if small civilian élite whose power lay in its wealth, mobility, education and foreign connections. Officers belonging to this class did not distinguish between their sense of duty as soldiers and as members of a social élite. Up till 1897 officers tended to act in unison with politicians to enforce constitutional reform or even to effect a change of regime. Both cases of major intervention in the nineteenth century (1843 and 1862) were planned together with civilians. Furthermore, the ability of officers to occupy political posts and ministerial positions while still in the service provided them with an outlet for their political aspirations.[37] In spite of

---

[34] Samuel Huntington, *The Soldier and the State*, Cambridge, MA: Harvard University Press, 1957, pp. 80-4.

[35] *Ibid.*, p. 95.

[36] *Ibid.*

efforts by the state to create a thoroughly professionalised army during this period, objective control became impossible because of the absence of a clear differentiation of roles among the military. Subjective civilian control on the other hand was invariably practised, with some success but also with occasional setbacks. However, this type of control could backfire whenever civilians were overwhelmed by a politicised army refusing to accept their authority.

The coup of 1909 was the first instance of independent military action against the political establishment. Although the architects of the movement were at first motivated by professional grievances, this was soon associated with more fundamental criticism and even contempt for many aspects of civilian society and of those circles that had traditionally exercised political control. Despite its ultimate subordination to Venizelos – a politician – the *coup* of 1909 later became a stereotypic reference used to justify military intervention against civilian corruption. The brief confrontation between military and civilian authority resulted in civilian supremacy since Venizelos assumed power.

After the Balkan wars, the social structure of the officer corps changed, increasing the dependence of officers on politicians. The large numbers of reserve officers granted regular commissions ushered in civilian attitudes and civilian patrons. Their susceptibility to political manipulation temporarily increased the subjective control of civilians and served further to politicise the army. However, the motive of individual self-interest aggravated by economic insecurity increased the inclination of the military to intervene:

> The army provided a means by which boys of lower middle class family or even poor family could rise to officer rank. Now there is no reason why the social aspirant, having come so far, would not wish to climb higher and gatecrash into the circles reserved for the social set itself, i.e. the circles of government.[38]

The initial attitude of Venizelos towards the military was far from being one that would encourage interventionism. In his first term he was strict in enforcing order when a few incidents of military opposition to his favourable treatment of the royal

[37] Mazarakis, p. 13.
[38] Finer, p. 56.

family took place.[39] According to Dousmanis, Venizelos did not fail to remind him of the vital role of politics in winning the war even after praising the army for its performance.[40] His subsequent decision to turn a blind eye to the actions of his followers was probably out of gratitude rather than out of weakness; however, by acting as a patron rather than as head of government he encouraged clientelism within the forces.

Whatever professionalism the army had attained was disrupted by the national schism. Up till 1922 the military did not question civilian supremacy, which King Constantine and Venizelos embodied in an almost paternal way. However, no institution or person inherited their personality cult, and between 1922 and 1927, when both these figures were missing from the political scene, the military challenged the authority of both republican and royalist politicians. However, in spite of the numerous upheavals between 1923 and 1926, the military did not supplant politicians; their level of interventions ranged from simple pressure and blackmail to replacing one set of civilians with another. Even the dictatorship of Pangalos can be viewed as the attempt of a retired general to embrace a political career and achieve legitimate power (his ministers, on the other hand, were all civilians). Officers such as Plastiras, Kondylis and Pangalos, once out of service, retained their ties with the officer corps, not because they wished to return to the army, but because they hoped to use them to improve their position in politics. With the possible exception of the members of the ESO, interwar political officers basically aspired, via either parliament or a dictatorship, to a status of civilian authority.

A number of political scientists have tried to fit the Greek case into a theoretical framework. But it is no use, for instance, to talk of the army as an agent of modernisation in contemporary Greece simply because – so it has been argued – armies have performed such a function in the emerging nations of Africa. Although there is some value in comparing such political analyses of the military in society as have been proposed by Pye, Johnson, Shils and Kourvetaris with the Greek case, the value of such a comparison when applied to the interwar period is questionable.[41] In the light

---

[39] D. Dakin, *The Unification of Greece*, London, Ernest Benn, 1972, pp. 188-9.
[40] V. Dousmanis, *Apomnimonevmata*, Athens, 1946, pp. 143-4.

of our analysis, Kourvetaris' contention that 'from the beginning of Greek nation building, the military has played a pivotal role in the process of...social modernisation' has to be considered an overstatement.[42]

The role of the military in interwar Greece conforms largely to that ascribed by Huntington to the soldier as guardian. In a society possessing civilian élites and a developed civilian culture, the military view themselves neither as the modernisers of society nor as the creators of a new political order but rather 'as the guardians and perhaps the purifiers of the existing order'.[43] Military involvement was therefore, as Finer puts it, limited to displacing one civilian order with another rather than permanently handing the government over to the army.[44]

[41] George Kourvetaris, 'Professional Self-Images and Political Perspectives in the Greek Military', paper presented at the American Sociological Association meeting, Washington, DC, September 1970, p. 1. See also J. Johnson (ed.), *The Role of the Military in Underdevelopped Countries*, Princeton University Press, 1962, pp. 17-22, 36-50, 87-152. Also G. Zacharopoulos, 'Politics and the Army in Post-War Greece' in Richard Clogg and G. Yannopoulos (eds), *Greece under Military Rule*, London: Secker and Warburg, 1972, pp. 17-34.

[42] George Kourvetaris, 'The Role of the Military in Greek Politics', paper prepared for the Political Sociology Section of the Illinois Sociological Association, October 1970, p. 7.

[43] Huntington, pp. 222, 225-6.

[44] In Finer's definition of countries having a mature, developed, low or minimal political culture, Greece would rank among those with a low political culture. 'In these countries... the political formula is feeble enough to allow the military to displace the civilian government by violence or the threat of it... But this does not mean that it is so feeble as to permit the military supplanting civilian government altogether, and ruling in its own name.' Finer, p. 118.

# 6

# THE SENSITIVE ISSUE OF
# THE ARMY LIST

The question of the Army List, which plagued civil-military relations throughout the interwar period, was introduced in 1917 by
the Venizelos government. According to Law 927 of that year,
officers who had fought with the 'National Defence' in Thessaloniki
were granted an extra ten months of service in their seniority
ranking – an extraordinary arrangement with far-reaching consequences in the officer corps. With the exception of the 1923
counter-*coup* directed against a military regime that had court-
martialled and executed members of the royalist cabinet responsible
for the Asia Minor debacle, most of the interwar *coups* reflected
professional grievances among the military rather than disputes
of an ideological nature. In an officer corps that had been purged
of its major royalist element after the failed 1923 attempt, Venizelist
officers were splintered into antagonistic groups that competed
for scarce commissions in a peacetime army that had naturally
contracted.

Some of the officers in the Thessaloniki government of 1916
and the subsequent protagonists of the 1922 military regime under
Colonel Nicolaos Plastiras re-emerged between 1923 and 1926
as arbiters of backstage politics and heads of patronage networks
that promised their clients security and promotion. With royalist
competition formally out of the way after the proclamation of
the republic in 1924, Venizelist officers shed all pretences of ideology and merely strove to improve their means of access to the
source of political power. Officers such as Georgios Kondylis and
Stylianos Gonatas retired from active service and pursued political
careers, while Plastiras, having retired, abstained from politics but
continued to exert influence in military affairs. Theodoros Pangalos
managed to usurp power briefly in 1925-6 and so became the

only military dictator of this turbulent interwar period, but he was overthrown by his own praetorians led by Kondylis and imprisoned. Alexandros Othonaios was forced to retire as a concession to the anti-Venizelists so that a government of reconciliation could be formed. The Pangalos dictatorship had not only reaped its own toll of blunders on the economic and foreign policy fronts, but it had also succeeded in alienating both republican and royalist politicians as well as excluding them from power. After the inconclusive elections of 1926, a widespread spirit of tolerance and moderation prevailed that led to the formation of a coalition government under the veteran politician Alexandros Zaimis, known as '*Ikoumeniki*', in which all the major parties had seats in the cabinet.

On 14 December 1926 the Minister of Army Affairs in the '*Ikoumeniki*' government, Alexandros Mazarakis, introduced a bill on the status of 2,836 officers dismissed from the army between 1922 and 1926, most precisely because of their anti-Venizelist activities. The Populist party deputies in the government made the rehabilitation of these officers a condition for reconciliation. The heated discussion of the bill in parliament showed the importance that both sides attached to the issue.[1] Populist deputies argued that since most officers had been dismissed *en masse* after the November 1923 *coup*, they should all be readmitted and judged in future, along with officers on active duty, by their professional competence rather than their political affiliations.[2] Liberal deputies retorted that the purpose of any decision on the question ought to be to prevent politically-minded officers from undermining the future unity of the army. Therefore, according to the Liberals, the degree of political involvement of the officers in question should be the sole criterion of whether they should be readmitted or not.[3] Valid as the argument of the Liberals may have been, there was no way of denying the Populist accusation that the officer corps then on active duty was dominated by elements that had been responsible for past republican *coups*. Because the records of republican officers were not also examined, the concern of the military establishment to keep political officers out of the

---

[1] *Ephimeris ton Syzitiseon tis Voulis* (Gazette of Parliamentary Debates), session of 7-14 December 1926, p. 91.

[2] *Ibid.*, p. 136.

[3] *Ibid.*, p. 141 (speech by Georgios Papandreou).

service revealed its intention to preserve the *status quo* of Liberal supremacy in the army. The Populists, anxious to improve their position in the corps, clamoured for impartial judgement. Although the lessons from the Pangalos dictatorship were still fresh, the initial resolution of politicians to desist from manipulating the army was weakened by the prospect of a royalist comeback. The '*Ikoumeniki*' government, which had been brought into being by a genuine effort to rid politics from military influence, faced its first crisis on precisely that issue.[4] On 26 May 1927 Venizelos, who had left politics in 1924 in disgust at military interventions, wrote to Plastiras:

> General Othonaios has informed me that the army is determined to resist the reinstatement of the dismissed officers. I have great confidence in his honesty and uprightness, and unless he is misinformed, the situation seems dangerous. He insists that both Papathanasiou and K. Manetas, together with the rest of the officers on active duty, are of the same opinion. He also believes that even you would admit that cooperation between reinstated officers and those already in the army would be impossible.[5]

Plastiras replied[6] that the fears of Othonaios were unfounded, and urged Venizelos to disregard them. On 31 May 1927 Tertikas, a close friend of Plastiras, wrote asking him to assume the leadership of Othonaios' movement, or at least not to oppose it. His letter reveals the annoyance of a republican officer on active duty at the effort by Plastiras to discourage those opposed to the reinstatement of royalists.[7]

On the whole, republican officers disapproved of the moves being made towards political reconciliation. Rumours that General Othonaios was plotting against the government not only affected prices on the stock market, but also strengthened the precarious solidarity between traditional opponents in parliament. Some deputies blamed the army for all the misfortunes visited on Greece, and others openly admitted their responsibility for past involvement

[4] Gazette of Parliamentary Debates, session of 7–14 December 1926, p. 157.
[5] The Plastiras papers in the Benaki museum.
[6] *Ibid.*
[7] *Ibid.*

in military *coups*. Information about exorbitant military costs was disclosed, proving that 35 per cent of an annual budget of 8,801,000,000 drachmas was absorbed by military expenses. (France allocated only 15 per cent of its annual budget, England 14 per cent, and Italy 18 per cent.) In Greece there was an officer for every twelve soldiers, compared to one for every twenty-four in France and one for every eighteen in Yugoslavia.[8]

On 20 December 1926, a bill was approved in parliament authorising a Higher Military Council to decide on the fate of the officers. The Council, headed by retired General A. Haralambis, was composed of five Army Corps commanders and four generals recalled from retirement. On 18 December 1927 the Council decided, first, to reinstate 325 officers with the rank they would have achieved by 1927 had they not been dismissed, and secondly to grant a pension to most of the dismissed officers who had not completed the years of service necessary for one. The decision caused an immediate outcry from Populist deputies led by P. Tsaldaris, who considered the number of readmitted officers too small, as well as from republican officers in the army who held the opposite view. Members of the Liberal camp made a slight concession to Tsaldaris by allowing another sixteen to be readmitted, but this increased the irritation of republicans, who had much to lose from the sudden influx of 341 officers.[9] Crowding the Army List meant slower promotions, greater competition for desirable positions, and the strengthening of the anti-republican ranks by such avowed royalists as Alexander Papagos. Republican reaction was headed by Othonaios who had been retired from active duty in order that Metaxas and Tsaldaris would agree to join the coalition. The influential commander of the 1st Army Corps, K. Manetas, who had been punished for spreading rumours that the republic was in danger, openly declared his solidarity with Othonaios. Although the Ministry of Army Affairs had given strict orders against the issuing of news bulletins by the Army Corps Intelligence Services without prior authorisation, Manetas made use of such bulletins to express his grievances. When Metaxas and Papanastasiou met the rebellious Othonaios and Manetas to

---

[8] Gazette of Paliamentary Debates, session 10-17 December 1926, pp. 148-9.

[9] *Ibid.*, pp. 157-8, 170, 171, 175.

discuss a compromise, the prestige of the government was seriously impaired.[10]

Georgios Kondylis was not a candidate in the 1926 elections. Conciliatory tactics were unappealing to his volatile temperament, since he believed that his political ambitions could be achieved only in a state of turmoil which would allow him to appear as a strong man defending order. He was against readmitting dismissed officers to the army. In a long letter to Venizelos he accused two ministers, G. Kaphandaris and A. Michalakopoulos, of failing to keep their promise never to allow royalist officers to return. He insinuated that Venizelos himself had become a victim of the illusion that the '*Ikoumeniki*' government would reconcile republicans with royalists, and Venizelists with anti-Venizelists. In Kondylis' estimation, the '*Ikoumeniki*' experiment was no more than an opportunity for the royalists to infiltrate the army.

> The reinstated 341 [mainly senior officers] will forever owe their comeback to the royalist politicians and their royalist friends in the army and will feel bitter against republican politicians and generals who opposed their reinstatement. These officers, though removed from service for such a long time, will be given commands and will decide the fate of their juniors who confronted and captured them in Nares and Kitheron.[...] With these facts in mind it is easy to estimate the future of the army. Ideological differences and old divisions rekindled by self-interest and the inherent instinct in every man of domination will instil discord in the ranks of the army which requires ties of mutual respect and cooperation in order to accomplish its high mission.[11]

Venizelos' reply was much too clear to allow Kondylis any margin for arbitrary interpretation.

---

[10] Georgios Vouros, *Panagis Tsaldaris*, Athens, 1955, pp. 105–11. Interview with Mrs Lina Tsaldari, Athens, August 1971. FO 371/12170/1357/786/19 from P. Loraine, despatch no. 3025, January 1927, 'Minister of Defence ordered First Army Corps to cease circulation of "Information Bulletins" spreading false rumours of Royalist movement', FO 371/12170/1363/786/19 from P. Loraine, despatch no. 40; 'General Manetas was blamed for the matter of the "Bulletins" and was removed from the First Army Corps for one month.' *The Times*, 18 January 1927.

[11] *Ethnikos Kiryx*, 'Eleven Years of Political Turmoil', by P. Katsambas, 20 November 1954, p. 4.

*Halepa (Crete), 7 May 1927*

My dear General,

The public's instinct supported the need for a coalition government before my own opinion that it was necessary ever became known. I was aware of the shortcomings of National Front governments before the present one was formed, and that is why its problems neither surprised me nor discouraged me. I am convinced that there are times when the task of common salvation cannot be handled by a partisan government, especially if it is weak. Instead a truce is necessary so that salvation can be achieved through common effort. Greece found itself in precisely that state after the holocaust of the Pangalos dictatorship.[...] Greece had been in a far worse state than France when Poincaré was invited to form a National Front government.

I am sorry of course that none of the objectives set by the government —settlement of the military question, voting of the [republican] constitution, economic reform — has yet been achieved. I am confident, however, that we are nearing their realisation.

The decision of the committee of generals...is, I think, fair and holds no dangers for the army of republican Greece. [...] In spite of the economic burden it may cause, it will be entirely justified if it achieves the recognition by the royalists in parliament that the military question has been permanently solved. Without such formal recognition I am confident that the republican leaders in parliament will not ratify the decision of the committee... As I understand the situation, I cannot see what alternative there is to the present arrangement. The National Front government will inevitably fall, or it will succeed, in which case its life will again be limited, having fulfilled the reasons for its existence. I think we should all hope that success will end its term rather than failure.[12]

In another letter to Othonaios sent on 14 May 1927, Venizelos expressed his approval of the commitee's decision. On the 24th, however, Othonaios visited Venizelos in Crete and apparently persuaded him to oppose readmission. Two days later Venizelos wrote to Kaphandaris and Mazarakis and asked them not to publish the tables of reinstated officers, giving the following reason for the request:

> [...] If it is confirmed that publication of the tables will cause military intervention, it is preferable to cancel it even if this means the unavoidable fall of the government. If the fall of

---

[12] The Kondylis papers, held by Photis Katsambas.

the National Front prevents a new military *coup* and allows the formation of a new government of politicians, that is preferable to an open confrontation.[13]

Venizelos refused to believe that the possibility of military intervention was remote until Plastiras assured him that he would personally prevent any attempt against the government. In a telegram sent on 30 May, Venizelos thanked Plastiras for his assistance and authorised him to put an end to the republican conspiracy. The President of the Republic, Admiral Koundouriotis, who had also been persuaded against the publication of the tables and had left Athens for his home in the island of Hydra, was rushed back to sign the document. At the same time, dissident officers such as the commander of the 1st Army Corps General K. Manetas, the Athens garrison commander Colonel A. Protosyngelos (a client of Kondylis), and the commanding officer of the 2nd Infantry Regiment, Colonel L. Spais, were all replaced.[14] Spais had been removed from his position in the Ministry of Defence and punished for publishing a threatening article in the newspaper *Eleftheros Logos*, but when ordered to leave his position in the 2nd Infantry Regiment, he appealed to his junior officers to rise against the government but was ignored and had to leave in disgrace.[15] Plastiras meanwhile summoned influential republican officers to his home and asked them to abstain from any armed intervention. He then took part in an emergency conference at the Ministry of Army Affairs and made a public statement that he would defend the government against any military threat. Although they held him responsible for the execution of the royalist politicians in 1923, Populist deputies were forced to welcome Plastiras' assistance because it was evident that without his influence there was little hope of the controversial bill being enforced.

[13] Vouros, p. 110. FO 371/12170/5309 P. Loraine to F.O. despatch no. 212, 2 June 1927.

[14] G. Daphnis, *I Ellas metaxy dyo polemon*, vol. A, Athens: Ikaros 1955, pp. 354–6. FO 371/12168/460 P. Loraine to F.O. despatch no. 447, 31 December 1927: 'Newspaper *Politeia* (supporting Metaxas) published the charter of a new league of officers of the Navy, Army and Gendarmerie, under the title "Republican Guard" Article 4 sets forth the objects of the league as being: (*a*) the safeguarding of the Republican regime, (*b*) protection of the officer corps in such a way so that entrance and removal would take place on the basis of the existing law concerning the status of officers, (*c*) exclusion of all officers who have been retired or dismissed since the counter-revolution of 1923.'

[15] L. Spais, *Peninta chronia stratiotis*, Athens, p. 185; Vouros, 1970, p. 113.

Faced with opposition on two fronts, Othonaios was obliged to drop his plan to launch an anti-government *coup*. According to officers of his circle[16], Venizelos persuaded Othonaios to desist from an armed conflict by promising to reinstate him in active duty when the opportunity arose. However, the preventive action by Plastiras was not forgiven by Othonaios' supporters, and this caused yet another feud among Venizelist officers. The significance of these personal quarrels proved far-reaching in the political developments of the following decade, especially during the 1935 *coup*. On 2 June 1927, Venizelos wrote to Plastiras thanking him for his services to the republic: '[I] regret that I took General Othonaios' advice and information seriously and was led to believe that we were on the brink of a revolution.[...] I am glad that you were not influenced by my own hesitation....'[17]

The motives of Plastiras in assisting the '*Ikoumeniki*' have remained open to conjecture. Rumours that Pangalos had been directing a new *coup* from his prison cell caused anxiety among republicans, who felt that support for the government was the only guarantee against a new dictatorship. Reports about his plans were contradictory. In his letters of 22 June and 7 July 1927, Major H. Papathanasopoulos wrote to Plastiras that Pangalist officers had tried to persuade republicans who disagreed with the reinstatement of anti-Venizelists to rise against the government. However, Diamesis, Spais, Dais and others who had been persecuted during the Pangalos regime claimed that the ex-dictator was in fact backing officers who were seeking readmission. Thus both Othonaios and Plastiras, by referring to a different set of evidence or rumours, could claim that they were opposing Pangalos.[18]

A letter dated 16 June 1927, written to Plastiras by Georgios Papandreou, may add yet another angle to Plastiras' motives. Papandreou, who had remained close to Plastiras since 1922, informed him that the Minister of Finance, Kaphandaris, was expecting the dissolution of the '*Ikoumeniki*' in the autumn of 1927 and would possibly be willing to back an all-Liberal government. 'Our cabinet will follow after the fall of the *Ikoumeniki*', wrote

---

[16] Kondylis papers.

[17] Plastiras papers.

[18] *The Times*, 21 April, 1 June 1927; Plastiras papers; FO 371/12170/2664 P. Loraine to FO despatch no. 111, 11 March 1927. FO 371/12170/3876 P. Loraine to F.O. despatch no 164, 20 April 1927.

Papandreou. 'Have a good rest this summer because there is a lot of work ahead.'[19] Whether Plastiras was influenced in his decision to aid the '*Ikoumeniki*' by being promised the prestigious post of 'Inspector-General of the Army' is difficult to confirm. However, it is certain that in 1927 several officers, among them Kondylis and Plastiras, decided to legitimise their influential position. As the country returned to consensual politics after years of confrontation, a number of Liberal retired officers made a concerted effort to enter parliamentary politics.

At first the legacy of the '*Ikoumeniki*' in restoring civilian supremacy was strengthened by the return of Venizelos to active politics in 1928. However, the military did not abstain from conspiracies for long. When Venizelos began to raise the spectre of a restoration of the monarchy in 1932, many republican officers who had always been susceptible to cries of alarm rallied to his side. First Othonaios and then Plastiras mobilised their followers[20] in support of the allegedly threatened republic, thus ending the brief period of military inertia.

---

[19] Plastiras papers.

[20] Othonaios was after all reinstated by Venizelos but he refused to reach an understanding with Plastiras in spite of the fact that both were promoting the same cause.

# 7

## THE SIGNIFICANCE OF THE MARCH 1935 *COUP* AND THE FORCES BEHIND ITS ORGANISATION

The indigenous anomalies that plagued Greek parliamentary life between 1915 and 1926 and the rise of authoritarian ideologies in Europe contributed to the ebbing away of democracy in the country. Although the opposition to the monarchy mounted after the Asia Minor catastrophe and the *coup* of 1923, republican fervour among the military was not combined with corresponding respect for parliamentary democracy. Such military strongmen of the republic as Kondylis, Pangalos, Plastiras, Othonaios *et al.* each savoured a personal version of authoritarian rule.[1]

From the end of 1922, '*Dimokratia*', with its double meaning of democracy and republic, had become a very inclusive term. For Venizelist Liberals '*Dimokratia*' had in fact been secured with the intervention of the army and the execution of the most prominent royalist leaders in 1922. To the republicans in the army between 1923-4 it signified the expulsion of the monarchy and its clientele. Only a few progressive intellectuals associated the term with social reform.[2] Regardless of whether they felt favourably inclined to it or not, the public were aware of its partisan character. Terminating a brief interlude of cooperation between the major parties (1927), the return to active politics of Venizelos in 1928 confirmed the impression that the republic was associated with his party.

Between 1926 and 1933 the credibility of parliamentary institutions was temporarily restored but the repercussions of economic recession in the rest of Europe caused serious turbulence.

---

[1] S. Maximos, *Koinovoulio i dictatoria?*, Athens: Stochastis, 1975.

[2] A. Papanastasiou, *Politika kimena*, vol. A, Athens: Byron, 1976, pp. 358, 383, 423.

In March 1935 a coalition of republican officers and civilians sought to overthrow the government of Panagis Tsaldaris (a moderate conservative), allegedly to avert an impending return of the monarchy. Of those involved in the *coup* of March 1935 who were interviewed between 1969 and 1971, not one admitted to having favoured the idea of insurrection at the time when it broke out. Some claimed to have been drawn into it unwittingly, others halfheartedly out of a sense of solidarity with their comrades. Retrospective denunciations are not uncommon in private accounts. What is interesting to note, however, is that republicans who opposed the *coup* chose to do so only on the practical grounds that they judged the action to be untimely. It can be doubted whether this opposition was sincere for two reasons.

First, because of the favourable position of republicans within the army and navy, rational forecasts gave the *coup* a good chance of success. And secondly, our observation is that most of the republican sense of outrage is directed against those who carried out the *coup* rather than against Eleftherios Venizelos, who gave the signal for it. Had the *coup* succeeded, feelings on the subject might well have been positive.

Making a distinction between civilian and military conspirators does not clarify at all the nature of the opposition that existed between the different groupings that made up the loose republican coalition responsible for the *coup* of 1935. Examining the different categories of the military who were implicated is more revealing. There were roughly three such categories. First, there was a group which played a minor role in the outbreak of the *coup*, made up of older retired officers who somehow felt, like Nicolaos Plastiras,[3] that an officer's mission does not cease with his career in the service. Generals Neokosmos Grigoriadis and Anastasios Papoulas, both members of 'Republican Defence', were two such cases. Secondly, there were officers who had been dismissed either at the fall of the dictator Theodoros Pangalos in 1926, like Napoleon Zervas and Andreas Kolialexis, or after the attempt by Plastiras to seize power in 1933, like Leonidas Spais, Ilias Diamesis and Miltiadis Kimisis, whose main motive was the desire to re-enter

---

[3] Plastiras fled the country after failing to prevent the Populist leader, P. Tsaldaris, from assuming office on the next day of the elections (6 March 1933). A number of his accomplices were dismissed from the army and navy. T. Veremis, 'Anekdota keimena gyro apo to kinima tis 6 Martiou 1933', *Mnimon*, Athens, 1975, pp. 81-100.

the army or navy. These officers formed the radical clique in 'Republican Defence'. Their obstinate faith in Plastiras and their impatience in pressing for action soon brought them at odds with the third group, the ESO ('*Eliniki Stratiotiki Organosis*' – Greek Military Organisation), which consisted up till 1934 of junior officers, graduates of the Military Academy, with ambitious plans to reform the army into an élitist institution, independent of politics.[4]

Although the *coup* was initially conceived by Venizelist politicians as a pre-emptive measure against the Populist government, the active participation of civilians in it was ultimately limited to Venizelos and a few of his close friends. Most of the politicians involved had made feeble attempts to direct different military groupings, and were either ignored by the officers or willingly dispensed with at various stages of the organisation. An account of the civilian role in the *coup* is necessary at this point.

On 29 June 1933 Venizelos was greeted in Thessaloniki by an enthusiastic crowd demonstrating against the government's halfhearted efforts to apprehend the criminals responsible for an attempt on his life. On 3 July 1933 five prominent Liberals (Venizelos, Mylonas, Alexandros Papanastasiou, Ioannis Sophianopoulos, Georgios Kaphandaris) met at the house of Alexandros Zannas in Thessaloniki. Kaphandaris pointed out that the republic had been seriously eroded by changes in the army and the police, effected by the Minister of Army Affairs, Georgios Kondylis. Fearing a royalist dictatorship, he proposed the formation of a military association to act as a safeguard for the republic. Mylonas and Sophianopoulos agreed, but Papanastasiou objected on the grounds that military organisations rarely kept their defensive character and easily went on to the offensive.[5] Kaphandaris' proposition that Zannas should study the matter on behalf of them all was finally accepted. Venizelos left for France with the assurance that

---

[4] Stephanos Saraphis, who dominated the ESO by March 1935, had a different view of the role of the military. He felt that the armed forces could direct policy from a distance, threatening politicians with strong measures if they failed to adhere to their wishes. His attachment to his patron, General Alexandros Othonaios, for whom he might have envisaged the presidency of the republic, brought him into direct collision with Plastiras, Othonaios' rival since 1927, and 'Republican Defence'. S. Saraphis, *Istorikes anamniseis*, vol. I, Athens 1952, p. 385.

[5] G. Daphnis, *I Ellas metaxy dyo polemon*, vol. II, Athens: Ikaros, 1955, p. 295. S. Gonatas, *Apomnimonevmata*, Athens 1958, pp. 357-8.

the organisation was under way.[6] Fifteen days later Kaphandaris, Papanastasiou, Zannas, Maris and Mylonas met at Mylonas' house in Kifissia; Zannas was officially appointed president of the prospective military organisation and a system of liaison between officers and politicians was established. Zannas accepted the presidency of the group, in spite of doubts, on condition that there would be total secrecy concerning the inner core of officers, that he would be given complete freedom of action, and that the republican politicians would actively support the effort.[7]

The first person initiated into the organisation by Zannas was an old hand in naval conspiracies, Captain Andreas Kolialexis. Although dismissed from the navy after the fall of Pangalos in 1926, he was respected by republican naval officers. Along with Saraphis (whom Zannas persuaded to join), Kolialexis and Zannas formed the first Revolutionary Committee. The latter had in the mean time succeeded in bringing together Venizelos and Plastiras after a year in which they had been totally estranged. Understandably, Plastiras nursed a grudge against his old patron for having abandoned him while executing his *coup* of March 1933 – a *coup* that Venizelos had initially appeared to encourage. Venizelos' initiative in asking for a reconciliation did not fail to flatter his client into agreeing to cooperate.

From the beginning of 1934 rumours of a Kondylis-Metaxas dictatorship were in the air, but by July the threat of an improvised uprising by 'Republican Defence' was far more serious. Plastiras, who had favoured such a *coup*, was reluctant to persuade the 'Defence' to postpone the date of action but Venizelos finally convinced him of the need for better coordination. On 1 August 1934 an agreement was signed by Zannas, Venizelos and Plastiras, but reconciliation between the two pillars of the republic brought no joy to 'Republican Defence' whose plans for an early *coup* were thus foiled. However, the Revolutionary Committee was

---

[6] The papers of Alexandros Zannas; A. Zannas, 'To moiraion kinima pou efere ton Eleftherio Venizelo ston tafo', *To Vima*, 25 January 1959.

[7] Interview with Mrs Virginia Zannas, Kifisia, summer 1970. Alexandros Zannas, Venizelos' most respected supporter in Thessaloniki, had been one of the architects of the 'National Defence' movement which instigated in 1916 a revolt against King Constantine's position. He later became a successful Air Minister in a cabinet under Venizelos. E. Kavadias, *O naftikos polemos tou 1940*, Athens 1950, p. 36.

reshaped to admit the representative of the 'Defence', retired General Prassos Vlachos.[8]

Periclis Argyropoulos was the foremost political adviser of 'Republican Defence'. In his memoirs he claimed to have originated the idea of pre-emptive action against the Populist government after the attempt on Venizelos, which the latter had not overruled when he suggested it. His insistence on precisely that strategy throughout 1934 caused much discord and confusion in the republican camp. Zannas, whom he accused of authoritarian tendencies and of satisfying personal ambitions, became his primary target from the outset. He also accused Zannas of trying to persuade Venizelos to assume the leadership of the *coup*, thus endangering his prestige in case of failure.[9]

The allegation is not altogether just: besides Zannas' testimony to the contrary, the latter's mother-in-law – that distinguished lady of Venizelism, Mrs Penelope Delta – had repeatedly appealed to Venizelos to abstain from official leadership of the conspiracy. Either because Zannas had approached their rival organisation of officers on active duty or because they suspected him of aiming at the leadership of the coup, 'Republican Defence' began to slander him to Plastiras. Exasperated by their offensive attitude, Zannas decided to resign from the organisation of the *coup*, and he finally broke with Argyropoulos when it became apparent that the latter had been preparing an uprising without previously consulting the Revolutionary Committee.[10] Argyropoulos, who was hoping to force the hand of officers on active duty to turn against the government, accused Zannas and Saraphis of foiling his plans –and Saraphis in particular, whom he considered a friend of Othonaios and hence opposed to Plastiras, of using the prestige of Venizelos in order to manipulate the views of officers on active duty.[11]

In August 1934 Venizelos wrote the following letter to Gonatas:

....Our friend Mr Zannas will bring you minutes of the agreement concluded with General Plastiras after long discussions through

---

[8] *To Vima*, 27 January 1959, p. 1. Article by A. Zannas.

[9] Interview with Mrs Marie Argyropoulos, Athens, October 1970; P. Argyropoulos, *Apomnimonevmata*, vol. I, Athens 1970, pp. 478-80.

[10] The A. Zannas papers, Daphnis, vol. II, p. 284.

[11] Argyropoulos, p. 480.

which we hope to avoid isolated and hasty uprisings by impatient republican elements. Choosing you was imperative after the overt enmity of the recalcitrant republicans towards Mr Zannas. There is no other person who combines the trust of both myself and the Leader [Plastiras].[12]

It was through the enclosed minutes of the agreement that Gonatas discovered he had already been chosen to replace Zannas.[13] Without bothering to consult him, Venizelos had decided that Gonatas would be the president of the Revolutionary Committee. Gonatas complained in his memoirs: '....Neither Vlachos nor Saraphis ever consulted me and the signatories of the agreement [Venizelos and Plastiras] kept corresponding and coming in contact directly with various revolutionary elements.'[14]

Saraphis contradicted Gonatas in his own memoirs, stating that he had consulted him on several occasions but that Gonatas had been indecisive.[15] Reluctant to involve himself directly, but too timid to refuse Venizelos, Gonatas tried on several occasions to dissuade his leader from carrying out the *coup*, but Venizelos had already been bound by a network of commitments which even he could not control. The removal of Zannas from the Revolu-

---

[12] Gonatas, pp. 365-6.

[13] Gonatas, pp. 366-7. 'Eleftherios Venizelos-Nicolaos Plastiras. Mr Zannas had informed us that impatient officers who had been dismissed from the army because of the events of 6 March 1933 had decided to stage a *coup* on a specific day. The operation was postponed because the units of northern Greece and officers in Athens were informed by Mr Zannas that Venizelos disapproved of the movement. To avoid similar isolated republican activities which might lead to disaster, the following decisions were reached: (1) The formation of a three-member committee consisting of Capt. Kolialexis, Col. Saraphis and Gonatas, who will be its president and without whose opinion no military action will be taken; (2) Efforts to reach an understanding with the government on the following points: Re-election of Zaimis [President of the Republic], return to the electoral system of proportional representation and a general amnesty for participants in the *coup* of 1933. Once the system of proportional representation is established Venizelos will not run for office again. [...] (3) If the government refuses the plea of the Senate for a joint session and attempts a second voting of its electoral bill only by parliament, the parties of the 'National Coalition' will organise demonstrations to protest against the infringement of their rights and demand that the unconstitutional bill be rejected by the President of the Republic. [...] If all the above are not taken into consideration and the government conducts elections with the unconstitutional electoral system, then the opposition will abstain and will protect the [republican] system in accordance with the final article of the constitution, trying to bring about the fall of the government by any means, including force.'

[14] Gonatas, p. 366.

[15] Saraphis, p. 347.

tionary Committee meant that the organisation of the *coup* lacked effective coordination.

By 1935, the conviction of Venizelos that the republican officers were still the servants of his political designs had been somewhat overtaken by events. His flight to Crete after friction with members of the government in parliament had deprived him of a clear view of newly emerging military groupings. Although old allies such as General Othonaios were still active in the army, the latter's staff officer Colonel Saraphis was now aiming to lead an organisation made up of junior officers. Contrary to what Venizelos may have thought, the members of the ESO had no intention of facilitating the return of officers who had been dismissed for collaborating with Plastiras in his *coup* of 1933. Between the members of the ESO, who were sophisticated Military Academy graduates, and the dismissed officers of the 'Republican Defence' there was no point of agreement other than their general desire to overthrow the Populist government. In fact, a large gap separated them, and Venizelos failed to realise that the goals of the two groups were incompatible. It was this very rivalry among hypothetical allies that undermined his *coup* of 1935.

The origins of the ESO can be placed sometime in early 1932 when Venizelos was threatening his Populist opponents with military intervention. With General Othonaios organising a clandestine 'Military League', insubordination had again become rampant. Younger officers such as Lieutenants Nicolaos Skanavis and Markos Kladakis, despite being Venizelists, felt indignant at the way political patrons were corrupting the professional ethos of officers and turning them into the familiar '*condottieri*' of the 1920s (Loufas, Karakoufas, Dertilis and others). By 1932 the percentage of Academy graduates among junior officers had risen. Those from Evelpidon, in whom professional pride was strong, formed a separate caste within the army. They read literature and psychology, discussed international affairs and despised their seniors who had risen from the ranks. Education was at a higher premium than reckless valour, and the independence of the army from politics was their most cherished goal.[16]

Late in 1932 Lieutenant Nikolaos Skanavis, leader of the class

---

[16] We have reached that conclusion after examining the attitude of fifty Academy graduates of that period.

of 1922, met Lieutenant Georgios Kostopoulos to discuss the formation of an association of junior graduates of the Academy. The need for it was based on three particular reasons. First, there was the grievance of remaining in the same rank indefinitely; all members of the class of 1922 were still lieutenants in 1933. On this issue they reiterated the relevance of the *pronunciamento* of 1909. It was necessary for officers who had been kept in the armed forces beyond the age-limit to be retired. Secondly, officers who had been involved with political action in the past and whose presence therefore caused controversy, should be retired also. They felt that political bigotry had divided the army and made it a prey to aspiring politicians. Finally there had been no significant acquisition of arms since 1925.[17]

Yannis Tsigantes, leader of the class of 1920, was the first captain to be initiated into the ESO. He was a dashing young man of thirty-five whose air of self-assurance betrayed his upper-middle-class background in Romania. In 1929 he had published a military manual with far greater pretensions than any previous literature.[18] It was a mixture of logic, psychology, sociology and biology and had the unusual feature of dealing with few subjects of specifically military concern. The book began by stating that the army had been the foremost school for democracy and that officers were entrusted with the task of transmitting national ideals as well as military training. There are chapters entitled 'Reasons for Human Psychological Differences' and 'The Relationship between Psychology and Physiology', and the bibliography included a note that the author consulted 500 documents in writing the book. This extravagant undertaking gives a good idea of the confusion in the minds of those who provided ESO with ideological directives. With this mixture of contemporary know-how and worldly arrogance Yannis Tsigantes became a model of the modern officer and probably the most prominent member of the ESO.[19]

The founders of the association were mainly Venizelist officers from the class of 1922 who made it a provision of the chapter that membership was limited to republican junior officers no more

[17] Interviews with Chris. Tsigantes, London, June 1970, and Athens, August 1970; Nicolaos Skanavis, Athens, August 1970; and Markos Kladakis, Athens, December 1970, September 1971 and October 1972.

[18] Y. Tsigantes, *I methodos ekpedefseos*, Athens 1929.

[19] Interview with Markos Kladakis.

senior than captains. Being a graduate of Evelpidon was not explicitly mentioned, but it was in fact a requirement for admission till 1933. The original charter did not provide for a leader and the position of the chairman was to rotate among its members. Meetings were called whenever one was thought necessary by a member. The ESO's loose organisation failed to protect it from ambitious strongmen and hindered its original aspiration for a system of democratic participation.

In 1933 Kladakis, who was in favour of a larger membership, suggested that the political position of officers should not be considered among the prerequisites for admission. The majority of members of the ESO agreed and the provision for 'confirmed republicanism' gave way to acceptance 'regardless of political conviction' (Kostopoulos disagreed with this and left the organisation). An alliance took place between officers with different party loyalties who joined forces to promote their occupational interests. Concern over promotion had temporarily convinced members of the ESO that political conflict did not serve their aims; thus all junior officers who shared a vague notion of reform, coupled with a very precise desire to see some of their seniors go, were welcome.[20] However, it was only a short honeymoon. In February 1933, shortly before Plastiras' coup in March, the leaders of the classes of 1920, 1921 and 1922 met to discuss the introduction of a clause in the charter requiring members to accept the republican system regardless of party preferences. The Populist party had already recognised the republic but some of its supporters in the army, preferring to keep their royalist sentiments alive, had left ESO. The leader of the class of 1921, Captain Ketseas, was the first such to go.

The leader of each class was the cadet with the highest overall average in lessons, conduct and personality. He was responsible for every collective activity of his class and in some cases even for the individual conduct of his classmates. Hence class leaders enjoyed considerable prestige and benefits throughout their career because the seniority of officers was determined not only by their year of graduation but also by the rank they held within their own class. Nevertheless, we have noticed how, with

---

[20] Markos Kladakis' private papers. Interview with Athanasios Tountas, Athens 1970. L. Spais, *Peninta chronia stratiotis*, Athens, 1970, p. 206.

few exceptions,[21] there had been no correlation between a man's academic rank and his subsequent achievement (or notoriety) in the army.

The ESO was opposed to the Plastiras *coup* of March 1933, and the Tsigantes brothers, along with many young Venizelist officers, had signed a protocol denouncing it.[22] Whether they were against Plastiras or the *coup* is not clear; what seems certain, however, is that the *coup* had been carried out by officers of the kind that the ESO would have been glad to get rid of. General Kimisis had persuaded Colonels Diamesis, Spais and Bizanis to join. Diamesis was known as the 'prince of the republic' because of his intense concern for its welfare, and Spais as the 'midwife' for his constant involvement in military politics.[23]

The abortive *coup* by Plastiras was followed by the dismissal of forty officers suspected of complicity. From this point till the March *coup* of 1935, these officers constantly conspired against the government. After the attempt on Venizelos' life, they joined 'Republican Defence', the arch-rival of the ESO, and were sarcastically termed by Venizelists the '*viastiki*', short for 'those in a hurry to regain their position'.

In 1934 the Minister of Army Affairs, Kondylis, raised the question of reforming the existing seniority in the Army List. Officers who had joined Venizelos on the side of the Entente in 1916 had been rewarded with a bonus of ten months' added seniority, and hence those who had chosen to remain stationed in Athens found themselves overtaken in seniority by some of their juniors.[24] The ESO agreed that the ten months' bonus be set aside but that the principle of promotion on the battlefield should remain. The ESO had obviously nothing to lose by Kondylis' proposed change since its oldest members had graduated from the Military Academy in 1920. By contrast Major Alkimos Bourdaras, a member of the 'National Defence' of 1916, had much to lose from the reform and was preparing his own private *coup* against the government. Yannis Tsigantes immediately suggested cooperating with Bourdaras but most officers, including Kladakis

---

[21] Pangalos, who had been the leader of the class of 1918, was such an exception.

[22] Information from Chr. Tsigantes.

[23] Information from Plastiras' adjutant Col. Mihalis Minioudakis, December 1971.

[24] Daphnis, vol. II, pp. 258-9. L. Paraskevopoulos, *Anamniseis*, vol. I, Athens, 1934, p. 310.

and Skanavis, overruled him. The idea of conspiring simply because Bourdaras' seniority was at stake did not appeal to anyone except Tsigantes, who thought this moment opportune to annex his organisation. The possible benefit did not seem worth the trouble involved and Tsigantes suffered a loss of prestige.[25]

In February 1934 Yannis Tsigantes proposed amending the charter in favour of admitting senior officers. Despite an initial reaction against the proposition, the decision was adopted, at the expense of the organisation's homogeneity. Along with the élitist junior officers of the Academy came officers with little formal military education and very specific political commitments based on their past activities. The association was henceforth marked by the very characteristic it was set up to oppose: allegiance to a civilian patron, in this instance Venizelos. Kladakis complained that Tsigantes had often kept the ESO uninformed about his activities while wrongly posing as leader of the organisation. His practice of taking unauthorised initiatives was furthered by Saraphis, who in turn claimed to be in charge. As a result of this influx of middle-ranking officers, the founders of ESO were increasingly ignored as a decision-making body, and the principles of their charter were contradicted.[26]

Throughout 1934 most officers in the ESO carried out an intensive recruitment of new members. Yannis Tsigantes had come into contact with Saraphis, and Kladakis initiated Colonel Spyros Giorgoulis into the organisation.[27] The reason for this urgency was that Othonaios had reported to Saraphis that he had been asked by an agent of Kondylis if he was interested in participating in a dictatorial triumvirate.

'Republican Defence', on the other hand, was officially authorised in 1932 as an association of retired officers and elderly civilians with strong feelings that the republic should be preserved. Its first president had been a leading officer in Venizelos' secessionist army of Thessaloniki in 1916 and later a senator under the republic,

---

[25] Markos Kladakis' papers.

[26] Interview with Chris. Tsigantes, London, June 1970.

[27] Officers who were initiated had to sign a protocol of 'honour': 'Faithful to our oath to defend our country and the republican regime, we, the undersigned, assume the responsibility upon our word of military honour ...to resist any attempt at establishing a dictatorship or the monarchy or any threat against the existing republican constitution. Keeping secret the content of the present document is also a question of honour for us.' This particular copy dated 24 April 1934 bears the signatures of fifteen members.

Neokosmos Grigoriadis. After Plastiras' coup and the attempt against Venizelos, the character of 'Republican Defence' changed from a social gathering of senior citizens into a centre of belligerent propaganda and conspiratorial activity; its ranks were revitalised by the entry of dismissed officers from the *coup* of March 1933. Its renaming as 'Panhellenic Republican Defence' was meant to emphasise its nation-wide appeal and following.

In May 1934 the presidency of the organisation was assumed by the one-time anti-Venizelist commander of the Greek forces in Asia Minor, Anastasios Papoulas. In a complete change of heart matched only by Kondylis and Admiral Hadjikyriakos,[28] Papoulas had been totally rehabilitated from his royalist past. During the trials of the Gounaris government in 1922 he had appeared as a witness for the prosecution, an act which earned him the everlasting hatred of the anti-Venizelist world, and his subsequent *volte face* may have been an effort to protect himself from the revenge of his ex-colleagues. Towards the end of 1933, Papoulas launched a journalistic onslaught against the government, and an article he published in the daily *Republican Struggle* of 11 October 1933 began: 'The reinstatement of the monarchy can only bring disaster and destruction.'

Two weeks later, in the same newspaper, he drew the public's attention to Kondylis' effort to change the Army List:

> The well-known plan for changing the republican composition of the army has been discussed in the Senate. It is imperative that all republican leaders and all the republican people remain on the alert. The republican officers must be ready to defend our republican regime. [...] These officers who have the great honour to play the leading part in establishing the republic should be aware – and they are aware – that with them lies the responsibility for protecting the republic. [...] The republican officers have written with their struggles one of the most glittering pages of contemporary Greek history. This history they must adorn with new struggles. We should not forget that during the hundred years of our independence the army has played a very important role in the democratisation of our political regime (1843, 1863, 1909). In 1922 the republican

---

[28] Both were fervent exponents of the republic in 1924, who joined the anti-Venizelist camp in 1932 as members of a Tsaldaris cabinet.

officers mitigated the Asia Minor disaster. [...] The great majority of Greek officers are from the working people. [...] which is why the people and the army will now defend the republic and will then march together to face new social struggles.[29]

Most of the newpaper was dominated by pictures of Plastiras, who was generally regarded as the leader of 'Republican Defence' *in absentia*. A reply to the *Republican Struggle* was the pro-government *Popular Struggle* with articles that even outdid its rival in its fanatical tone: 'Greece will never rest until the miserable old man from Halepa [Venizelos] is led like a common criminal to the gallows or to the madhouse.'[30]

Venizelos himself tried to keep Papoulas in line:

.... You have to try and avoid all misunderstanding about your organisation. Make it clear so that everyone will understand ...that your organisation has no other purpose but the defence of the republic, if it is endangered. The government may remain in power as long as parliament supports it. Under these terms I will declare that I agree to the 'Panhellenic Republican Defence' and give it my blessing....[31]

The 'National Republican Sentinel of Northern Greece' was founded in August 1933 in Thessaloniki and its charter was approved by a court on 11 November 1933. The stated reasons for its foundation were that the Senate was threatened with extinction, that distinguished members of the Populist party had formed royalist clubs with the sole purpose of restoring the monarchy, that the most dangerous of these organisations, the 'National Political Association', enjoyed the favour of the government itself, that members of the said organisation had paraded in central streets in Athens accompanied by a naval band, that two ministers had been present at one of the organisation's rallies applauding royalist slogans, that ministers had threatened directors of republican clubs with exile, that unconstitutional laws were being put into effect which threatened the position of republican officers in the army, and that an attempt had been made on the life of Venizelos.[32]

---

[29] *Dimokratikos Agon* (newspaper), 25 October 1933.

[30] *Laikos Agon* (newspaper), 13 December 1933.

[31] Y. Benekos, *To kinima tou 1935* (The *coup* of 1935), Athens 1958, p. 70.

[32] *Ibid.*, p. 71.

Papoulas established close ties with the 'National Republican Sentinel of Northern Greece', which became a branch of 'Republican Defence'. At a solemn ceremony in Thessaloniki, he made a clear insinuation about the intentions of 'Defence' while presenting the organisation with a Greek flag, pointing out that 'this is a battle standard, not something you hang outside a club'.[33]Although the second article of its statute stated its intent to observe the law, the organisation had already tasted the success of unauthorised activity. On 25 October 1934 armed members of 'Defence' had apprehended the bandit Karathanasis, who had been hired to kill Venizelos, and handed him over to the police. Although Karathanasis was a wanted man, government newspapers protested strongly against the arbitrary action taken by 'Republican Defence'.[34]

Alarm was caused by the election of Kotzias, a royalist, as Mayor of Athens, and officers on active duty gathered at the home of Lieut.-Colonel Christodoulos Tsigantes to decide how the ESO would go into action. A staff was organised on the lines of the official military model, but without deciding who would head it. The 1st Bureau was responsible for its organisation and command and would itself be under the direction of Lieut.-Colonel Giorgoulis with the assistance of Lieut.-Colonel Hondros. The 2nd Bureau, headed by Colonel Petros Grigorakis and Tsigantes, would deal with information and intelligence, and the 3rd Bureau, under Colonel Saraphis, was concerned with operations and communications. Captain Yannis Tsigantes would act as general coordinator of all the three Bureaux. The organisation would have as its representatives Major Thomas Sfetsios in Thessaloniki, Lieut.-Colonel Hondros in Serres, and Lieut.-Colonel Psarros in Veria. The introduction of higher-ranking officers into the ESO all but obliterated the influence of the junior officers who had founded it. Their last independent activity was the planning of a *coup* in the spring of 1934. However, General Delagrammatis, Director of the Military Academy, used his influence to avert the uprising.[35]

Meanwhile, 'Republican Defence' was dismayed to observe the growing influence of Saraphis over Venizelos. Advised by Zannas, Venizelos was increasingly favouring the more useful

---

[33] *Ibid.*, p. 74.

[34] *Epikaira* (magazine), 30 January 1970, pp. 62-3, 72.

[35] Kladakis' papers. Saraphis, p. 341.

officers on active duty instead of those who had been dismissed and were thus powerless. When Diamesis accused Saraphis of trying to prevent dismissed officers from returning to the army, Saraphis replied rather vaguely that, for reasons of security, more than one organisation was necessary. According to Kladakis, Saraphis had deliberately exaggerated the numbers of the ESO to Venizelos, and by claiming that there were 1,400 members rather than the actual number of 244 (of whom 90 per cent were staff officers), he made a *coup* seem much more feasible. What he wanted was the prestigious blessing of a patron with the calibre of Venizelos and at the same time to prevent 'Republican Defence' from playing any serious role in a prospective operation against the government.[36]

In July 1934 Saraphis was informed by the Athens garrison that Diamesis was planning to launch a *coup* with Zervas (the military adventurist of the Pangalos dictatorship who had been dismissed from the army in 1927):

> I sent a message that no one was to move and that they [officers friendly to Diamesis and Zervas] were only to obey orders given by officers on active duty. I informed Zannas of the events and went to Kifissia to inform George Ventiris and General Skandalis that it was necessary to summon Papanastasiou, Kaphandaris *et al.*, to use all their influence to prevent such a foolish action. At the same time I informed them [Diamesis and Zervas] directly that not only did I disagree.... but that I would join their opponents to save the republican officers from the consequences of their failure.[37]

It is interesting to note that politicians could still wield such influence over the military that they could dissuade them from carrying out their decision to rise.

When word came that the *coup* had been approved and blessed by Plastiras (Papathanasopoulos informed Saraphis of this), Zannas decided to go to France and attempt a reconciliation between Saraphis and Venizelos to make sure of effective coordination of any activities in the future. The positive result of that effort has already been discussed.

---

[36] Interview with Marcos Kladakis, Athens, November 1971.

[37] Saraphis, p. 345.

In August 1934 Venizelos invited members of the ESO to Crete, and pointed out to Saraphis, Giorgoulis and Chr. Trigantes the danger of a restoration of the monarchy, urging them to act on the same lines as the officers of the *pronunciamento* of 1909.[38] Saraphis replied that if circumstances led to a revolution they would wish to have Venizelos as their leader, but without the company of councillors such as Maris and Vourloumis, who had brought the republican camp into disrepute. It was the first time that the military protégé of Venizelos dared to impose conditions on his patron, but the significance of the incident escaped the old statesman who, since the meeting of July 1933, had retained the illusion that the army was still prepared to do his bidding.[39]

Unwittingly the ESO helped to diminish the prestige of the Venizelist political leadership, but otherwise it achieved little as an organisation. The aspirations of its founders to give it a corporate structure by emphasising criteria of professional merit rather than patronage relations came into conflict with the prevailing client system. The ESO had thus been condemned by the very aims of its founding charter. Since most of its articles set out a position contrary to the traditional operation of client networks, the charter fell into disuse while such active members as Saraphis and Yannis Tsigantes took the initiative in recruiting allies on the basis of their personal grievances and ambitions. Principles such as a clear separation between civilian and military authority, professional integrity and meritocracy were replaced by personal criteria.

The participation of Venizelist officers on active duty in the 1935 *coup* was almost total. Two significant exceptions were General Alexander Othonaios and naval Captain Ioannis Karavidas, who refused to participate for reasons other than ideological opposition.[40] Pending the presidential elections in the autumn of 1934, the republican Othonaios (head of the 2nd Branch of Army Inspection) had gone to northern Greece to prepare garrisons for possible action against the government. The reluctance of Tsaldaris to withdraw a controversial electoral law had linked politicians and

---

[38] Venizelos hoped that the military would limit their intervention to an overthrow of the existing government and that he would subsequently be summoned to step in. Interview with Spyros Giorgoulis, October 1972.

[39] Saraphis, pp. 346-7.

[40] Interview with N. Karavidas, Athens, October 1970.

officers disturbed by Kondylis' military reforms in a common opposition to the Populist party in power.

News of efforts at conciliation by Gonatas, serving the interests of politicians rather than the officers, reached Othonaios while he was delivering fiery speeches in support of the endangered republic. The general, who had been led to believe that the Venizelist camp was determined to resist any compromise over the government's intention to alter the republican *status quo* in the army, expressed his disgust with politicians and vowed to abstain from any future venture instigated by republicans. When later asked by Venizelos himself to accept the leadership of the March *coup*, he refused but promised to join in a provisional cabinet if the *coup* succeeded.[41]

A letter by Venizelos sent to Othonaios on 20 February sought to touch the General's feelings where they were most sensitive:

.... You are aware that a year ago I suggested that republican officers should organise in such a way as to be able to defend the system if confronted with an attempted restoration or the establishment of a dictatorship by Kondylis or Metaxas. Since that time conditions have changed significantly. The alteration of the Army List threatens to destroy permanently the very soul of the army. I was also informed that with General T. Manetas' removal from the 2nd Army Corps, the majority of the Supreme Military Council is with the government. There is no guarantee any longer against further purges of republican elements in the army.[...] I believe it is imperative that the republican world should take pre-emptive action.[42]

Othonaios delivered a written refusal, expressing his mistrust of politicians, on 25 February.

Othonaios had correctly assessed the reluctance of politicians to take part in an armed rebellion. Once their basic demand of withdrawal of the electoral law had been satisfied, the pertinent paragraph in the Plastiras-Venizelos agreement of August 1934 had lost its relevance for them.[43] This was: 'If the government conducts elections under the unconstitutional electoral system,

---

[41] Saraphis, pp. 348-9.

[42] Daphnis, vol I, Athens, p. 292.

[43] Interview with Pyrros Othonaios (brother of the general), Athens, August 1971.

then the opposition will abstain and will protect the [republican] regime in accordance with the final article of the constitution, pursuing the fall of the government by any means, including force.'[44] With the major threat against their interests gone, the signatories of the agreement of 3 July 1933, Papanastasiou and Mylonas, willingly detached themselves from the organisation of the *coup*. Gonatas did his best to forestall the outbreak, and although in his memoirs he mentions that Kaphandaris tried to persuade Venizelos to accelerate the process (in January 1935), there is no other evidence of the elder statesman's involvement.[45]

The second officer who refused to participate was the Director of the Naval Staff College, Captain Ioannis Karavidas. On 10 February 1935 Venizelos wrote a long letter to Lieut.-Commander Zangas, taking pains to explain the reasons that had driven him to decide on the *coup*. He was counting on Zangas to pass on the information to his superior officer in the Staff College. However, Zangas did more than merely initiate Karavidas into the organisation. Along with Argyropoulos, who was influential in naval circles, Zangas proposed that Karavidas should take on the leadership of the entire movement in the navy. Karavidas eagerly presented his own plan for capturing the fleet and for a large-scale operation against Athens. He proposed using part of the fleet to blockade the city and the rest to transport troops from Crete to capture it. His insistence on attacking the centre directly rather than moving in upon it from the periphery was founded on mistakes of past *coups* and was fundamentally sound, but his eccentric personality made relations with his colleagues difficult.

Karavidas claimed to this author that at the time when he accepted the leadership of the *coup* he had not been informed that a parallel organisation existed in the navy headed by Kolialexis. Argyropoulos had reassured him that his appointment was authorised by Venizelos, who was the unofficial leader of the operations. 'Of course Venizelos supports and finances the *coup*,' he was told; 'where else could Plastiras find the money for transport?'[46] However, when Karavidas learned of Kolialexis' posi-

[44] Gonatas, *Apomnimonevmata*, pp. 366-7.

[45] Gonatas, p. 367. In his letter of 6 December 1934, Gonatas tried to convey to Plastiras the discord existing among the rival factions of the republican camp. 'He who will attack first will be beaten.[...] it is exactly what Kondylis is hoping for. Desist therefore from unwittingly becoming Kondylis' ally in his plans.' Plastiras papers.

tion and the rejection of his own plan to capture Athens, he withdrew his support and was followed by Zangas.[47]

Kondylis meanwhile had been making provocative statements about the Venizelists. In his interview with *Estia* on 13 February 1935, he said that the people had given him the power to organise the country for war regardless of whether the enemy was external or internal. According to his biographer Stamatis Mercouris, the Minister of Army Affairs had been repeatedly urged to overthrow the moderate Tsaldaris and establish his own dictatorship. To Mercouris, the chief advocate of this plan, he replied: 'A dictatorship is untimely. [...] We have against us the organised party of Venizelos ... and the largest part of the Populist party. Stay calm and have confidence in me. Let our enemies make the first move with revolutionary and violent action, and rest assured that we will enforce order. Then, when everyone has seen their insane plans for themselves, we will again discuss the question of the regime and a dictatorship.'[48]

There is little doubt that Kondylis welcomed a Venizelist *coup*. If he suppressed it, as he did, he would emerge with increased prestige and power to do what he pleased. If, on the other hand, the *coup* showed early signs of success, he could allow himself ample time to join it. There is some evidence that Saraphis was on cordial terms with Colonel A. Protosyngelos, Director of the Ministry of Army Affairs and a friend of Kondylis, but it is difficult to prove that he had any sound reason to believe that Kondylis would cooperate. Kondylis had played a waiting game at the start of the *coup*, which enabled his enemies to accuse him of opportunism. In spite of government efforts to trace his whereabouts, he was nowhere to be found; he appeared and crushed the insurgents only after word had come that the garrisons of Thessaloniki and northern Greece had failed to move against the government.[49]

Be that as it may, Venizelos was annoyed at the public declarations by Kondylis. In a cable to Zannas on 27 February 1935 he wrote:

---

[46] Interview with Karavidas, Athens, October 1970. Notes of Karavidas to Zannas in latter's papers.

[47] Interview with Athanassios Zangas, Athens, December 1970. Papers of Air Marshal S. Papaspyros.

[48] Stamatis Mercouris, *Georgios Kondylis*, Athens 1954, p. 112.

[49] Argyropoulos, p. 483, Also Saraphis, p. 352.

It is obvious that we are confronted with the beginning of an unconcealed attempt to restore the hated throne. And because I am convinced you have nothing to gain from your appeal to the President of the Republic, I advise constant vigilance and that you enlighten the people so that they are prepared to defend the republican system in keeping with the final article of the constitution.[50]

Parallel to the preparations for the uprising, efforts were made to dissuade Venizelos from his plans. Late in 1934 Philipas, an air force captain, visited him in Crete and convinced him that the conspiracy should be abandoned. S. Papaspyros, also a Venizelist, confirms this, and adds that Venizelos gave up his idea of aiding the *coup* out of disgust with the disagreements among his followers.[51] In January 1935 Gonatas had also tried to dissuade him from attempting the *coup*. The Cretan once more gave the impression of bowing to reason and implied that he would take a trip to Japan, but far from intending to abandon his plans he had decided on the spur of the moment to follow the advice of Argyropoulos and appear neutral at the moment of the outbreak. To Argyropoulos' dismay, the insistence of Saraphis that his presence and commitment were the *sine qua non* of the entire enterprise made Venizelos reverse his decision to leave Greece.[52]

The correspondence between Plastiras and members of 'Republican Defence' shows the confusion prevailing among republican conspirators. In his first letter to Plastiras, Argyropoulos belatedly congratulated him on his attempted *coup* in March 1933 and expressed regret at its failure. He complained bitterly of the officers on active duty, particularly Saraphis, who had forestalled the republican plans for a *coup* on 24 July 1934.

In his letter of 19 October 1934 the republican Philotas complained about Saraphis and Zannas to Plastiras and expressed doubts about their sincerity. In another letter he suggested that Argyropoulos become the leader of the undertaking since the 'tin-pan soldiers' (officers on active duty) were fighting among themselves. Argyropoulos' letter of 12 November implied that he had been appointed by Plastiras as his spokesman in Greece. 'After our

---

[50] The A. Zannas papers.

[51] Letter by S. Papaspyros in the possession of the author.

[52] Saraphis, p. 355.

success... it is the opinion of V [Venizelos] that you must act as the watchdog of the republic. [...] Saraphis' organisation is very conservative ... and hostile to you ... Kolialexis is with them. They do not want either you or the Premier [Venizelos]. [...] General Vlachos also seems to be with them. B and B [the Bourdaras brothers] ought to be made your representatives in Macedonia.'[53]

In his letter of 16 December 1934 to Plastiras, Zannas denounced those who accused him: 'I try not to notice the scum of Republican Defence—my contempt is sufficient for them.' He also did not spare Plastiras for having lent a sympathetic ear to Papoulas, whom Zannas considered responsible for spreading slander against him.[54]

Hostility between officers on active duty and 'Republican Defence' grew worse with the successive failures of Plastiras to land in Greece. His first attempt in November 1934, planned by Papoulas and 'Republican Defence', failed because his ship developed engine trouble and had to return to port. Once the attempt was disclosed, officers on active duty protested furiously at not being told about the operation. 'Defence' also considered Othonaios a potential threat to Plastiras, because in 1927 the two men had quarrelled over the attempt by Othonaios to overthrow the government. As head of the emergency cabinet following the abortive *coup* of March 1933, Othonaios repaid Plastiras in the same coin by omitting to grant him amnesty. Argyropoulos, who trusted neither Othonaios nor his protégé Saraphis, secretly organised Plastiras' return to coincide with the date of the *coup* set by the Revolutionary Committee to occur on 18 January. Plastiras reached Sofia by rail under an assumed identity and waited for Argyropoulos' signal to cross into Greece.[55]

Saraphis claimed that he was informed of Plastiras' whereabouts by Protosyngelos, who indirectly warned him that the government was aware of Argyropoulos' plot. The Central Committee of ESO authorised Giorgoulis to inform 'Republican Defence' that further unauthorised activity would not be tolerated. N. Roussos, a friend of both Venizelos and Plastiras, expressed his fears to the

---

[53] In his letter of 12 November, Argyropoulos conceals the names of friends (by using a capital initial) but makes no such effort for antagonists such as Saraphis, Kolialexis *et al.*

[54] All letters mentioned are taken from the Plastiras papers.

[55] Benekos, *To kinima tou 1935*, p. 83. See also C. Kalligas, *Proti Martiou 1935*, Athens 1974.

latter that ESO would go as far as to betray him to the police. His friends' admonitions forced the general to abandon his plans and return to France, especially after word came from ESO that the police had been aware of his movements. Argyropoulos, who had sent a telegram to Plastiras that the police had been informed of his presence in Bulgaria, later wrote in his memoirs: 'Saraphis admitted later ... that everything about the police was made up, but that the army was simply unprepared to make its move.'[56] This, of course, was not publicly admitted, and officially the *coup* of January 1935 was postponed because officers serving in the submarines had not yet given their reply as to whether they would participate.[57]

The postponement of the *coup* caused anger in the 'Republican Defence' and relations between Plastiras and Saraphis became strained. The former, in a letter delivered to Roussos, demanded the enlargement of the Revolutionary Committee to include at least four additional members (all friends of his – Zannas, Argyropoulos, Kimisis, Demestichas), and accused Saraphis of having acquired the conservative mentality of a colonel in the hope of being promoted to general. On 10 February the Committee replied to Plastiras that Venizelos had authorised the existing three-member directorate and that a reversal of the decision should only come from Venizelos himself. Having no choice but to comply, the exiled general once more accepted Venizelos' authority.[58] In a letter of 10 February to Venizelos, the Revolutionary Committee expressed doubts about Plastiras' leadership. Saraphis wrote: 'Although you prefer the option of having General Plastiras, all will depend on the specific circumstances of the final days.'

Amazingly, there are some indications that even Kondylis had been unsuccessfully approached by the Committee.[59] The latter's procrastination due to unresolved rivalries with 'Republican Defence' annoyed Venizelos. On 10 February S. Pistolakis brought a message from Crete urging the Committee to take immediate action. Fears were expressed that impending elections to the Senate would give the government a majority in the joint session of the

[56] Argyropoulos, p. 483.

[57] Saraphis, pp. 352-3; Kladakis papers; article by K. Vovolinis, *Eleftheros Kosmos*, 2 December 1969; Argyropoulos, p. 491.

[58] Saraphis, pp. 354-5.

[59] Daphnis, pp. 300-5.

two houses. 'Of course the Committee will decide on the date of the *coup* ... but it should keep in mind ... that this ought to take place three or four weeks before the elections.' In his final letter to the Committee (dated 27 February), Venizelos expressed optimism about the outcome of the *coup* and suggested that the undertaking should appear to take place under the exclusive initiative of the military.

> You know how much I insist that at first the revolution should have a purely military character. I hope that you too will realise this. If I personally assume the leadership, that will of course inspire the republicans but, on the other hand, it will inflame the passions of our enemies.[60]

Venizelos sought once more to use the officers without endangering his own image. His decision may be attributed to his concern for his reputation as guardian of normal parliamentary practices.

With Othonaios' refusal to become the leader, the position was passed on the Commander of the 4th Army Corps, General Kammenos. A person with far less prestige than the original choice, Kammenos was viewed merely as a temporary replacement for Plastiras although he had confided that he was opposed to Othonaios' and Plastiras' involvement.

On the evening of 26 February 1935 the final planning of the *coup* took place in the house of the retired Major Eustratiou, with the participation of Saraphis, Vlachos, Kolialexis, Demestichas, Diamesis, Spais, Gravaris, Nikolaou and Papathanasopoulos. Only three of the officers present were on active duty; the vanguard of ESO was missing, and thus it is safe to assume that the real planning of the *coup* had already been done at an earlier meeting of the officers on active duty. The meeting in Eustratiou's house was therefore probably a sham to keep retired and dismissed officers out of mischief. ESO, on the other hand, knew nothing of Saraphis' contact with 'Republican Defence'. According to Kladakis, Saraphis and J. Tsigantes were the only members of ESO who knew of the existence of the Revolutionary Committee. Colonel Giorgoulis, the most respected of the senior officers in the organisation, had also not been informed of this meeting.[61]

---

[60] Zannas papers.
[61] Interview with M. Kladakis.

The *coup* would begin with the capture of the fleet in Piraeus by Captain Kolialexis and Admiral Demestichas, assisted by officers in the navy. Part of the captured fleet would then sail to Thessaloniki where a simultaneous revolt of the garrison would ensure the takeover of the city. The entire 4th Army Corps was expected to march to Thassalonoki and join up with the rebels, along with garrisons in northern Greece that would side with the uprising. Venizelos forbade any movement in Athens because of the weakness of local Venizelist forces. The government had carefully arranged for the capital, as the nerve-centre of the armed forces, to be manned by officers known for their loyalty to the Populist party. However, diversionary activity was deemed necessary to help in the capture of the fleet and to eliminate a battery of guns covering the entrance to the harbour at Piraeus. In order to divert the attention of the authorities and give time for Kolialexis and Demestichas to achieve their objective, it was agreed that groups of conspirators would capture the regiment of Evzones in Makriyanni, occupy the Military Academy, capture armoured cars and use them against the government, take over the power station in Keratsini and cut off the electrical power of the city, silence the gun on Lycabettus hill overlooking Athens which gave the emergency signal, and gain control of an infantry regiment.[62]

The reluctant Saraphis had pressure put on him to assign as many positions as possible to members of 'Republican Defence'. Therefore, General Vlachos was given the leadership of the operation in the Military Academy with J. Tsigantes as second in command (Skanavis and Kladakis were informed two hours before the operation). Colonel Diamesis (dismissed in 1933) insisted on being given command of the group that would capture the armoured cars. Other dismissed officers such as Zervas and Dertilis (dismissed in 1926) would assist him. Spais was asked to capture the infantry regiment but, according to Saraphis, he demanded funds to bribe officers who would otherwise refuse to participate.[63] Saraphis refused as a matter of principle to give Spais money, but Chr. Tsigantes mentioned to this author several cases of bribery that proved the best guarantee of action. Captain Christos Triantafyllidis, who allowed Saraphis and Chr.

[62] Daphnis, pp. 306-8; Saraphis, pp. 357-9.
[63] Benekos, pp. 85-6.

Tsigantes to reach his unit in Makriyanni, was one such. According to Chr. Tsigantes, a long list of allocations of funds was drawn up including the amounts paid to specific officers.'Only members of ESO worked for nothing,' he claimed.[64] Mrs Elena Venizelos had deposited a large sum in a Greek bank for that purpose. Members of the Revolutionary Committee had full access to the money and *carte blanche* to use it as they thought best.[65]

The *coup* of 1935 had the unusual feature of being the only one of its kind to have been disclosed in detail by a newspaper before it occurred. Three days beforehand, the Communist newspaper *Rizospastis* gave a detailed and basically accurate account of the whole venture.[66] The 'leak' was later attributed to a numerous group of Venizelist officers who became leftist during the German occupation (Bakirtzis, Athinellis, Zoulas, Makridis), but although the legend of the 'Red Colonel' informer became the popular explanation of the phenomenon, there is evidence that Damianos Mathesis, an air force technician trained in Moscow, had overheard the plans from friendly officers and passed them on to the newspaper.[67] Communist hostility to the *coup* was later lamented by party members with belated regrets that efforts had not been made to secure a popular front with the Venizelists. 'Today, in view of recent experience, we see that our fire ought to have concentrated against the forces of monarchical reaction....'[68]

Plastiras was a tireless correspondent. Besides many letters from members of the 'Defence', his papers contain advice and opinions from people who had no formal position in the organisation of the *coup*. For example, there is a letter from Sir Arthur Crosfield (dated 14 January 1935) expressing his dismay at the situation in Greece, and two letters from Sophoclis Venizelos. In one of these, dated 3 January 1935, Sophoclis advises great care: 'We are playing our last card.' In his other (undated) letter, he points

[64] Information disclosed by Chr. Tsigantes, confirmed by M. Kladakis.

[65] A highly speculative list of contributors to the *coup* is mentioned in court testimony by a police agent. The industrialists Fix, Papastratos, Georgis and Koumantaros, the bankers Kostopoulos and Iliaskos, the newspaper proprietor Lambrakis, and the bank directors Tsouderos, Gontikas and Diomidis are included in the list. The court testimony, dated 30 March 1935 and signed by the Gendarmerie NCO, D. Antonakos, was taken from the archive of A. Diomidis.

[66] Letter published in *Rizospastis*, 26 February 1935.

[67] Article, 'To kinima tou 1935', *Akropolis*, 14 February 1970.

[68] S. Zorbalas, *I simaia tou laou 1917-1936*, Belgrade 1966, p. 243.

out that the operations should be concentrated in Athens rather than carrying the conflict to the strategically sensitive border area.[69] Never was a clandestine undertaking so widely publicised and discussed in advance. Thus the extensive use of assumed names (often more than one) for security reasons seems superfluous; Venizelos appeared as Halepas, Eustratios and Minos, Zannas as Evraios, Philippas and Vatrachos, Gonatas as Aivaliotis and Gonidis, industrialist Fix as Xanthos, Argyropoulos as Argyriou, Papathanasopoulos as Karolidis and Plastiras as Neos.[70]

Major Thomas Sfetsios was given his instructions by Saraphis on 27 February. He was to alert the troops in northern Greece on the day of the *coup* (1 March) if the insurgents in Athens made their move. General Vlachos gave him 30,000 drachmas, an amount sent by Venizelos to Vokos of the 'Defence' chapter in Thessaloniki to cover its local expenses. Sfetsios had been afraid to assume such enormous responsibility alone and asked Saraphis to go with him. After many reassurances, Sfetsios left with the impression that Saraphis would call him at Zannas' home in Thessaloniki if the *coup* was to take place: if Saraphis did not call, he was to assume that it had been postponed. Saraphis' plan had been exactly the opposite of that which Sfetsios had understood. Saraphis, who had tried to accompany Sfetsios, was recognised by officers at the railway station and had to turn back. Meanwhile, he kept Othonaios fully informed of the movement's progress and the general in turn gave him as much advice as he could.

Sfetsios failed to give the signal for the launching of the *coup*. Instead he informed the whole of Macedonia that it had been postponed. He later insisted in his own defence that Saraphis had promised to contact him only if the *coup* was to take place.[71] One could give Sfetsios the benefit of the doubt and blame Saraphis for not issuing clear orders, were it not for a letter addressed to Zannas by A. Papachristopoulos, dated March 1936. The writer informed Zannas that the order for the *coup*'s

---

[69] Daphnis notes in his biography of Sophoclis Venizelos that the latter had learned about the organisation of the *coup* at the end of February 1935 from the dismissed naval Captain Toumbas who had been sent to Paris by the Revolutionary Committee to inform Plastiras of the date of the *coup*. His letter of 3 January proves that S. Venizelos had known before that time. G. Daphnis, *S.E. Venizelos*, Athens: Ikaros, 1970, p. 142.

[70] A. Zannas papers.

[71] Saraphis, p. 361; K. Vovolinis, 'The Coup of 1935', *Eleftheros Kosmos*, 7 December 1966.

postponement was issued in Thessaloniki on the morning of 1 March 1935, a few hours after Sfetsios' arrival by train. There was hardly time for a telephone call from Saraphis, assuming that Sfetsios had genuinely understood that the decision to rise would be confirmed by Athens. Evidently the major delivered the money to Vokos' house as soon as he arrived and was confronted there with a general unwillingness to act. Generals Manousos and Spano-poulos asked for a postponement because two captains in their confidence had suddenly been transferred from an important unit in the city. Sfetsios must have given the order for postponement while in a state of panic. During the confusion that followed, he was taken to Zannas' house by Papachristopoulos for a clear confirmation of his order. At that point Zannas was called by Saraphis and informed that the *coup* had begun in Athens.[72]

The day of the uprising had been announced in advance to all the important participants in northern Greece, and the postponement therefore caused great confusion. The order was transmitted by the headquarters of the 4th Army Corps commander, Kammenos, and his staff officers, A. Bourdaras and E. Bakirtzis. He and his staff were later blamed by members of ESO for their lack of concern to confirm Sfetsios' order. Chr. Tsigantes claimed that, according to a letter found in Bourdaras' abandoned archive, the delayed reaction from Kammenos had been planned by officers opposed to ESO in order to eliminate future rivals. Although the accusation has not been substantiated, it serves to illustrate the suspicion and antagonism among republican officers.[73]

On the evening of 1 March, Lieut.-Colonel A. Tountas had been left in charge of the 7th Division in Drama. Its commander, General Delagrammatis, was on leave and Tountas ignored an order for his transfer to a unit in Athens and secretly prepared his soldiers for the attack on Thessaloniki. He had previously sent on leave all officers who disagreed with the objectives of the *coup* but who had given their word that they would do nothing to oppose it. Those who refused to accept his terms he imprisoned. At 9 p.m. he called Kammenos for instructions and discovered to his surprise that the 4th Army Corps was not even

---

[72] A. Zannas papers.
[73] Bourdaras, along with Kammenos and his staff, fled to Bulgaria after their own belated *coup* collapsed. Colonel Panayotou, shattered by remorse, committed suicide on the way.

in a state of alert. Bourdaras informed him that the *coup* had been cancelled but Tountas protested that rumours of the uprising in Athens had already reached Macedonia despite Sfetsios' alleged message. However, Kammenos had left camp after receiving the order of postponement and was nowhere to be found. At about 10 p.m. Tountas dispersed his mobilised troops and released the imprisoned officers. By 11 p.m. the government had placed the entire army on alert.[74]

Orders for postponement reached Kammenos at 10 a.m. on 1 March, but by midnight he was convinced that the *coup* had been launched in Athens and in the fleet. Thus, instead of taking immediate action, he transmitted appeals to the President of the Republic to interfere. It was only when Kammenos received orders to give up his command and appear before the Minister of Army Affairs that he finally decided to make his move. On the morning of 3 March the 4th Army Corps rebelled[75] and its commander issued the following statement:

> ...The decision of the government to give emergency ministries to Metaxas, a notorious exponent of dictatorship, and Admiral Dousmanis [replacing Hadjikyriakos], a royalist... these blatant acts of tyranny... have left the army no alternative but to oppose the destruction of the republic...[76]

The cohesion among naval officers helped them play their part in the *coup* without a breakdown in communications. Their undertaking to capture the fleet had been a total success. However, on board the flagship *Averoff*, Kolialexis and Demestichas differed over whether to sail to Crete or to Thessaloniki, where the garrison had failed to rise. Information about the latter reinforced Demestichas' original decision to join Venizelos. However, Kolialexis could see no point in a fruitless trip to Crete, so he retired to his cabin and would not make any further effort to dissuade Demestichas. The strength of the fleet was therefore lost to the republican cause. Had it joined up with Kammenos, the outcome of the *coup* might have been different.

The uprising in Athens was significant merely as a diversionary

---

[74] Interview with A. Tountas. January 1972.
[75] P. Demestichas, 'Pos katelava ton stolo', *Ta Nea*, 19 October 1953.
[76] Benekos, p. 138.

move to give naval officers time to capture the fleet, and because the naval operation suceeded, one might conclude that it achieved its objective. However, a closer look at the details gives an impression of total chaos in communication and organisation. Saraphis drew up his own list of individuals who failed to participate: Diamesis, Zervas and Dertilis failed to reach the armoured cars in time; General Vlachos was late for his rendezvous at the Academy and then returned home when he saw that the building had been recaptured by government forces; Lieut.-Colonel A. Pyriochos, instead of capturing the infantry unit assigned to him, appeared in his own unit when the alert was sounded; and Papathanasopoulos did not even attempt to destroy the power station that supplied Athens.[77] Saraphis claimed that officers loyal to Plastiras had conspired to leave him and the Tsigantes brothers without cover: 'The Plastirists felt that the coup would in any case succeed and it was therefore their chance to get rid of me.'[78] But this allegation is not altogether justified. Pyriochos was Saraphis' own choice and both Colonels Papamantelos and Hadjistavris, who joined Saraphis and Chr. Tsigantes at the Evzone battalion, were loyal to Plastiras.[79] To Saraphis' list of failures one could add Colonel Floulis who failed to move against the Ministry of Foreign Affairs, the air force officers Dimakis and Hadjinikolis who joined the naval officers instead of sabotaging air planes (the cruiser *Averoff* was attacked by government planes), and the dismal failure of 'Republican Defence' to mobilise refugees. Instead of the 300 civilians who were supposed to join Saraphis at the Evzone unit, only eight appeared. All in all 'Republican Defence' proved to be a hindrance to the execution of the *coup* rather than a help.

The *coup* in Macedonia took an even worse course. Officers from units in Larissa and Kozani, Serres and Thessaloniki failed to move (the only exception was Tountas in Drama, who was on alert on the night of the coup). Lieut.-Colonel Psaros, a strong supporter of armed insurrection, had gone to the cinema after news of a delay became known, and his unit in Veria remained inactive. Colonel Flengas committed suicide when he realised that he was alone in opposing the government in his Serres unit.

---

[77] Saraphis, pp. 383-5.

[78] *Ibid.*, p. 385.

[79] Saraphis (p. 385) clearly expressed his plans to discard Plastiras' followers if the *coup* succeeded: 'That was our second objective after the victory of the coup.'

The *coup* greatly enhanced the reputation of such anti-Venizelist officers as Admiral Sakellariou, who captured part of the rebel fleet, and especially of General Kondylis who prevented the faltering Tsaldaris from giving in to Venizelos' blackmail. He justified his nickname 'Thunderbolt' by outmanoeuvering the defences of Kammenos in Macedonia, on the banks of the river Strymon. In this he was greatly helped by the 1st and 3rd Army Corps commanders, Generals Petritis and Panayotakos.[80] In Athens Kondylis had relied on a close circle of clients such as Colonels Kousindas and Trepeklis and Captain Kourouklis to put down the uprising. On the other hand, the boisterous Navy Minister Admiral Hadjikyriakos found his reputation in ruins and retired from public life in disgrace. Distrust between Metaxas and Kondylis persisted throughout the *coup*. Fearful that the activities of the newly-appointed minister Metaxas might take some of the shine off his ultimate triumph, Kondylis ordered the guards to refuse his rival entry into the Ministry of Foreign Affairs. Frustrated by this affront, Metaxas handed in his resignation.

The morale of the insurgents in Macedonia was greatly affected by the failure of either Venizelos or Plastiras to appear. Lieut.-Commander Toumbas had been sent to Paris to inform Plastiras that he would have to be in Greece on either 1 or 2 March. Sophoclis and Kyriakos Venizelos, who were responsible for arranging for the general to be flown in, failed to secure a plane in time. Simultaneously, the Italian authorities refused Plastiras permission to leave their country. With their leader absent, most members of 'Republican Defence' remained inactive.

Venizelos had lost control of the *coup* from the outset. His message calling for its postponement was ignored; the fleet, confusing his instructions, arrived on his doorstep in Crete instead of sailing to Thessaloniki, and General Kammenos delayed his rebellion. On the whole, Venizelist officers did not take advantage of the element of surprise and reverted to defensive tactics, hoping perhaps that the government would collapse before the fighting began. In spite of his disappointment, Venizelos handled the political aspect of the *coup* with dexterity. He capitalised on the goverment's error in proclaiming martial law, and at the same time he reassured

---

[80] To secure Panayotakos' cooperation and prevent other officers from turning against the government, Tsaldaris had vowed that the republic had never been in danger under his regime. K. Mayer, *Istoria tou ellinikou typou*, vol. II, Athens 1959, p. 310.

the people that the *coup* was a harmless incident. Venizelos rightly pointed out that the government either had to admit that it faced a serious external threat, in which case only parliament could decide if martial law was the correct response, or it had to accept that it had acted unconstitutionally.[81] The 2 March issue of *Kathimerini* admitted openly that dictatorship was no longer a theoretical question but the only way of facing the danger of revolution. Formally, therefore, Venizelos appeared to be opposing a government which had infringed the constitution. His proclamation in favour of the insurgents rekindled anti-Venizelist hysteria. His effigy was burned in public, petitions were signed against him, and the more fanatical newspapers called him a 'mad dog' and demanded that he be shut up in an asylum.[82] Georgios Vlachos, owner of *Kathimerini* and his avowed enemy, wrote on 2 March: 'The republic and the imaginary perils of the republic are concoctions of the old man from Halepa and his criminal mob whose sole preoccupation is to seize power.'[83] In this anti-Venizelist frenzy, all those held in prison for the attempt on the life of Venizelos in 1933 (including the ex-police commissioner Polychronopoulos), were released.

In spite of the large number of people who were mobilised, the *coup* of 1935 was relatively bloodless. No more than four or five soldiers and civilians were killed and several officers were wounded. Two officers committed suicide and three more were court-martialled and executed. Among them were leading figures of 'Republican Defence', Generals A. Papoulas and M. Kimissis, who had done nothing during the evening of 1 March 1935. By the time the *coup* erupted, Saraphis and Tsigantes had severed all their contacts with its leaders. Their death sentence was an act of anti-Venizelist vengeance. Both Papoulas (a royalist before 1922) and Kimissis had in different ways been instrumental in the execution of the six prominent royalists in 1922. Cavalry Major S. Volanis, who was left to rebel alone against the authorities of Thessaloniki, was also executed. Between 10 March and 14 May,

---

[81] According to Article 97 of the 1927 constitution, martial law could only be proclaimed in case of war or if the country were faced with an external danger. The Chamber of Deputies and the Senate would have to give their approval. Daphnis, *I Ellas metaxy....*, vol. II, p. 321.

[82] *O Typos* (newspaper), 1 March 1935.

[83] G. Vlachos, *Politika arthra*, Athens: Galaxias, 1961, p. 61.

when martial law was finally lifted, 1,130 officers and civilians were tried. Sixty were sentenced to death, of whom fifty-five – including Venizelos and Plastiras – had been abroad, and two were pardoned. Fifty-seven were sentenced to life imprisonment and seventy-six were given light terms.[84]

Curiously, more active participants such as the Tsigantes brothers, Saraphis, Stephanakos and Kladakis escaped execution. There were rumours that Kondylis himself took an interest in the welfare of Saraphis either because the two had made an agreement before the *coup*, or because Kondylis received his political backing from Saraphis' home town. To have stood by while a fellow-townsman was being executed would have been a strain on the reputation of Kondylis. Argyropoulos, along with many other civilian members of the 'Defence', fled the country. Zannas was imprisoned and there were wholesale purges of the civil service and army. About 1,500 officers were dismissed from all three armed services.[85]

The failure of the *coup* has been attributed to a variety of reasons. Undertakings on a large scale require the kind of organisation which was almost impossible to sustain in Greece. Given the traditional competitiveness between factions at all levels of Greek society, Venizelos should not have delegated authority to so many participants. Zannas failed because each group demanded autonomy of action and refused to submit its plans to the scrutiny of a coordinator. Venizelos was the only figure commanding sufficient authority to act as leader of the operation, but by 1935 he was an old man, and instead of assuming absolute command over a limited number of conspirators, he decided to mobilise all anti-government forces to act on his behalf. The different groupings involved (with some overlapping) were the following: ESO; Saraphis and Tsigantes acting without the knowledge of ESO; the Revolutionary Committee which was the result of Zannas' efforts to coordinate the various groupings consisting of Saraphis, Kolialexis and Vlachos who represented respectively officers on active duty, the navy and 'Republican Defence'; 'Republican Defence', a loose organisation made up of civilians and of dismissed and retired officers; Periclis Argyropoulos, a member

---

of the 'Defence', who derived his authority from his connections in the navy – with members of the 'Defence' he championed the cause of Plastiras and kept in contact with him; Kolialexis and Demestichas, though not on the best of terms, who represented the navy; Karavidas and officers such as Zangas, who had drawn up their own plans for cooperation between navy and army; Kammenos and Bourdaras in Macedonia, who were presumably following orders directly from Venizelos; Gonatas, who had been isolated, trying to act as moderator; and finally Venizelos and his Cretan political clients Pistolakis, Maris, Koundouros, Moatsos and Roussos. The network of conflicts between groups and individuals was made up of many combinations: Zannas as a coordinator *vs.* Argyropoulos who wanted to take his initiatives; Saraphis and ESO *vs.* Plastiras and dismissed officers; Kammenos and Bourdaras *vs.* ESO; Zannas and ESO *vs.* 'Republican Defence'; members of ESO such as Giorgoulis, Kladakis and Skanavis vs. Saraphis and Tsigantes; Kolialexis *vs.* Demestichas; Karavidas *vs.* the revolutionary organisation of the navy under Kolialexis; and junior officers of ESO *vs.* senior officers who were not of Military Academy origin. There were also varying degrees of attachment to Venizelos, who was the general point of reference. Zannas, Argyropoulos and the navy were loyal to him whereas the loyalty of ESO, Saraphis and Tsigantes was questionable.

The absence of strong common ideological grounds among the various groups was thinly disguised by a republican front. Diversity of aims and motives hampered cooperation and impaired the outcome of the *coup*. In addition to their allegiance to Venizelos, groups or individuals strove to further the interests of different and often conflicting patrons. ESO's effort to destroy the traditional clientage arrangement in the army and replace it with a professional meritocracy failed dismally. Saraphis was the client of Othonaios and the Tsigantes brothers had been attached to Pangalos in the past. The dismissed officers of the 'Defence' depended on future patronage from Plastiras to return to the army; and the navy, basically loyal to Venizelos, was divided between Demestichas and Kolialexis.

The March uprising, like most military anomalies of the interwar period, was essentially a Greek affair. The British government viewed the *coup* as a struggle between 'ins' and 'outs', while Italy, though friendly towards Venizelos' foreign policy, nevertheless refused Plastiras passage through Italian territory, and the Bari radio station prevented the insurgents' declarations from being broadcast. A minimum of statements concerning the *coup* were issued by foreign embassies, most of which favoured the victorious government.[86] However, the *coup* had profound implications for both internal and external Greek affairs. The restoration of King George II in 1935, which came about partly in consequence of a purge of Venizelists from the army following the *coup,* had a direct impact on Greek foreign policy up till the Second World War.

The reinstatement of Venizelist officers who had been dismissed for their connection with the 1935 *coup* preoccupied Venizelos in his self-exile shortly before his death in 1936. King George was prepared to use their reinstatement as a way of securing Venizelist compliance to his rule, but, as it turned out, the dictatorship of Metaxas inaugurated on 4 August 1936 made this compromise unnecessary. With almost 1,500 Venizelists out of the armed forces, the 5,000-strong officer corps under Metaxas (or, more appropriately, under King George) was ideologically the most homogeneous that twentieth-century Greece ever had.

Metaxas was advised on military questions by the National Defence Council chaired by the Chief of the Army General Staff in 1937, Alexander Papagos, but he held the ministerial portofolios of the three armed forces himself. Metaxas was also responsible for drafting the strategy of resistance against an Italian attack, but had no illusions that the King was the figure to whom the army owed its ultimate loyalty.[87]

Papagos was close to the King through family ties, yet his initial pro-Kondylis position in the anti-Venizelos camp had com-

---

[86] There was much British speculation over Italian involvement in the Venizelist *coup.* Reports from Waterlow in Athens and Henderson in Belgrade during the first few days of the *coup* hinted at Italian complicity in favour of the rebels. Henderson's Yugoslav sources attributed Italy's support of the *coup* against the Greek government to the Greek refusal to help Italy break up the Balkan Pact by accepting an Italian proposition of a tripartite pact which would also include Turkey. According to Barros: 'When this message arrived in London, one of the members of the Foreign Office, D'Arcy Patrick Reilly, minuted that Henderson's information "had been confirmed from Athens". He pointed out that the previous year it was suspected that "M. Venizelos' opposition to the Balkan Pact was due to Italian instigation".' James Barros, 'Sanctions and the Small State: Greece and the Italo-Ethiopian Crisis, 1935-1936', Ms., chapter II.

[87] D.H. Close, 'The Power-Base of the Metaxas Dictatorship' in R. Higham and T. Veremis (eds), *Aspects of Greece, 1936-1940: The Metaxas Dictatorship*, Athens:, ELIAMEP-Vryonis Center, 1993, pp. 29-31.

promised him with Metaxas. As Minister of Army Affairs in the Demertzis caretaker government, he visited the King on 5 March 1936 with the ultimatum that the armed forces and security services would not tolerate any deal between either of the two large parties and the Communists. After this, the King immediately replaced him by Metaxas and thus established his authority on a potentially rebellious segment of his own military followers.[88] After being disciplined by the King, the future army chief was used by him in his delicate balance of influence in the armed forces.

On the whole, officers were kept content with the regime. 'Their loyalty was strengthened by the great increase in all types of military expenditure under Metaxas: pay, arms, uniforms and barracks as well as roads and defense works.'[89] The gap left behind by Venizelist officers was partly closed through intensive training and the entry of additional cadets to the Academies. This period influenced an entire generation of post-war officers, not least the April 1967 Colonels.

Opposition in the armed forces to the mainstream of the 4th August dictatorship was insignificant. General Platis, a germanophile commander, was dismissed by Metaxas, and a conspiracy by the 'Fighters for Popular Liberties' was nipped in the bud with a purge of the Athens garrison in March 1938.[90] The better-known rising of 28 July 1938 in Chania, Crete, which included the Venizelist politician Emmanuel Tsouderos, Periclis Argyropoulos, Aristomenis Mitsotakis and a host of cashiered Venizelist officers, was mainly inspired by nostalgia for 1935, but with less fury and no consequences.[91]

The war found the officer corps on active duty in relative harmony with the political authorities. The persistent petitions from cashiered Venizelist officers to be allowed a place of glory in future history books were mostly ignored.

---

[88] John S. Koliopoulos, *Greece and the British Connection, 1935-1941*, Oxford: Clarendon Press, 1977, p. 40. The appointment of Metaxas elicited much enthusiasm from Venizelos who saw it as a prelude to the reinstatement of his cashiered military followers. See Daphnis, *I Ellas metaxy dyo polemon*, vol. II, pp. 406-7.

[89] Close, p. 31.

[90] *Ibid.*, p. 33.

[91] Koliopoulos, p. 80-1.

# 8

# THE WAR AND CIVIL WAR CAULDRON

Between 1936 and 1940 King George II, the force behind the Metaxas dictatorship, exerted his personal control on an ideologically homogeneous and compliant officer corps which had been purged of all prominent Venizelists in 1935. With the occupation of Greece in 1941, the King and his government fled to London and Cairo. Traditional political leaders who stayed behind exhibited a singular inability to come to terms with new realities.[1] Preoccupied with the constitutional question after liberation, they abandoned the business of armed resistance against the Germans to the EAM (*Ethnikon Apeleftherotikon Metopon* – the Communist-dominated National Liberation Front) and the British and smaller guerrilla bands and organisations. Of the old politicians only a few chose to collaborate with the occupation forces. Some took leading roles in the government in exile, but the great majority did little else besides preserve themselves for a brighter parliamentary future. George Kaphandaris, the most respected of interwar Liberals, discouraged his followers from becoming involved with the resistance because he genuinely believed that Greece had given more than its share to the war effort and should desist from further activities that would lead to its obliteration as a nation.

Curiously, the one principle that united politicians of the Liberal and Populist camps was an anti-monarchist manifesto demanding a post-war plebiscite to decide the monarchy's fate. The document was signed by leading Liberal figures (Themistocles Sophoulis, George Kaphandaris, George Papandreou and Alexander Mylonas) and Populists (Petros Rallis, Stephanos Stephanopoulos and G. Chloros).[2] This exhibition of anti-monarchical sentiment by

---

[1] John Petropulos, 'The Traditional Political Parties of Greece during the Axis Occupation' in John Iatrides (ed.), *Greece in the 1940s*, Hanover, NH: University Press of New England, 1981, pp. 27-8.

[2] *Ibid.*, p. 30.

politicians of both camps was intended partly to compensate for their relative passivity during the Metaxas dictatorship.

The breakdown of political authority in Greece had a profound effect on the military. Whether retired since 1935 or heroes of the Albanian front now made idle by the demobilisation of the Greek armed forces at home, officers who had been accustomed to political control and direction were suddenly faced with a vacuum of legitimate authority. A significant reorientation of their attitudes was dictated by the spirit of defiance bred by the resistance and the war effort. Some chose to join with the forces in the Middle East and North Africa, but the majority remained in Greece and became part of the resistance or the Security Battalions, or did nothing.

The interwar cleavage between royalists and Venizelists was forcibly resolved in the aftermath of the 1935 *coup* with a wholesale purge of active republican officers. The army's royalist monopoly became the guarantee of the dictatorship backed by King George. Thus it follows that the position of royalists in the Middle East forces of the Greek government in exile was no more legitimate than that of their opponents who had been cashiered for seeking to overthrow a popularly elected government in 1935.[3] The latter were forced to remain idle during Greece's finest hour, while their rivals in the officer corps reaped the glory of the Albanian campaign. Their readmission by the Tsouderos government in 1941 was charged with feelings of mutual hostility.

In October 1941 the Greek 1st Brigade included 6,000 men, of whom 400 were officers. This ratio was upset by the continuous arrival of officers from occupied Greece and exceeded the 10 per cent limit set by the government in exile. Rivalries in the officer corps were exacerbated by the ever-growing scarcity of commissions. Since royalists had reached the Middle East first, most important commissions were held by them, but a significant exception to this rule was the army's Supreme Commander, General Emmanuel Tzanakakis, a Venizelist of 1935 who had been readmitted and given his command by Prime Minister Emmanuel Tsouderos (also a Venizelist) as a gesture of reconciliation of old feuds.

---

[3] Hagen Fleischer's, 'The "Anomalies" in the Greek Middle East Forces, 1941-44', *Journal of the Hellenic Diaspora*, vol. V, no. 3, 1978, is the most comprehensive and thought-provoking round-up of a complicated subject. See also Lena Divani, *I politiki ton exoriston ellinikon kiverniseon, 1941-44*, Athens: Sakkoulas, 1992, pp. 70-80.

Soon royalists and Liberals congregated in separate clubs, and members of the former's secret society, '*Nemesis*', threatened the authorities with mass resignations if their opponents were not dismissed from active duty. In October 1941 Liberals and republicans formed their own society, the 'Anti-Fascist Military Organisation' (ASO), with chapters in the navy and air force. Their goal was to rid the forces of royalists who refused to support the war effort, and ultimately to bring about a republican regime in liberated Greece. Supporters of ASO, in and out of the forces, exhibited (or rather harboured) a variety of political positions ranging from traditional Liberal-Venizelism to republicanism and Communism. Among these many variants Yannis Salas, a young Communist who had escaped from the notorious Greek prison of Akronafplia in 1941 and joined VESMA (the Royal Hellenic Army of the Middle East) as a corporal, became the moving force of the organisation.[4]

Although the British War Office and the Foreign Office expressed their concern over developments in VESMA, the Foreign Secretary, Anthony Eden, and Tsouderos signed on 2 March 1942 the final accord concerning the organisation and use of the Greek forces. Panayiotis Kanellopoulos, a young Liberal politician who had just arrived from Greece, became Deputy Prime Minister in May 1942 and Defence Minister as well a month later. Kanellopoulos, a political innocent with honourable intentions, initially made headway in improving the performance of the armed forces. He placed a Venizelist, Pausanias Katsotas, in command of the 1st Brigade and another Venizelist, Alcibiades Bourdaras, of the newly-formed 2nd Brigade. He court-martialled some of the '*Nemesis*' officers who had handed in their resignation, and took credit for the 1st Brigade's extraordinary contribution to the battle of El Alamein in October 1941.[5] Ultimately Kanellopoulos became a universal target. King George considered his Liberal inclinations dangerous to the crown, the royalist officers viewed him as their enemy, and even the republicans began to turn against him when he placed both the 1st and 2nd Brigades under the overall command

---

[4] For details on Salas see Yannis Chiotakis, *Politikes Thielles*, Athens, 1981, pp. 68-9; Giorgis Athanasiadis, *I proti praxi tis ellinikis tragodias,* Athens, 1975, p. 56; and Vassilis Nefeloudis, *I ethniki antistasi sti mesi Anatoli*, Athens: Themelio, 1981, vol. A, pp. 339-48.

[5] P. Kanellopoulos, *Imerologio*, Athens: Kedros, 1977, p. 121.

of the conservative and hero of the Albanian war, General C. Zygouris.

When Kanellopoulos decided to clamp down on the turbulent Liberals, ASO members took swift action against him. Katsotas presented him with ASO's demand that he purge the army of 'reactionary' elements and restructure the cabinet to include the old Venizelist politician G. Roussos and a republican former officer, Byron Karapanayiotis. Caught between Liberal-left criticism and royalist displeasure, Kannelopoulos resigned in March 1943 and became the first serious casualty of those who strove to preserve the armed forces for the liberation of Greece.[6] The changes in the cabinet precipitated by the action of ASO gave it a decidedly Liberal colouring. Roussos became Deputy Prime Minister and Karapanayotis Minister of Defence.

The ASO left-wingers criticised these changes as mere window-dressing, but Salas preferred to bide his time. 'I am aware that a government with only centrist elements after the revolutionary action of the anti-fascist forces is a rightist deviation,... [However] a leftist deviation would be the equivalent of a leap into chaos. A rightist deviation gives you the chance to return to the right track.'[7] Less flexible and obsessed with his own grievances against Tsouderos, Karapanayotis – shortly before assuming office – prodded Salas into forcing the Prime Minister's resignation, but was rebuffed. Salas reminded him that his (Karapanayotis') differences with Tsouderos were certainly less substantial than those between the two of them (Salas and Karapanayotis) and pointed out that he was not prepared to provoke the British into a reaction at that juncture.[8] It appears that Salas considered Tsouderos' presence in the government a divisive influence among Liberals and therefore useful to his own designs.

In July 1943 Karapanayotis was faced with renewed trouble in the 2nd Brigade and an escalation of ASO demands. His countermeasures effectively incapacitated the brigade as a fighting force but failed to put down ASO.[9] In August the EAM representatives P. Roussos, A. Tzimas and K. Despotopoulos, along with E.

---

[6] *Ibid.*, pp. 381-4, 390-8.

[7] Athanasiadis, p. 116.

[8] *Ibid.*, p. 118.

[9] Alexis Kitroeff, 'Anglo-Greek Relations and the Greek Situation in Egypt, 1941-44', unpubl. MA thesis, University of Keele, 1979, p. 88.

Tsirimokos, came to Cairo bearing a message from Greece with wider political appeal. They asked that the King's return after liberation be deferred until the issue of the monarchy could be decided by a plebiscite. The representatives also instructed ASO to abstain from activities that would provoke British intervention and the army's dissolution.[10] News of the formation of PEEA (Politiki Epitropi Ethnikis Apeleutherosis – Political Committee of National Liberation) in the Greek mountains, however, made ASO more defiant. In the spring of 1944 the final act of the military troubles in the Middle East was played out. A delegation of officers representing a society called EASDO (National Military Liberation Organisation) requested Tsouderos to form a government according to PEEA principles, and its members were promptly arrested. ASO mobilised its forces against the Prime Minister and caused his replacement by Sophocles Venizelos. April proved to be the cruellest month for the Greek army. Renewed demands by EASDO and the spread of rebellion into the navy brought the British into the picture. On April 7 the commander of the British forces, General Sir Bernard Paget, informed the Greek Minister of Defence that he had assumed command of the Greek army and would quell the rebellion. Salas rose to the occasion[11] by sending two soldiers, Andriotes and Tsamatoulides, to spread the uprising to the hitherto peaceful 1st Brigade. The brigade was preparing to embark for the Allied offensive in Italy but never reached its destination. Representatives of ASO presented its commander, Brigadier Pappas, with a demand that he declare the unit in favour of PEEA and, when he refused, raised the flag of rebellion. British action put an end to the uprising as well as to the Greek army as a credible force to liberate Greece and play a role in subsequent political developments.

In the Lebanon conference of May 1944 the representatives of PEEA, EAM and KKE (Greek Communist party) unanimously condemned the uprisings that had incapacitated the armed forces. Zahariades later intimated that the entire affair was planned by the British, but Andriotes and, more significantly, Salas dismissed the theory of British implication.[12] Salas wrote in his report to

[10] Fleischer, p. 24.

[11] Procopis Papastratis, *British Policy towards Greece during the Second World War 1941-44*, Cambridge University Press, 1984, pp. 165-6.

[12] Nefeloudis, pp. 312-22. 318.

the KKE's Political Bureau in March 1946: 'Comrade Zahariades claimed...that the coup was the work of the British. Again I must tell you that this is not correct. The uprising was the choice of the "Kathothigisi" and first of all my own choice.'[13] Salas and the extraordinary influence of his group on ASO were indicative of a new development in Greek civil-military relations. Whereas the initial skirmishes between royalist and Venizelist officers in VESMA were inspired by the old royalist-Liberal schism and directed towards the settling of professional scores, the new clash between right and left was based on entirely different premises. Privates and NCOs of ASO were often members of EAM or sympathetic to its cause, and viewed their conflict with the Greek government in exile as part of a universal class struggle. Their hold on ASO, in spite of being secret, exceeded the scope of 'subjective' control exerted on the Greek military by the traditional parties. Probably most officers of ASO had no clear picture of the real power structure of the organisation, but those that did submitted to the supremacy of ASO's political leadership – although after a while it became clear that this was in the hands of privates and NCOs. Nonetheless, anti-royalist sentiment among Venizelist officers facilitated their transition from the old to the new cleavage.

At the time of the armistice of April 1941 there were 4,390 Greek officers on active duty. These were subsequently retired by the occupation forces,[14] and old feuds within their ranks or between certain groups of officers and political figures of the past, determined their future allegiances. Some officers with an axe to grind against Metaxas and the King indirectly supported the position of the collaborationist Quisling government by criticising the dictatorship's administration of the Albanian campaign. A respected Venizelist general, Dimitrios Katheniotis, who was refused permission to go on active service in 1940, was one of several officers asked by the government of General Tsolakoglou to draft a report on the conduct of the war. In the summer of 1941 they were given access to reports from commanders on the front, and Katheniotis gathered his material to publish (albeit belatedly) his own scathing conclusions under the titles *Istorikon polemikon*

---

[13] *Ibid.*, p. 348.

[14] For statistics on the various categories of officers see Andre Gerolymatos, 'The Role of the Greek Officer Corps in the Resistance', *Journal of the Hellenic Diaspora*, vol. XI, no. 3, fall 1984, pp. 69-79.

*epichiriseon, 1940-41* (A History of the Military Operations, 1940-41), and *Ai Kyrioterai stratigikai faseis tou polemou, 1940-41* (The Most Important Strategic Phases of the War, 1940-41).[15] Tsolako-glou's motive for commissioning such works was to prove the ineptitude of the royal General Staff and exonerate himself for having signed the armistice without orders from his superiors. The motives of such important commanders of the war as Bakos, Katsimitros and Demestichas in joining the Tsolakoglou govern-ment are less clear. It is possible that they genuinely believed in the ultimate victory of the Axis powers and wanted to spare their compatriots further suffering.

Dismissed republicans who joined the Security Battalions founded by Prime Minister Ioannis Rallis in the spring of 1943 were among the least respected of the Venizelist adherents. Their past in the army was marked with political intrigue and their view of professional security was more mercenary than the average. In spite of their initially declared republicanism they were clearly interested in making a new career in the army, which would have been impossible under a royalist goverment.[16] There were recruits such as Colonel Haralambos Papathanasopoulos, an old royalist conveniently turned fanatical Venizelist and a client of Plastiras in the 1920s; Vassilios Dertilis of the notorious Republican Battalions which brought Pangalos to power in 1925 and toppled him in 1926; and the ex-dictator himself who, while not joining the Battalions, urged some of his followers to do so. They were disoriented after several years in jail and isolation from political discourse, and rather than emphasising their dubious repub-licanism, it is perhaps more relevant to point out their availability to almost any form of recruitment. As it turned out, their declared anti-Communism served them better in the long run than anti-royalism.

When small resistance organisations were disbanded by ELAS (*Ethnikos Laikos Apeleftherotikos Stratos* – National Popular Libera-tion Army), some of their members chose to take revenge by throwing in their lot with the Security Battalions. In June 1943

---

[15] The two mentioned works by Katheniotis were published in Athens in, respectively, 1945 and 1946. See also Yannis Koliopoulos, *Palinorthosi, dictatoria, polemos 1936-41*, Athens: Kollaros, 1984, pp. 196-8.

[16] Andre Gerolymatos, 'The Security Battalions and the Civil War', *Journal of the Hellenic Diaspora*, vol. XII, no. 1, spring 1985, p. 17.

the organisation of the Athenian EDES (*Ethnikos Dimokratikos Ellinikos Syndesmos* – National Democratic Hellenic League) disintegrated 'and one faction led by Voulpiotis and Tavoularis played a prominent role in the development of the Security Battalions'.[17]

By the spring of 1944 the republican cause was collapsing on several fronts. Zervas, leader of EDES, reconciled himself with the monarchy, officers in the Security Battalions realised that their allegiance to the King would become their guarantee of safety and legitimacy after the war, VESMA was purged of almost all republican elements after the 1944 upheaval, and old republican politicians began to view the left wing as their main future adversary.

Several factors contributed to the breakdown of the appeal of traditional parliamentary ideology to wartime Greek society. The Metaxas dictatorship had prepared the way by disrupting for a prolonged period the channels of communication between political parties and their constituencies, and more significantly it deprived them of the ability to dispense patronage. The hardships of occupation and the collapse of the economy had an unprecedented radicalising effect on a nation of small property-owners who in the past had always resisted joining corporate movements.[18] Such developments could only increase the prestige and power of EAM-ELAS. As Svoronos points out,

> EAM's resistance activities, both political and military, as well as its social welfare efforts during the years of famine that decimated the urban population, attracted an ever-widening social spectrum. Its program and activities responded to the demands of a large segment of the working-class and petit bourgeois groups that were becoming more and more socially aware and radicalised. Moreover, in the countryside the political and cultural activities of EAM contributed to the politicisation of the peasants.[19]

The majority of officers who joined ELAS had been cashiered by the Populist party in 1935 and were kept out of the Albanian war by Metaxas.[20] Most of them hated the dictator because his

---

[17] Gerolymatos, 'Security Battalions ....', p. 19.

[18] On the transformation of pre-war liberalism see Constantine Tsoucalas, 'The Ideological Impact of the Civil War' in Iatrides, pp. 321-2.

[19] Nicolas Svoronos, 'Greek History, 1940-'50: The Main Problems' in Iatrides, p. 11.

[20] Grigoriadis claims that 1,500 retired officers were kept out of the war because they

regime was sponsored by the King – the traditional opponent of their political camp – and not out of a strong commitment to parliamentary democracy. Several belonged to clandestine organisations that had tried to topple the dictatorship, and were therefore prepared for underground activities. Even before the outbreak of the Greek-Italian war, the British SOE (Special Operations Executive) had established contact with disgruntled retired or cashiered officers to prepare for resistance against a potential occupation of Greece by Axis forces. Colonel E. Bakirdzis, a leading Venizelist officer who had been implicated in several interwar *coups*, became an early link between the SOE and officers organising resistance groups.[21] For such officers occupation amounted to a change of guard from one authoritarian regime to another, but presented an opportunity for a wide patriotic front against it because the oppressors were now foreigners. Furthermore, for these republican officers 'an allied defeat would have left them professionally in the same position outside the armed forces. [...] Professionally they had nothing to lose and everything to gain by joining the resistance.'[22]

Initially only a few officers joined ELAS. When Stephanos Saraphis, a republican well known because of his role in the abortive *coup* of 1935, was persuaded to assume the military command of ELAS and Mandakas and Bakirdzis joined its ranks, many retired Liberals as well as officers who had been on active duty during the 1940-1 war followed suit. By the end of 1943 ELAS included 1,250 of the first category and 600 of the second and a large number of reservists.[23] At about the same time EDES included a total of 900 officers – some of whom had been cashiered in 1935. Feeble and belated efforts to organise conservatives into a unified resistance movement came to nothing, as General Alexander Papagos and a few high-ranking commanders of the Albanian campaign were arrested by the Germans and spent the rest of the war in a prison camp.[24]

---

were considered dangerous to the regime. *Syntomi istoria tis ethnikis antistasis, 1941-45*, Athens, 1981, p. 116.

[21] Gerolymatos, 'The Role of the Greek Officer Corps', p. 71.

[22] *Ibid.*, p. 72.

[23] *Ibid.*, p. 75. These numbers represented 31 per cent of officers who remained in Greece and 21 per cent of the entire officer corps.

[24] *Ibid.*

Liberation and its bloody aftermath precipitated new developments in Greek society and the armed forces. After December 1944 EAM-ELAS lost its strategic advantage as well as the near-monopoly of armed power, and was in time debarred from the political discourse. New formidable factors militated against its influence, besides British arms or secret agreements between great powers. Resistance in the mountains and covert activities in the urban centres had been the natural element of EAM-ELAS, while peacetime posed altogether new challenges. Like snails after heavy rainfall, political parties made their appearance and slowly reconstituted their power-bases. In the immense enterprise of reconstruction there were jobs, contracts, loans and patronage to be dispensed to a war-ravaged populace. The Americans ultimately controlled the purse strings.

The December 1944 confrontation had an effect on the future of the armed forces not dissimilar to that brought about by the upheavals in VESMA. A gradual weeding-out of leftist, republican and ultimately Liberal elements forged a homogeneous and loyalist officer corps. On the 'under side' of this metamorphosis, imprisoned members of the Security Battalions were released and the less conspicuous were admitted in the national guard. Shortly after the Varkiza agreement, military committees set up by the Plastiras government to elect officers for the national army appointed 228 who had served with the battalions and 221 from ELAS.[25] However, the Greek General Staff placed the latter on a list of inactive officers and paid them until the time of their retirement.[26]

In the winter of 1945 the Holy Bond of Greek Officers (IDEA) was founded. This was a secret organisation of conservatives and royalists dedicated to principles not dissimilar from those that inspired the devotees of the 4th August regime. A dispute over the third article of the organisation's charter, which professed overt anti-Communism, was settled in favour of keeping the article intact.[27] The fifth article disavowed party affiliations and promised that the organisation would remain an instrument of the nation.[28]

---

[25] George Alexander, *The Prelude to the Truman Doctrine*, Oxford: Clarendon Press, 1982, p. 162.

[26] *Ibid.*, p. 138.

[27] George Karayannis, *1940-'52. To drama tis Ellados. Epi, athliotites*, Athens, 1963, pp. 206-9.

[28] *Ibid.*, p. 207.

A promise embedded in that very article was less innocuous than it appeared at the time. The strange assortment of officers who came in out of the cauldron of war, resistance and collaboration were united in the new army by their often belated commitment to the royalist and anti-Communist cause. In spite of their apparent dedication to the state they served, there were those who mistrusted and even despised politicians. Some replaced native political patronage with that dispensed by the power across the Atlantic. Twenty-two years after the foundation of IDEA, its political heirs in the army found their chance to emancipate themselves from the tutelage of politicians.

The upheavals in VESMA and the subsequent December 1944 uprising in Athens determined the political orientation of the officers that were selected to lead the Greek National Army (GNA) after the war. The defeat of EAM-ELAS in 1944, though far from decisive, gave the political parties a chance to reconstitute their power-bases and assume control of the state. By 1945 a right-wing backlash was evident among the military. Henceforth IDEA officers sought to infiltrate high positions and weed out what remained of Liberal elements in the officer corps. The Civil War that raged between 1946 and 1949 made the task possible and secured them powerful allies. When the Liberal Prime Minister Sophoulis attempted in 1947 to replace rightist commanders, he was faced with the reluctance of Anglo-American officials who held the key to military supplies.[29]

From the start of the Civil War, the GNA lacked seasoned and able commanders. A variety of factors had deprived the senior ranks of the army of its best elements. Of the conservative commanders who had distinguished themselves in the Albanian war many were either killed or discredited for participating in the collaborationist Tsolakoglou government of 1941. Venizelists of some repute who became entangled in the Middle East incidents and officers who joined ELAS were also kept out of action throughout the Civil War.

---

[29] Lawrence S. Wittner, *American Intervention in Greece, 1943-49*, New York: Columbia University Press, 1982, pp. 240-1. For a detailed account of the irregular as well as the regular forces that took part in the 1946-9 war, see David Close and Thanos Veremis, 'The Military Struggle' in David Close (ed.), *The Greek Civil War, 1943-1950*, London: Routledge, 1993, pp. 97-128.

Three of the highest-ranking officers left their mark during the fratricidal strife of 1946-9 – Generals Vendiris, Tsakalotos and Papagos. Constantine Vendiris, a close friend of Eleftherios Venizelos, was one of the precious few Liberals who held major posts in the GNA during the Civil War and was often the target of attacks in right-wing newspapers for his anti-royalist past.[30] He became Commander-in-Chief briefly after the liberation, was appointed Chief of the General Staff in 1947 and finally commander of the 1st and 2nd Corps combined during the last phase of the Civil War in 1949. Thrasyvoulos Tsakalotos, a royalist of the 'national schism' era, managed to survive the army purges of the interwar period and made his name as commander of the Greek Mountain brigade at the battle of Rimini in Italy.[31] He was commander of the 3rd Corps in 1946 and became deputy to the Commander-in-Chief in 1947, and commander of the 1st Corps, combined with responsibility for the 2nd Corps, in 1948. He conducted a successful mopping-up operation in the Peloponnese before handing over the command to General Th. Pentzopoulos. In 1949 he led the final assault against Mount Grammos in what was known as 'Operation Torch'.[32] Tsakalotos was an idiosyncratic commander who could instill enthusiasm in the ranks and lead complex operations. According to Woodhouse: 'The disharmony between Papagos and Tsakalotos was rather like that between Eisenhower and Montgomery. [...] Tsakalotos was a brilliant field commander, egoistic and impetuous, always convinced that the crux of any strategic problem was where he happened to be in command. Papagos was a superlative staff officer, impeccable in logistic planning and exact calculation, a master of the politics and diplomacy of war, with little experience of high command in battle.'[33] General Alexander Papagos, Commander-in-Chief of the Greek forces in the 1940-1 war against Italy and Germany, became the *deus ex machina* to extract the GNA from its inertia and lead it to victory in 1949. An officer with a distinguished

---

[30] For more details concerning Vendiris' Venizelist past see his correspondence with Plastiras, Thanos Veremis, *I epemvasis tou stratou stin elliniki politiki*, Athens: Odysseas, 1983, pp. 280-98.

[31] Th. Tsakalotos, *Saranta chronia stratiotis tis Ellados*, Athens, 1960, vol. A, pp. 52, 68.

[32] C.M. Woodhouse, *The Struggle for Greece 1941-49*, London: Hart-Davis, MacGibbon, 1976, pp. 199, 205-10, 239-40, 261-76.

[33] *Ibid.*, p. 270.

family background, he remained unswervingly loyal to the crown throughout its period of tribulations.

There are certain patterns in the organisational shortcomings of the GNA forces, their failure to assume the initiative and the dearth of effective leadership, which persisted throughout most of 1946-9. From the outset of the struggle the GNA had a clear advantage in numbers and equipment. Between the summer and winter of 1946 the GNA forces attained a strength of 90,000 men, and the Gendarmerie of 30,000. They were equipped with tanks, armoured cars, artillery and motor transport but failed to take advantage of their superiority in men and arms till the last months of the war. The rebels of the Democratic Army (DA) seized and retained the initiative and forced the GNA to dance to its tune. By shifting their operations from the cities to the mountains and country towns they used hit-and-run tactics that kept the government troops off-balance and prevented them from using their resources to the full. Furthermore, the training provided by the British Army missions was not anti-guerrilla warfare. Men called up for service had mostly been soldiers before the war, and although they had seen action in Albania they were reluctant to stay away from their homes and livelihoods for long periods. Poor leadership and political patronage that favoured officers with party connections rather than proven merit was initially the rule rather than the exception.[34]

The rebels were able to move with relative ease in rough terrain of their own choice, while the GNA could only use the few mined roads leading to the mountains. The rebel forces consisted basically of light infantry units, and obliged the GNA to use comparable forces against them. However, it was the GNA's ability to recruit soldiers in large numbers that proved to be its decisive advantage in the long run.

A persistent theme throughout the Civil War was the constant pressure exerted by the Greek authorities on the British and then the Americans to maintain aid for substantial increases in manpower and supplies. In November 1946 the Chief of the General Staff, Spiliotopoulos, went to London to press for the GNA's strength to be increased to 135,000. Along with Vendiris who succeeded him in February 1947, they created new static, mobile

---

[34] *Ibid.*, pp. 186-7.

and commando units. Non-Communist resistance leaders such as Tsaous Anton and Mihalagas were allowed to re-form their bands with the hope that they would beat the rebels in their own game and Zervas, commander of the second largest resistance organisation during the occupation period, was made Minister of Public Order. The GNA was organised in seven divisions and seven independent brigades and by the end of 1947 its forces became 120,000 strong.[35] In the mean time three generals – Spiliotopoulos, Vendiris and Giantzis – alternated in the position of Chief of the General Staff. But in spite of everything, morale in the GNA remained low and this was testified by a secret report written by the Director of Military Operations, Thomas Pentzopoulos, and published in the Communist newspaper *Rizospastis* on 19 April 1947.

The arrival of United States liaison officers in October and the formation of the Joint US Military Advisory and Planning Group (JUSMAPG) to coordinate operations, injected the senior commanders of the GNA with a much needed improvement in morale.[36] The real change in GNA tactics was put into effect by General James Van Fleet who was appointed head of JUSMAPG in January 1948. The new plan of the US mission was to initiate operations against the rebels instead of waiting for their next strike. With 147,000 troops in 1948, the GNA appeared equal to the task. However, events were to prove otherwise.

In April 1948 the GNA began a systematic operation to sweep south-central Greece and reach the DA's northern strongholds. The nationalist forces advanced but failed to encircle the guerrillas. The campaign culminated at Mount Grammos on the Greek-Albanian border. At the end of June 50,000 government troops attempted to storm the positions of 15,000 DA troops who managed to defend themselves for two and a half months before withdrawing into Albania. Soon the rebel forces regrouped and appeared in the Mount Vitsi area, north-east of Grammos. This unexpected reversal and the GNA's failure to dislodge the rebels from their new location did great damage to the morale of the government troops. Soldiers who had exerted themselves to breaking-point realised that there was no end to a war with an adversary who

---

[35] D. Zaphiropoulos, *O anti-symmoriakos agonas, 1945-1949*, Athens, 1956, pp. 94-5.

[36] Edgar O'Ballance, *The Greek Civil War, 1944-49*, London: Faber and Faber, 1966, p. 156.

could seek sanctuary on foreign soil and return at will. Meanwhile guerrilla activities in southern Greece became unmanageable and by mid-winter the DA re-established itself at Mount Grammos.[37]

Following the events of 1948, the Greek government, the British military mission and JUSMAPG called for dramatic increases in the strength of the Greek armed forces. Whereas US military expenditure for 1948 in Greece did not exceed $150 million, Van Fleet submitted two military budgets, of $450 and $541 million, for the next fiscal year.[38]

The strength of the guerrilla forces was in inverse proportion to the state of the national economy. As long as there was no improvement in the social problems caused by occupation, the Communist party could draw support among the population to build a more just and equitable system. Since the state continued to plough considerable resources into the war, reconstruction was inevitably postponed. US aid became a strategic factor in the Civil War since it allowed the Greek government to free funds for productive investment and relief.

Henry Grady, the US ambassador, was not supportive of Van Fleet's proposals. When George Marshall, the Secretary of State, flew to Athens in October he realised that without effective leadership the government forces could not win the conflict, however large the amount of aid received. The idea of centralising the command of the GNA finally focused on General Papagos, but the former Commander-in-Chief set firm conditions for accepting it: an increase in the forces from 147,000 to 250,000 men and a free hand in military decisions. By mid-January 1949 a compromise between Papagos and the Americans settled the appointment of the new commander of the Greek armed forces.[39]

Between 1945 and 1949 the Supreme Council of National Defence (ASEA), which included the three war ministers, the chiefs of the three branches of the armed forces and the chiefs of the British and later US military missions (without a vote), operated under the chairmanship of the Prime Minister. The

[37] J.C. Murray, 'The Anti-Bandit War', *Marine Corps Gazette*, in three monthly parts: vol. 38, Jan.-March 1954, pp. 17-18.

[38] Wittner, p. 245.

[39] *Ibid.*, p. 248. G. Karayannis in his book about IDEA claims for the secret organisation some of the credit for convincing the Prime Minister, Sophoulis, to choose Papagos. Karayannis, *To drama tis Ellados, op. cit.*, pp. 256-7.

ASEA dealt with the drafting of defence policy, the selection of the military high command, and allocation of military expenditure. With the appointment of Papagos the ASEA was replaced by a cosmetic war council while the Commander-in-Chief himself was given complete authority over all military issues. 'His suggestions, which could even include the imposition of martial law, were binding on the Minister of Defence. Papagos' extraordinary powers, granted due to the emergency conditions caused by the Civil War, concentrated authority over military decisions and facilitated the establishment of American influence, unhindered by political opposition.'[40]

On the eve of the final confrontation in Vitsi and Grammos the GNA forces presented the following picture. The combat arms of the army consisted of infantry, artillery, armoured reconnaissance, tanks and engineers. A division was composed of infantry, headquarters and signal elements. Supporting arms were under the control of various directorates of the General Staff, but were established to provide certain attachments. A mountain division was normally reinforced by a cavalry squadron, a machine-gun company, engineers and a regiment of mountain artillery. Field divisions were similarly reinforced, except that armoured cavalry and field artillery replaced cavalry and mountain artillery. Six types of infantry were employed by the government: Mountain, Field, Commando, National Defence Corps (light infantry), Gendarmerie and armed civilian components. The National Defence Corps battalions were formed from old classes of reservists to provide static defences for lines of communication, towns and vital installations. As the army became more active, National Defence units were used as light infantry in searching operations. The Gendarmerie continued to assist in military operations by conducting searches to ensure that areas were cleared of guerrillas. Armoured cavalry and tanks did not play a significant offensive role in the Civil War, but were mainly used for the defence of towns and cities.[41]

The GNA had certain significant advantages over the DA. It could field balanced forces of combat arms, while the guerrillas

---

[40] T. Veremis, 'Security Considerations and Civil-Military Relations in Post-War Greece' in R. Clogg (ed.), *Greece in the 1980s*, London: Macmillan, 1983, p. 178.

[41] Murray, 'The Anti-Bandit War', *Marine Corps Gazette*, February 1954, pp. 53–5.

could oppose it with infantry units alone. The government forces were supported by supply and service elements, which provided them with strategic mobility and staying power. Finally, the government could recruit conscripts without harassment and draw from the plentiful supplies of urban manpower.[42]

GOVERNMENT FORCES, JULY 1949 [43]

| | |
|---|---|
| Greek National Army | 150,000 |
| National Defence Corps | 50,000 |
| Gendarmerie | 25,000 |
| Civil police | 7,500 |
| | 232,500 |

The victory of the GNA in the struggle for control of Greece was only partly due to military reform and Papagos' skill as a staff officer. More significant factors were Tito's break with the Cominform and his final break with Stalin. These paved the way for the eventual closure of the Yugoslav borders to Greek guerrillas on 10 July 1949. Furthermore, Zahariadis' decision to sack Markos Vafiadis both as commander of the DA and head of the 'Democratic Government' during the fifth session of the Central Committee of the KKE (30 and 31 January 1949) precipitated a shift in Communist strategy from guerrilla tactics to positional warfare.[44]

In the summer of 1949 Zahariadis concentrated his DA forces on the Vitsi and Grammos area and dug in for the final confrontation. The attack of the GNA against Vitsi began on 10 August and within three days the DA positions had been overrun. Out of a garrison of 7,000 almost 5,000 fled to Albania. In the Grammos operation launched on 24 August, the 200 square miles of the area were occupied by government troops in five days, and 4,000 guerillas withdrew into Albania.

The Civil War had finished but, as with the evil that men do, its destructive effects persisted long afterwards.

---

[42] *Ibid.*, Feb. 1954, p. 55.

[43] *Ibid.*, January 1954, p. 23.

[44] O' Ballance, pp. 179-97.

# 9

# THE POST-WAR LEGACY

The American Mission for Aid to Greece (AMAG) in 1947 signified the changing of the guard from Britain to the United States in sustaining the lifeline of pro-Western Greek governments, which had been confronted by civil strife since 1946. Members of foreign missions were interested only in seeing the defeat of the leftist forces – often at the expense of an orderly revival of democratic institutions in the war-torn country. The operations of the Greek Army were effectively coordinated and supervised by the Joint United States Military Advisory and Planning Group (JUSMAPG), and the overriding priority of winning the war dictated its support for cabinets which were not diverted from their main objective by liberal sensibilities. Thus British and American officials averted the attempt by Prime Minister Sophoulis to replace certain right-wing commanders with republicans, and ignored his contention that the former had already become a state within a state.[1] In February 1948, representatives of the US and British embassies and AMAG persuaded the Greek cabinet to accept their presence at all meetings of the Supreme Council of National Defence and to empower the Chief of the General Staff to take important decisions on the conduct of operations. Although in practice the government had already abdicated its control over the war effort, the concessions of February 1948 signified an official transfer of authority to the Greek military and their American counterpart.[2]

By 1949 the Greek army had become an enclave of American influence, and members of the US mission often set a negative example to their military protégés by expressing their disdain for

---

[1] Lawrence S. Wittner, *American Interventions in Greece, 1943-1949*, New York: Columbia University Press, 1982, p. 240.

[2] *Ibid.*, p. 241. See also D. Kondis, *I angloamericaniki politiki kai to elliniko provlima, 1945-1949*, Thessaloniki: Paratiritis, 1984.

Greek politicians and members of the government. The extraordinary circumstances of the Civil War and the function of foreign missions put a distance between the military and civil society in Greece. Furthermore, the ideological ossification of officers, due to their special training, encouraged their claim to a certain autonomy in relation to politicians and civilians in general who, according to military perceptions, failed to understand the nature of the enemy.

The emergence of Papagos as a major figure of the right-wing camp was soon perceived by the Greek royal family as a threat to their own monopoly of influence in the armed forces. Although the rift between the King and Papagos was never brought to public attention, the marshal's supporters were determined, in one way or another, to install their hero in power. Such officers belonged to the clandestine military organisation IDEA, the product of a combination of royalist (ENA) and nationalist organisations that arose during the war in the Middle East.[3] By 1950, through a gradual process, IDEA had shifted its loyalty from the King to Papagos and had become the rallying point of officers whose professional ambitions were frustrated by the King's socially prominent military clients. IDEA members attempted to overthrow the government on 31 May 1951 after Papagos resigned as head of the army following a disagreement with the court. Although Papagos had not discouraged his admirers from criticising his opponents, he in fact prevented their *coup* from taking over. His interwar record of involvement in military interventions was overshadowed by his stature after the Civil War, which secured for him a position in parliamentary politics.

The IDEA officers who took part in the attempted *coup* were cashiered, only to be reinstated after the resounding electoral victory won by Papagos in 1952. Panayotis Kanellopoulos, who served as Minister of Defence in several post-war cabinets, refers to the covert influence of IDEA members on promotions and vital appointments throughout the 1950s and early 1960s.[4] The most significant such appointment because of its far-reaching consequences was the choice of General V. Kardamakis as head of the General Military Staff. According to Kanellopoulos (then Deputy

---

[3] Karayannis, *To drama tis Ellados, op. cit.*

[4] Panayotis Kanellopoulos, *Istorika dokimia*, Athens, 1975, pp. 26–44.

Prime Minister in the Karamanlis government), Kardamakis became the rallying point of young IDEA followers and the springboard of their rise to conspiratorial prominence.[5]

The National Union of Young Officers, an offshoot of IDEA, was founded in 1958 and headed by the future dictator George Papadopoulos. Its ideology combined fervent nationalism and anti-Communism with contempt for parliamentary democracy. No less important in the make-up of such military associations, a sense of social inferiority drove the least endowed officers to join its ranks.[6] Although no systematic research has yet verified this contention, it is our suspicion that interest in conspiracies and clandestine societies was in inverse proportion to an officer's ability and professional prospects. Membership of secret organisations that expounded nationalist orthodoxy but also promoted the corporate interests of its followers became a guarantee of success and indeed of survival for the least prominent and able elements in the army. Furthermore, IDEA was a symptom of growing factionalism in what, after the Civil War, had been an ideologically monolithic officer corps.

The *coup* of 21 April 1967 came about through a variety of factors.[7] International détente reduced the significance of the army as guarantor of internal order and guardian of the state against external challenges. The furious efforts of the 1967 junta to justify its overthrow of parliamentary democracy were based mainly on the allegation of a Communist threat. Yet in later statements the military contradicted this allegation by boasting that the Communists were a negligible danger in Greece.[8] The only conceivable claim of legitimacy which the conspirators could invoke was Article 91 of the constitution, which empowered the King to suspend a number of articles under extraordinary circumstances; however,

---

[5] *Ibid.*, pp. 41-3.

[6] N. Stavrou, 'Pressure Groups in the Greek Political Setting', Ph.D. thesis, George Washington University, 1970.

[7] Dimitris Haralambis, *Stratos kai politiki exousia*, Athens: Exantas, 1985. Haralambis views the evolving role of the Greek military within the context of a 'bourgeois emergency regime'. According to him, efforts of a modernising segment of the middle class are invariably cancelled out by countervailing conservative forces. The military are seen as a primary instrument in impeding change.

[8] Richard Clogg and George Yannopoulos (eds), *Greece under Military Rule*, London: Secker and Warburg, 1972, pp. 38-9.

a recommendation to this effect was required from the Council of Ministers and of course was never made.[9]

Besides producing a justification for its takeover, the junta hoped to exert control over networks that had ceased to be of the same mind by rekindling a spectre of the past and thus rejuvenating the military national mission. The decisive spark in the tinderbox was the conflict between parliament and the monarchy exemplified by the break between Prime Minister George Papandreou and King Constantine II in 1965. During most of the post-war period, the cooperation of the crown and the majority party had kept the military out of political disputes, but the conflict over control of the armed forces, which was at the centre of the Papandreou-Constantine confrontation, resulted in the gradual emancipation of certain officers from political and royal tutelage.

Professional grievances were also an important force behind the *coup* of 1967. The army's sudden expansion during the Civil War and the reduced promotional opportunities in its aftermath caused congestion in the middle ranks, and the problem of orderly professional advancement was aggravated by political and royal favouritism which distributed promotion not according to merit but by proof of loyalty. Some officers became willing clients of the 1967 regime, knowing that their escape upwards depended on mass dismissals.

The counter-*coup* against the junta on 13 December 1967 was in fact spurred by rumours that significant numbers of high-ranking commanders loyal to the King would be retired. Its failure created crucial vacancies which were predictably filled by friends of the regime. Some 3,000 officers were retired or dismissed between 1967 and 1972, but since military-politicos rarely have time to improve their professional skills, the promotions of 1967-72 seriously undermined the competence and preparedness of the armed forces. In 1974 lieutenants and captains formed 43 per cent of the entire corps, while no less than 54 per cent were majors and colonels.[10]

---

[9] King Constantine's 'acquiescence was therefore even more questionable than that of his uncle, George II, towards the dictatorship of General Metaxas in 1936, for Metaxas was at least himself the Prime Minister who recommended the partial suspension of the Constitution'. C.M. Woodhouse, *The Rise and Fall of the Greek Colonels*, London: Granada, 1985, p. 29.

[10] N. Stavrou, *Allied Policy and Military Interventions : The Political Role of the Greek Military*,

The 1960s in Greece were characterised by rapid economic growth and a corresponding liberalisation of society after two decades of austerity and constraints on civil liberties. The revolution of expectations generated during the liberal administration of Papandreou posed no real threat to the established social order other than to those whose task it was to police the state. As Mouzelis put it, 'The political mobilisation and Papandreou's liberalisation measures were [more] threatening to those occupying key posts in the repressive state and army apparatus ... than to the economic establishment of the country and to those politicians representing their interests in parliament.'[11] Thus it is not surprising that the Colonels, despite the initial compliance of the masses, failed to win wide support even in the conservative sector of society. Their eventual control of the army, however, was made much easier by a trump-card which no civilian group could easily counter: the approval of the United States.

We have already mentioned the influence exerted by American military missions on the post-war Greek officer corps. Officers of the Civil War period shared the view that for the sake of operational efficiency the Greek armed forces should become an autonomous enclave which would be answerable only to its foreign advisers. This conviction persisted many years after the end of the emergency that inspired it. American influence became the most stable element in the Greek forces and continued undiminished throughout the 1950s and '60s. According to US Department of Defense statistics, the total number of Greeks trained in the United States under the Military Assistance Program (MAP) between 1950 and 1969 was 11,229. An additional 1,965 students were trained under the MAP in overseas installations. These figures became very important, as Couloumbis put it, 'in terms of United States' modernising input to the Greek armed forces'.[12] In 1967 members of the junta encouraged their wavering colleagues by propagating rumours of American complicity in order to secure

Athens: Papazissis, 1976, p. 214. See also unpublished memoirs of a protagonist of the 13 December 1967 counter-*coup*, General Orestis Vidalis, *Chronia ekpatrismou*, file 4, documentation no. 2; N. Pantelakis, 'L'armée dans la société grecque contemporaine', unpubl. Ph.D. thesis, Université René Descartes (Paris V), 1980, pp. 74, 75.

[11] Nicos Mouzelis, *Modern Greece: Facets of Underdevelopment*, London: Macmillan, 1978, p. 113.

[12] Theodore Couloumbis, 'The Greek Junta Phenomenon', *Polity*, vol. VI, no. 3, spring 1974, p. 353.

wider support. Officers who looked to the United States for signs of active disapproval were disappointed and therefore discouraged from opposing the military regime.[13] By relying on what they interpreted as American backing, the Colonels could sever the umbilical cord which attached them to conservative politicians who had failed to stay in power and had few chances of winning the elections expected in May 1967.[14]

The introduction of certain institutional novelties in the command structure of the armed forces was indicative of the Colonels' determination to preserve an enclave of military autonomy even after the return to some form of civilian rule. Before the rule of the junta, the armed forces were governed by Law 2387 of 1953, whereby each Chief of Staff (Army, Navy and Air Force) was separately responsible for his own branch to the Minister of Defence, who in turn was vested with the highest authority over military matters. The General Staff of National Defence coordinated the activities of the three services without, in fact, having any authority over them. The dictator George Papadopoulos created the position of Chief of the Armed Forces, thus depriving the Minister of Defence of his authority and the Chiefs of Staff of any autonomy within their separate branches. By concentrating power, Papadopoulos was in a better position to control it and was confident that he would also be able to entrust the legacy of the Chief of the Armed Forces to the military guardians of any future regime.[15] The Cyprus crisis of 1974 proved that the concentration of authority caused an incapacity in decision-making at a time of emergency.[16]

In 1973 Papadopoulos decided to seek a way out of his isolation through the legitimacy of civilian rule. A partial and controlled transfer of responsibilities to politicians was seen as the beginning of a transformation that would turn the *homo militaris* into a *homo civilis*. His clumsy effort to civilianise the authority of the military included a series of trials of dissidents, aimed at adding a touch

---

[13] T. Veremis, *Greek Security: Issues and Politics*, Adelphi Paper no. 179, London: IISS, 1962, p. 18.

[14] The allegation of American complicity was also promoted by Andreas Papandreou, who believed that the US embassy favoured the Colonels' plot and had advised the King to accept the *fait accompli*. Andreas Papandreou, *Democracy at Gunpoint: The Greek Front*, London: Deutsch, 1971, pp. 192-3.

[15] A. Spanidis, articles in daily *Kathimerini*, 16 March 1975 and 18 January 1976.

[16] The Act of August 1977, revising the command structure of the armed forces, abolished the innovations of the military regime.

of legal refinement to his arbitrary tactics. However, the trials provided a podium for the critics of the regime and further diminished its legitimacy in those civilian quarters that would presumably help to extract it from its isolation.[17]

On 1 June 1973 the dictator proclaimed the birth of a presidential parliamentary republic, and this was ratified by a referendum. Under the new constitution, the President was entrusted with wide legislative and executive authority, with exclusive control over foreign affairs, public order and questions of national security. He was, in fact, vested with power that diminished the authority granted to the armed forces by the previous constitution.[18] The *coup* of Brigadier Ioannides which overthrew Papadopoulos that same year represented officers reluctant to give up their influence in public affairs.

The Greek military have never acted as agents of modernisation but rather as sources of political turmoil. Their professional grievances were aggravated by their sense of isolation from the rest of society. This isolation was partly due to the 'total institutional life'[19] set up for their benefit, but also to the widening gap between their social origins and those of the more prominent civilian technocrats of the 1950s. From this, however, one cannot assume that the officers' social origin determined their class allegiances, or that their lower middle-class and peasant background entailed an automatic identification with these classes. The great majority of Greek officers of 1967 identified with the values and interests of the prevailing middle class, and their humble upbringing was in fact supportive of the nationalist creed which looks to the simple people for devotion to the fatherland, as well as of the *laissez-faire* ideal in which hard work and merit lead to success. Equally important as an element of their identity was a traditional individualism which tends to protect the family from the malfunctions of a cumbersome state mechanism and allows for socially acceptable infractions of legality. As Nordlinger points out, 'given the self-image of the officer corps as leading nationalists they are commonly able to rationalise away or sincerely justify even their

---

[17] N. Alivizatos, *I politiki thesmi se krisi 1922-1974*, Ahens: Themelio, 1983, pp. 636-8.

[18] *Ibid.*, p. 312.

[19] Keith Legg, *Politics in Modern Greece*, Stanford University Press, 1969, pp. 191-2.

predatory actions'.[20] While charging politicians with offences against the national interest, the Colonels nevertheless aspired to establish themselves in prominent civilian positions.

Nordlinger's basic observation on military interventions appears relevant to the Greek case. The Colonels' regime did not promote modernisation simply because the officers possessed neither the necessary skills nor the influence of a vanguard of society. Once firmly in control they tended to follow the example of traditional party bosses by extending patronage to their kin and to the ever-growing number of their clients. The absence of public criticism and official opposition soon made the regime a paragon of corruption. Even the professional competence and preparedness of the armed forces fell short of the most moderate expectations, as the Cyprus crisis showed all too clearly.

The weakening of parliamentary institutions in the mid-1960s as a result of the clash between the head of state and the head of the government encouraged a group of officers who had come of age during the Civil War period to fill the temporary power vacuum. Such factors as professional grievances and their relative isolation from civilian society combined with the identity of a guardian of the established order. However, in a country where constitutional and parliamentary institutions have long been established and civilian authority cannot be disputed (or at least only temporarily), the military must seek to legitimise their intervention either by handing over power to civilians or through a metamorphosis which will transform them into widely accepted political figures. The Colonels of 1967 failed on both counts.

---

[20] Eric Nordlinger, *Soldiers in Politics, Military Coups and Governments*, Englewood Cliffs, NJ: Prentice-Hall, 1977, p. 65.

# 10

# THE COLONELS UNLEASHED

The Colonels came to power with no clear policies, no coherent ideology of their own, and no consistent views on the shape of the regime or the nature of its future options. Having first secured his own personal rule, Papadopoulos did, however, embark on a more ambitious programme – that of rejuvenating Greece. His plan provided for no less than a total purge of the decadent Western influences which he saw as responsible for the spread of anarchy in Greek society and as threatening the very foundations of 'Hellenic-Christian civilisation'.[1] In the dictator's improvised utopia, social classes would be abolished and general consensus on vital issues would be arrived at through systematic training in whatever was deemed expedient for the nation. But the realisation of this nebulous scheme, under the supervision of the military, was soon found to need more time than had been foreseen, so that promises of a speedy return to parliamentary politics were postponed indefinitely.

The pretensions of the junta were initially limited to setting society in order rather than coping with the complex problems of development. Yet it eventually decided that running a state was not so difficult after all, and it was aware too that if it failed to diversify its activities it would soon run out of excuses for holding on to power. Such terms as 'growth' and 'development' began to feature prominently in their discourse, and became part of an effort to modernise the image of the military. The new posture was also encouraged by a timely proliferation of published works on military sociology, which argued that the organisational strength and monopoly of force wielded by the officer corps qualified it for resolving problems of development. These ideas

---

[1] Clogg and Yannopoulos (eds), *Greece under Military Rule,*, pp. 19-21, 81-93.

were adopted by a small circle of advisers to the junta, and provided a theoretical mantle for Papadopoulos' budding aspirations.[2] Having patronised works which emphasised the role of officers as modernisers, the dictator was in turn convinced by his own rationalisations and propaganda that his was the task not merely of policing the state but of modernising it.[3] However, the reality of military rule in Greece was close to the role ascribed by Huntington to the 'guardian' soldier,[4] while Stepan's refutation of theories that viewed the military as agents of development in Brazil could equally be applied to the polity of the Greek Colonels: 'The Brazilian experience indicates that ... the pattern of civil–military relations which the military attempted to impose after 1964 has left the military internally divided, increasingly isolated from civilians, reliant upon torture as a mechanism of political control, and without a creative programme of social development.'[5]

The actual exercise of power by the Greek junta was largely based on clientelistic networks and kinship, and restricted to reliable army officers and their relatives and associates. Apart from the decision to relieve farmers of their bank debts, announced in advance of the 1968 constitutional referendum, the regime made little effort to attract civilian support, still less to create a viable political base. Their anti-Communism may have tempered any aspirations to a programme of social reform, while the Colonels were never widely popular outside the army and seem to have had an inexhaustible capacity for alienating even those party leaders who might otherwise have been expected to show sympathy for at least some of their aims. Not long after the *coup* the former conservative Prime Minister, Karamanlis, denounced the regime as 'tyrannical', calling on the army itself to remove it, while his later intervention in April 1973 was an unequivocal demand for

[2] A. Stepan, *The Military in Politics: Changing Patterns in Brazil*, Princeton University Press, 1971, p. 5.

[3] Issue no. 7-8 (Jan.-June 1971) of the state-supervised *Review of Social Research* was dedicated to the proceedings of a conference on military sociology which stressed the contribution of the military to development. Jean Siotis' article 'Some Notes on the Military in Greek Politics' was the exception in pointing out that the Greek officers have been agents of political turmoil rather than champions of development; the article appeared with the others, although the author had refused to grant permission for publication.

[4] Samuel Huntington, *The Soldier and the State*, Cambridge, MA: Harvard University Press, 1957, pp. 222, 225-6.

[5] Stepan, p. 5.

the military to quit government altogether. Much of the old middle class remained implacably hostile to military rule right to the end. And the extensive purge of unreliable or opposition elements within the civil service, their replacement by soldiers and their kin, and the introduction into each ministry or bureau of a military 'watchdog' all led to increasing friction between officers and the civil service.

From the outset the real and effective base of the junta was in the army, whose cadres made disproportionate gains both socially and materially from the 1967 coup and subsequent military rule, and could be said in that sense to constitute a new and privileged establishment. Officers not forcibly retired benefited from higher salaries, loans for cars and houses, improved promotion prospects, and discounts in shops. They therefore had little incentive to return power to the civilians. Meanwhile the purge of senior officers, which soon extended downwards, offered accelerated promotion to those at the bottom of the hierarchy, while with the military in government there were ample opportunities for patronage. In time, however, rapid promotion would bring new blockages and frustrations, compounded by the declining reputation of the military and mounting criticism of its administration. Even within the army, the regime betrayed its origins in the factional struggles of the previous decade, as the more dependable units, commanded by those close to the junta, were favoured with arms and other equipment and came increasingly to be deployed in the Athens region. The navy and air force, traditionally the 'aristocracy' of the services, had no part in the 1967 *coup* and played no very significant role in the ensuing government, and naval officers were implicated in an unsuccessful *coup* discovered in May 1973.

The purge in the armed forces and the civil service of enemies of the regime and those suspected or accused of left-wing sympathies or background gave ample opportunities for the regime's political pay-offs. In the autumn of 1967 King Constantine was presented with a list of officers – originally estimated at some 400 but later said to have been reduced to 144 – earmarked for early retirement. Since most of them were friends of the crown, Constantine, who had failed to make a stand against the Colonels in April, was belatedly faced with the dilemma of either playing his hand against the Colonels or losing what influence he still had within the army. The Colonels' inept handling of a crisis in Cyprus not only threatened the island with a Turkish invasion that year, but also provided the King with an excellent opportunity for stepping in to oust the junta. As it turned out, it was he who had to abandon his office and flee the country.

The King's abortive *coup* proved that his loyal senior officers, though professionally the more competent, were no match for the Colonels in conspiratorial skills. After his flight to Italy, the officer corps was purged of all royalist elements to an extent that adversely affected the operational capabilities of the armed forces. Between 1967 and 1968 one-sixth were cashiered or retired.[6]

We have suggested that the regime of 21 April was gradually shaped after Papadopoulos' own vision. When the royal threat was out of the way, the dictator assumed at different times a variety of combinations of offices which included those of Prime Minister, as well as Minister of Foreign Affairs, National Defence and Education. In March 1972 he became Regent, before proclaiming the republic and assuming the presidency the following year. Although his prototypes were those furnished him by the right-wing parliamentary governments of the 1950s and early '60s, he also sought to establish the army as the guarantor of future regimes. The constitution of 1968 bears witness to Papadopoulos' idea of the political regime best suited for Greece. A committee of jurists who toiled between May and December 1967 presented the government with a draft constitution which the regime ultimately ignored. Instead the officers produced their own draft between March and August 1968, and had it ratified by plebiscite in a country still under a state of emergency. The new constitution approved by 92 per cent of the voters provided a picture of the mentality of those in power. Civil rights were excluded from the document, and the emasculated legislature that emerged from it had no say on issues of defence and foreign policy. The Prime Minister, who was the only member of the government to have a seat in parliament, was accountable to the King in this 'crowned democracy', but the King was deprived of his former ties with the armed forces. These new constitutional elements were invented to secure the exercise of fundamental powers by the military: the

[6] C.M. Woodhouse, *The Rise and Fall of the Greek Colonels*, London: Granada, 1985, pp. 44-8.

Constitutional Court and the provisions which vested the armed forces with extraordinary authority. Much of the authority of the Defence Minister was transferred to the leadership of the armed forces, and promotions, retirements and commissions became the exclusive preserve of the military. Furthermore, there was explicit reference in the document to the army's right to safeguard the integrity of the existing political and social order. Politically motivated strikes were outlawed.[7]

Provision was made for a parliament which would be elected by universal and secret ballot, and divided into two sections. 'Most of the key articles of the constitution, however, were to remain inoperative indefinitely.'[8] All the same, Papadopoulos tried to consolidate his own position, basing his authority increasingly on the constitution and at the same time trying to ease the army out of the government. He presented the regime not as a dictatorship but as a 'parenthesis' that was 'necessary to put things straight'. The Revolutionary Committee that had acted as the conscience of the regime and met regularly during the first year seems to have been disbanded once the constitution was approved. By May 1970 Papadopoulos had emerged as the undisputed leader of the junta.

In 1971 the governmental structure was radically revised. The country was divided into seven administrative districts, each to be supervised by a governor with the rank of Deputy Minister. Far from attempting to decentralise the administration, as the government claimed, the new system in fact tightened the grip of central authority upon the periphery.[9] Such measures, like the fifteen-year Development Plan announced in 1972, had long-term implications for the flow of authority while indicating Papadopoulos' own plans for a protracted term in power. The decision to dig in for a more permanent stay in office presupposed a substantial investment in the means of mass repression. Thus the budget of the Ministry of Public Order increased by about 40 per cent from 1,798 million drachmas in 1966 to 2,520 million in 1968. Simultaneously, the military expanded its range of activities by assuming a greater share of internal security. The notorious

---

[7] R. Clogg, 'I dictatoria tis 21is Apriliou' in *Ellada. Istoria kai politismos*, vol. 6, Thessaloniki: Malliaris, 1982, p. 249.

[8] G. Kousoulas, *Modern Greece: Profile of a Nation*, New York: Scribner, 1974, p. 283.

[9] Clogg and Yannopoulos, p. 16.

military police, a ubiquitous unit under Colonel Dimitrios Ioannides, became a veritable state within a state.[10] By 1969 the Defence Ministry absorbed 49.8 per cent of all government expenditure, while the budget for education fell from 15 per cent in 1966 to 13.1 per cent in 1969.[11] Greek military expenditure averaged 4.8 per cent of GNP between 1967 and 1970, a high percentage compared with the NATO average of 3.5 per cent for the same period.[12]

Despite the prodigious growth in military expenses, few arms purchases were made while the junta was in power, and the large 1974 order was not delivered till after the regime's fall. Most of the extra funds were apparently allocated to propaganda or used for internal security purposes. The deplorable state of discipline and morale among the conscripts during the Cyprus crisis of 1974 betrayed the dictatorship's neglect of the army's battle-readiness. Such neglect could have stemmed from adoption by the Colonels of a doctrine concerning the country's defence posture which had originated in the late 1940s. According to an American National Security Report of 1949, Greece ought to have 'a military establishment capable of maintaining internal security in order to avoid communist domination', while Turkey was intended to have military capabilities 'of sufficient size and effectiveness to insure [its] continued resistance to Soviet pressures'.[13] The splinter group within the junta that engineered the attempt on the life of Archbishop Makarios, the President of Cyprus, in the summer of 1974 did not for a moment doubt that the United States would avert any Turkish reaction that might result in war with Greece.[14]

In May 1973 a group of naval officers loyal to the King launched their *coup* against Papadopoulos. The spectacular mutiny on the

[10] *Ibid.*, p. 17.

[11] *Ibid.*

[12] John Pesmazoglou, 'The Greek Economy after 1967' in Clogg and Yannopoulos, p. 181.

[13] Y. Roubatis, 'The United States and the Operational Responsibilities of the Greek Armed Forces, 1947-1987', *Journal of the Hellenic Diaspora*, 6, spring 1979, p. 46.

[14] On the evening of Karamanlis' return to Greece (24 July 1974), the author struck up a street conversation with a group of what proved to be ESA soldiers. These junta praetorians did not hesitate to express their conviction that the United States had deliberately misled Ioannides into believing that the Turks would remain passive in the event of an attempt against Makarios' life.

destroyer *Velos* indicated to the rest of Europe that the regime had failed to secure the passivity of the entire officer corps. Since the King had traditionally commanded the loyalty of the navy, the dictator accused Constantine of instigating the *coup* from his self-imposed exile in Rome. On 1 June he declared the King deposed and proclaimed the creation of a 'presidential parliamentary republic', subject to popular approval. Papadopoulos now appeared to be completely in control, with nothing to prevent him from assuming the presidency. According to the new regime, the President would be elected by direct popular vote for an eight-year term and would have wide legislative and executive authority, with control over foreign affairs, public order and national security matters. The plebiscite of July 1973 was held while martial law was still in force, and served a double purpose: to ratify the amendments to the 1968 constitution and to elect Papadopoulos as President of the Republic. The dictator assumed the presidential office with a 78 per cent 'yes' vote, 3,843,000 being in favour and 1,050,000 against.[15]

Since the plebiscite was conducted under repressive conditions, an analysis of its outcome and voting patterns can only be speculative. Unlike the previous plebiscite of 1968, however, this one provoked vociferous criticism from various quarters. Political leaders began to regroup and voice their anger after several years of muffled opposition and underground activities. Politicians of the right, centre and left, who had been bitter opponents before 1967, met again in prison cells, police headquarters and the islands to which they had been exiled. Their hatred of the junta became a point of consensus which led to a reappraisal of past errors, some modification of political passions, and an outright dismissal of the Civil War legacy of polarisation. Thus the ground was laid for a post-regime process of civilian renewal.

It was precisely because Papadopoulos had realised that he could no longer appeal to virulent anti-Communism for support that he sought a wider mandate by transforming his rule eventually into a sort of parliamentary system or 'directed democracy'. While the President alone was responsible for foreign policy, defence and internal security, and remained the sole source of power under the constitution until a parliament was elected, he did

[15] Clogg, p. 253.

appear ready for the first time to delegate some of his responsibilities to the Prime Minister and an all-civilian government. His choice of Prime Minister in October 1973 fell upon Spyros Markezinis, a one-time Minister for Coordination under Papagos and a leader of the small Progressive party in parliament. Markezinis was almost alone among former politicians in having kept silent about the regime in public, while privately offering himself as a possible 'bridge' between the dictatorship and some more democratic system of rule.

At the same time Papadopoulos acted to remove his remaining military colleagues from the government, in spite of their support for and participation in the *coup* of 1967 and their undoubtedly 'revolutionary' credentials. While there was a display of disaffection from some of those involved, a far more serious threat to the government was growing discontent within the army itself, arising from a combination of corporate and other grievances. Officers were sensitive not only to the problem of promotional blockages, but also to the charges of ineptitude and corruption made against the regime, which served to discredit the military as a whole. Complaints of one-man rule and electoral manipulation were coupled with acute resentment by some senior officers of the President's recent overtures to old-time politicians to participate in the parliamentary elections promised before the end of 1974. Not only had the regime lost contact with its original ideals, but it was becoming increasingly divorced from its military constituency, which was also its only political base.

The President could not make conciliatory moves towards the politicians and parties without risking the loss of military backing, notably from the military police under Brigadier Ioannides who controlled the security apparatus that kept him in power. Ioannides had not only refused all offers of a government position, but had successfully resisted the lifting of martial law, an amnesty for political prisoners and attempts to dismantle the security apparatus following the July plebiscite – all intended to signal a relaxation of the repression. Paradoxically, as Papadopoulos moved up the hierarchy of state offices, he became increasingly dependent on Ioannides to ensure the continuing loyalty of the army, and in particular that of the seven crack units stationed in and around Athens. Ioannides was not among those officers who may have shared the President's conviction that the future of the military regime was best assured by an accommodation with the political forces.

Nor were the party leaders in a mood to cooperate with the government, or convinced that the 'half-democracy' offered by the President was better than none. Their threat to boycott elections in 1974 was, in the circumstances, as serious a challenge to the President as the hard line being taken by an important section of the army. Moreover, one result of the attempt to 'unfreeze' the authoritarian regime was an increase in the level of criticism that managed to find its way to the public, leading in turn to a revolt of university students – that most sensitive barometer of political change. The re-imposition of martial law and the brutal suppression of the Athens Polytechnic uprising in November 1973 popularised the cause of the students across the nation. On 25 November a bloodless *coup* led by Ioannides overthrew Papadopoulos on the grounds that he had adulterated the principles of 21 April 1967. General Phaedon Gizikis was installed as President, and a civilian puppet government set up. While some of the newly-promoted commanders may earlier have favoured the return of Karamanlis from self-imposed exile as the best remaining option for the military, that does not seem to have been the view of Ioannides, who wanted no truck with the former politicians. The more puritanical faction of the junta not only attempted to put the lid on the boiling cauldron of internal dissent, but also blundered into a disastrous course in its foreign policy. The attempted assassination of President Makarios of Cyprus at the behest of Ioannides on 15 July 1974 precipitated the Turkish invasion of the island and the collapse of the military regime in Greece. The move against Makarios had been intended, at least partly, to improve the prestige of the regime and to restore the reputation of the military in Greece itself. However, the Turkish reaction meant that the junta had either to declare war and risk the consequences, or back down and face public humiliation. Unable or unwilling to choose the former, it preferred to stand down in favour of the politicians. Faced with an ultimatum by the 3rd Army Corps in northern Greece, and by the hostility of troops caught up in a chaotic general mobilisation, the junta transferred its authority to the very political leaders against whom it had risen in 1967 – and faded quickly into the background.

The dictatorship of 21 April 1967 shares with other military regimes certain features that invite generalisation. As often occurs with actual regimes, the Greek experience is a mixture derived from specific conditions, which fails to conform entirely with the requirements of any ideal type. While in the past the Greek military had always been subordinate to civilian governments, the 1967-74 regime most closely resembles the 'veto' type.[16] At the same time, it lacked the degree of military unity usually associated with this type, and from its origins as a factional *coup* directed against royalist senior officers as well as against democratic politicians, it degenerated in many respects to the level of a factional regime. The Revolutionary Council of twelve colonels that launched the *coup* was eventually superseded by George Papadopoulos' personalised rule and his aspiration to achieve the crowning glory of civilian legitimacy. The effort by Papadopoulos to transfer limited authority to a government of makeshift politicians provoked the wrath of Ioannides, the strongman of the military police, who sought to prevent the 'Revolution' from straying into political corruption. The regime thus possessed neither the military unity nor the civilian clientele necessary for the transformation into authoritarian clientelism.

The high level of autonomy enjoyed by the military and the perceived threats from civil society would also rank the Greek case with other 'veto' regimes. Whether real or imaginary, the perceived threat to the social order which prompted the Colonels to act was of a high level. The Greek officers chose to intervene, however, at a time when international détente threatened to make their position as guardians of the nationalist order redundant. In structural terms, the officers upheld middle-class interests, a choice highlighted by their role in the Civil War of 1946-9. Yet the Colonels viewed their power as unrelated to the outcome of economic class conflict, and insisted that theirs was a system that favoured the least privileged.[17] This supposed detachment from

---

[16] 'Veto Regimes: These are characterised by high unity, fairly high differentiation (though allowing for association between the military and centralist political groups), high threat and medium or high autonomy. This is, of course, a recipe for military regimes of the most systematically repressive kind, as in Chile and Argentina, since it pits the military directly against strongly organised civilian political structures' (Christopher Claphau and George Philip (eds), *The Political Dilemmas of Military Regimes*, London: Croom Helm, 1985, pp. 8-9.

[17] According to Stepan, the military is a situational and not a class élite, which will take action 'against those aspects of middle- and upper-class life which threaten their institutional

narrow class interests served to protect them from accusations of self-seeking behaviour, while providing them with a justification for extending their term in power. In fact the ethos of Greek officers does not differ from the stereotype military virtues of discipline, efficiency and valour, and their *esprit de corps* thinly veiled their awareness that the opportunities to improve their social status within the confines of their profession were indeed limited.

Although the military regime sought to elevate the officer corps to the position of guarantor of the social order, the members of the junta basically aspired to acquire the legitimacy that was inseparable from civilian authority. The protagonists of military intervention therefore tried to shed their corporate identity and assume the more respected civilian garb, thus confirming the fragility of their professional self-image. It is this absence of a strong corporate identity which, more than anything else, differentiated the Greek military from their colleagues in some emerging states.[18] The vital task of modernisation – a major source of pride for the military in certain developing societies – was not one for which the Greek military were well suited. Greek officers have more often been identified with political turmoil than with orderly change and social innovation, while their declining position in the social order generated a sense of isolation which before 1967 contributed to their hostility towards the ruling political élite, and reinforced their desire for social acceptance.[19]

position'. Stepan, pp. 269-70.

[18] T. Couloumbis, *Provlimata ellinoamerikanikon scheseon*, Athens: Kollaros, 1978, pp. 95-103.

[19] See the brief but penetrating social analysis of the Greek military by William H. McNeill, *The Metamorphosis of Greece since World War II*, Oxford: Basil Blackwell, 1978, pp. 22-7. According to Kleomenis S. Koutsoukis, 'As the military leaders were looking constantly for widening the bridge with the rest of society, and increasing the base of their legitimacy, they kept open the exchange of civilians with cabinet posts.' 'Cabinet Elite Recruitment during the Military Regime in Greece (1967-73)', Dept. of Political Science, State University of New York, Binghampton, NY, 1973, p. 180.

# 11

## FROM DICTATORSHIP TO
## DEMOCRACY AND AFTER

The anomalous circumstances that brought about the collapse of the military regime were caused by Ioannides' *coup* against the Cypriot President, Archbishop Makarios, and the subsequent invasion of Cyprus by Turkish forces. The disastrous intervention in the affairs of a foreign state was the responsibility of hard-core supporters of military corporatism who continued to refuse a transfer of authority to civilians even after the crisis. On 22 July 1974 officers of the powerful 3rd Army Corps in northern Greece signed a petition demanding the formation of a 'National Salvation' council with mixed civilian and military membership, and the mandate to elect Constantine Karamanlis as its president.

The directive of this body would be to restore parliamentary democracy, face the crisis in Cyprus, and get rid of the junta legacy. The commander of the 3rd Army Corps, General Ioannis Davos, communicated the declaration in the form of an ultimatum to the President of the Republic General Phaedon Gizikis, the commander of the armed forces, and the heads of the three branches. Furthermore, the general mobilisation which followed the outbreak of the crisis caused young reserve officers to take command of battle-ready units, and placed air force and naval officers, who were 'unreliable' in terms of their loyalty to the junta, in the front line of a prospective operation in Cyprus. Thus the bargaining position of junta opponents was greatly enhanced by the events of July while the resolve of Ioannides' followers to resist change quickly dissipated. It was the leaders of the navy and air force, the branches of the armed forces least penetrated by the junta, who informed Ioannides of their decision to transfer power to civilians. When the more prominent political leaders were invited by the President of the Republic to manage the crisis, they demanded and secured full authority. They invited former Prime

Minister Karamanlis to return from his self-imposed exile in Paris and assume the leadership of the government. He was sworn into office in the early hours of 24 July and formed his first civilian cabinet, consisting of Conservative and Liberal politicians as well as figures of the resistance against the junta. In twenty-four hours the military were replaced by civilians in the administration of the state. On 11 August the Prime Minister had all armoured divisions and crack units removed from Attica, and eight days later he retired most senior commanders in the armed forces.[1] The collapse of the military regime was facilitated by the resolve of moderate elements within the armed forces for political disengagement, and the initiative of civilians who took advantage of the confusion surrounding the general mobilisation to put pressure on the regime to relinquish power.

Karamanlis' goal of regenerating a democratic polity from the ruins of the discredited military dictatorship was aided by the fact that, unlike their counterparts in Spain and Portugal, Greek politicians had, not too long before, operated a workable parliamentary system. Moreover, the authority of Karamanlis was reinforced by the threat of war with Turkey which placed the youth of the country under arms and enabled the government to transfer units to the north, thereby breaking up the powerful military apparatus in the capital. By declaring the 1968/73 constitution null and void and revitalising the 1952 constitution on a temporary basis, he was able to suspend the junta's emergency measures which restricted the freedom of speech and the press, and legalised the Communist party. Despite military resistance, a constitutional amendment (coupled with a legislative decree) was adopted that made the political authorities responsible for appointments to key military commands. Army commanders associated with the junta were removed and the position of Chief of the National Defence General Staff was given to General Dionysios Arbouzis, who had been purged by the 1967 *coup*. Junta legislation that touched on the nature of the political regime, as well as the 'state of siege', was cancelled by the decrees of 23

---

[1] Constantine Danopoulos, *Warriors and Politicians in Modern Greece*, Chapel Hill, NC: Documentary Publications, 1984, pp. 126-9, and Potis Paraskevopoulos, *Andreas Papandreou. I politiki poria tou 1960-1995*, Athens: Synchroni Elliniki Istoria, 1995, p. 58.

September and 9 October, and civil servants dismissed by the military were recalled.[2]

The most pressing task for Karamanlis' government of 'National Salvation' was to stir Greece out of its diplomatic isolation and upgrade the country's defence in order to face the Cyprus crisis. Karamanlis, a conservative who had always maintained good relations with the United States, realised that public sentiment to the left and right of the political spectrum was running high against US support for the junta, as well as against Henry Kissinger's role during the invasion of Cyprus, especially the second wave of the Turkish invasion in mid-August that brought nearly 40 per cent of Cypriot territory under Turkish control and forced nearly 200,000 Greek Cypriots to flee to the southern part of the island. Arguing that the North Atlantic Treaty Organisation (NATO) was of little value for Greek security if it was not capable of preventing an armed clash between two of its members, Karamanlis withdrew the Greek armed forces from its military command structure. Although he ruled out a military solution and had to admit that Greece could not intervene to evict Turkish occupation troops from Cyprus, tension between Greece and Turkey persisted long after the invasion. For several months Karamanlis had to walk the tightrope between threats of a still active junta establishment in the army, demands for retribution and justice from the public, and security considerations that militated against a sudden purge that would undermine the defence capability of the armed forces.[3]

The 17 November 1974 elections gave Karamanlis' New Democracy party a resounding 54.4 per cent of the vote. Three weeks later a referendum to determine the future of the monarchy yielded a vote of over 69 per cent against its restoration.

The most important influence in this transitional period came from the Defence Minister, Evangelos Averoff. By soft-pedalling the government's changes in the military hierarchy, he sought to

---

[2] T. Veremis, 'Greece: Veto and Impasse, 1967-74' in Christopher Clapham and George Philip (eds), *The Political Dilemmas of Military Regimes*, London: Croom Helm, 1985, pp. 40-1. Nicos Alivizatos, *I politiki thesmi se krisi. 1922-1974*, Athens: Themelio, 1983, p. 682.

[3] For an account of post-dictatorial developments in Greece, see Richard Clogg, *A Short History of Modern Greece*, Cambridge University Press, 1979, pp. 200-5. See also T.A. Couloumbis and P. Yannas, 'The Stability Quotient of Greece's Post-1974 Democratic Institutions', *Journal of Modern Greek Studies*, vol. 1, no. 2, October 1983.

avert a backlash from the insecure former admirers of the junta. His assertion that he would not judge officers on the basis of past attitudes but on future performance and behaviour evoked criticism from opposition quarters but secured a relatively smooth transition to a democratic polity in Greece.

On 24 February 1975 the government announced that it had uncovered what was described as a minor conspiracy of *'Kadafiki'* (i.e. resembling Libya's Colonel Qaddafi in their extremism) supporters of Ioannides. Thirty-seven officers were arrested and charged with attempting to restore the military dictatorship and overthrow President Makarios, who had resumed his office in Cyprus in 1975. As it turned out, the conspiracy was the fourth of its kind following the return of Karamanlis, and the Prime Minister had to move from his home on several occasions to avoid the possibility of assassination. Sixty officers were dismissed and the review board procedures examining the records of serving officers were expedited. The subsequent trials of the 21 April *coup* protagonists ended with death sentences for its three leaders – George Papadopoulos, Stylianos Patakos and Nicolaos Makarezos – soon commuted to life imprisonment. Eight others, including Ioannides, received life terms. The number of cashiered officers, disclosed by Averoff to C.L. Sulzberger, was 500 and another 6-800 were transferred to less sensitive posts.[4] By the end of 1975 the parliamentary regime was safe from military challenges –a state of affairs that persists till today.

During the years of conservative rule (1974-81) the officer corps was treated with caution by the press while an effort was made by the state to re-educate young officers. Benefits received by officers were increased. This provoked a wry remark by the well-known Athenian cartoonist, Ioannou, who drew a general's wife asking her husband 'How long will they have to pay us for the junta?' In fact, the rehabilitation of the officer corps and the concern of the government for their morale could also be explained by the protracted tension in Greek-Turkish relations. Throughout the late 1970s and early '80s, Greece had the highest percentage of defence share in GDP in NATO (6.8 per cent

---

[4] Quoted by Danopoulos, p. 135. The total number of officers in the army in 1974 was 15,000.

compared to NATO's average of 3.8 per cent in 1984),[5] in spite of a *per capita* income among the lowest in the Alliance. The officer corps therefore acquired a vital role in the defence of the country that it had lost in the middle and late 1960s due to international détente. Furthermore, the major reason for right-wing extremism in the officer corps had dissipated after seven years of hollow warnings of a communist threat by the junta.

The junta significantly transformed the institutional structure of the armed forces (as mentioned in Chapter 9). Papadopoulos created the position of Chief of the Armed Forces, thus depriving the Minister of Defence of his authority and the Chiefs of Staff of any autonomy within their separate branches. This concentration of military control ultimately contributed to the decline of morale and initiative in the separate General Staffs. Their poor performance during the Cyprus emergency leaves little doubt about the failure of the system.

Law 660 of August 1977, reshaping the command structure in the armed forces, did away with the experimentations of the junta. By this law the government (the civilian authority) was alone responsible for national defence. The Supreme Council of National Defence (ASEA; later KYSEA), consisting of the Prime Minister, the Deputy Prime Minister, the Ministers of Defence, Finance, Foreign Affairs and Public Order, and the Chief of the General Staff, besides drafting defence policy, appointed the next Chief of the General Staff and the Chiefs of Staff, and made most other important military assignments. The decisions of ASEA were based on recommendations of the Defence Minister, who was in turn advised by the Chief of the General Staff (officially titled Chief of the Hellenic National Defence General Staff). Since the minister had no direct experience of the problems of the armed forces, his decisions were obviously influenced by military advisers, i.e. the Chiefs of Staff. This was seen by some as creating spheres of autonomy for the military that could prove dangerous for the future of the parliamentary regime, but others, who had fought for the dissolution of the junta's military institutions, argued that such autonomy for the three branches of the armed forces would

---

[5] Fotis Kikiras, 'Europe's Contribution to the Defence of the Western Alliance: an Ongoing Discussion,' *Yearbook 1988*, Athens: ELIAMEP, 1988, pp. 27-30.

guarantee the development of a more professional mentality among officers and would be a deterrent against joint conspiracies.[6]

The elections of 18 October 1981 gave the Panhellenic Socialist Movement (PASOK) of Andreas Papandreou 48 per cent of the vote and a clear majority of seats in parliament. This was the first time in Greek history that a Socialist party had won elections,[7] a fact that became the ultimate test of democratic consolidation in Greece. The towering presence of Karamanlis as President of the Republic helped cushion the new government from right-wing criticism, but what proved attractive to many officers was PASOK's nationalistic stance in relation to the great powers and its unyielding attitude towards Turkey. While in opposition (1974-81), Papandreou had promised that when he came to power he would withdraw Greece from NATO and remove United States bases from Greek soil. He had also opposed Greece's attempts to enter the European Community. However, unlike other fields of government policy under PASOK, Papandreou's defence policy did not deviate substantially from that of his predecessors. Although the country returned to the military structure of NATO in 1980, its relations with the Alliance were strained. Shortly after taking office, Papandreou asked NATO to guarantee Greece's borders from every threat, from whatever direction it emanated – the implication of a potential Turkish threat was clear. His administration partly froze the Rogers agreement of October 1980 which reintegrated Greece into NATO's military structure but did not withdraw from the Alliance. Greece repeatedly cancelled its participation in NATO exercises in the Aegean, refusing to accept the exclusion of the Lemnos airfield from NATO scenarios, which had been a constant Turkish demand. In an effort to break the Lemnos deadlock, Papandreou attempted another approach at the

---

[6] Nicos Alivizatos, *I syntagmatiki thesi ton enoplon dynameon*, Athens: Sakkoulas, 1987. The author is among the critics of the 1977 law. He pointed out that functional autonomy of the Chiefs of General Staffs towards the Defence Minister could prove dangerous for democracy. 'Unfortunately, ...two fundamental institutional means to ensure civilian supremacy over the military were almost ignored. That was the case with the cabinet's accountability before Parliament on defense issues and with the Chamber's exclusive competence to fix the strength of the armed forces and its budget'; Nicos Alivizatos, 'Civilian Supremacy over the Military. The Case of Modern Greece.' *Revue de droit militaire et de droit de la guerre*, vol. XXX, 1991, p. 18.

[7] This, however, was not the first time that a Socialist Prime Minister headed a Greek government. Alexander Papanastasiou led a mixed government of Liberal and centrist forces in 1924.

end of 1984. Greece officially announced the presence of its forces on the island in the Defence Planning Questionnaire (DPQ) and asked that they be placed under NATO command, but it did not succeed in overriding Turkey's veto.[8]

On the bilateral front, the negotiations initiated by Karamanlis in 1975 on the future of the US installations in Greece were concluded by Papandreou, and in September 1983 a Defence and Economic Cooperation Agreement (DECA) was signed which replaced the 1953 US-Greece Defence Agreement and other bilateral security arrangements.[9] The new document limited some of the privileges US forces had enjoyed in Greece over the previous thirty years. Greek and American officials disagreed over the interpretation of the agreement's final article which stated that the whole arrangement would be subject to termination on 30 December 1988. Papandreou argued that the DECA provided for the removal of the US bases, while American officials maintained that it was not clear from the treaty text whether after five years privileges would be terminated as opposed to being 'terminable' in accordance with the agreement's wording. On 10 November 1986 a new DICA (Defence and Industrial Cooperation Agreement) was signed between Greece and the United States that was to last for five years but would be subject to renewal. The DICA was indirectly linked to the DECA, and its conclusion was widely interpreted as an indication that a new DECA would also be negotiated and signed.[10] The entire policy of PASOK towards the United States and NATO cannot be divorced from the fact that American aid to Greece, which in the 1950s and '60s had been among the highest in global terms, declined thereafter along with overall US military involvement.[11]

The circumstances of the junta's collapse and the perceived

[8] G. Tsitsopoulos and T. Veremis, 'Oi ellinotourkikes amyntikes scheseis' in T. Veremis (ed.), *Oi ellinotourkikes scheseis, 1923-1989*, Athens: ELIAMEP-Gnosi, 1988, pp. 205-6.

[9] Antonis Bredimas, 'The U.S. Bases in Greece: The Legal Aspects' in *U.S. Bases in the Mediterranean: The Cases of Greece and Spain*, Athens: ELIAMEP, 1989, pp. 27-39.

[10] T. Veremis, 'Greece and NATO: Continuity and Change' in John Chipman (ed.), *NATO's Southern Allies: Internal and External Challenges*, London: Routledge, 1988, pp. 270-1.

[11] For a thorough analysis of US aid and the nature of American influence in Greece in the 1950s see Basil Kapetanyannis, 'Socio-Political Conflicts and Military Intervention. The Case of Greece: 1950-1967', unpubl. Ph.D. thesis, Birkbeck College, University of London, 1986, pp. 6-35.

threat from Turkey remained the major factors that guaranteed the unity of the armed forces throughout the latter half of the 1970s. Never had the Greek officer corps been less involved in party politics and more dedicated to its professional pursuits. Averoff, the Defence Minister, was advised against reinstating retired officers, and therefore promotions proceeded smoothly without external hindrance. Between 1974 and 1981 the over-whelming majority of army and navy officers, though kept aloof from party politics, remained conservative in their outlook, while the air force appeared to be the most politicised of the three services. After 1981 PASOK did not discourage its followers within the military from declaring their party preferences. However, the absence of PASOK adherents, or even Liberals, in the higher ranks made most military appointments in Papandreou's first term politically inconspicuous. The Chief of the Hellenic National Defence General Staff, Admiral Theodore Deyannis, was a moderate and the other Chiefs of General Staffs were of conservative inclinations, but PASOK encouraged its lower-ranking admirers by retiring a considerable number of senior and middle-ranking officers. By this means it allowed junior officers to rise through the ranks.

Although Papandreou had been critical of right-wing elements in the armed forces, he was always careful to distinguish between the 'few traitors' and the great majority of patriotic officers. On several occasions he even insinuated that the officers who, according to his populist parlance, were part of the people had been deceived by political patrons and misguided by corrupt politicians. As Defence Minister during his first premiership, he replaced certain senior officers in the military and security apparatus with men loyal to himself.

The practice of appointing retired officers to ministerial positions was initiated by New Democracy with retired General Ioannis Katsadimas as Deputy Defence Minister, and Solon Gikas as Min-ister of Public Order, and followed by PASOK with Ioannis Haralambopoulos as Defence Minister and Antonis Drosoyannis as Deputy Defence Minister. In the New Democracy cabinet of 1990, retired Admiral Alexandros Papadongonas was the Al-ternate Minister of Defence, and Ioannis Stathopoulos and Spilios Spiliotopoulos were Deputy Ministers. Both parties included officers with an anti-junta record among their members, and by doing so helped to reinstate the military in the esteem of the public.

The other side of the reintegration of the military in civil society was the gradual involvement of party politics in promotions and retirements. In 1982 the Chief of the Navy, Admiral Odysseas Kapetos, clashed with Deputy Defence Minister Drosoyannis over politically motivated appointments to the senior staff and resigned after holding his post for less than two months. By the end of PASOK's second term in office (1989) 20 per cent of army and navy officers and close to half of the air force officer corps were PASOK sympathisers.

The return of New Democracy in 1990 after eight years out of power was charged with feelings of recrimination against PASOK. The air force hierarchy had been a prime target of the new government, and Defence Minister Ioannis Varvitsiotis recalled retired air force General Thanassis Stathias and appointed him Chief of the Air Force. The recall of retired officers had always been a measure which disrupted the orderly process of promotion and therefore provoked negative reactions among officers on active duty. The return of Stathias through an administrative act was declared by the high court to be irregular on formal grounds, and the government was obliged to pass a law in parliament that retroactively legalised the posting of the air force general. By doing so New Democracy paved the way for future abuse of this practice.

A few months after its 1993 electoral victory, PASOK passed a law allowing the recall of retired officers to active duty within six months of its publication in the *Government Gazette* (Law 2171, 6 December 1993). The law was followed by presidential decrees replacing the entire leadership of the armed forces with retired officers recalled to active duty. Among them Admiral Christos Lymberis, who had been a prominent member of PASOK, was made Chief of the Hellenic National Defence General Staff. A total of thirteen high-ranking officers were recalled by Defence Minister Gerasimos Arsenis. This caused an outcry in the military community and the resignation of all ten lieutenant-generals, two rear-admirals and one air commodore. The resignations, according to their protagonists, prevented further recalls that would cripple the chain of command.[12] Whether it was the intention of the government to recall more officers or not, the credibility of the civil authorities has been severely tried. (At the time of writing, the constitutionality of the government's practice of recalling retired officers [under Law 2171] is pending before the Supreme Administrative Court.) If New Democracy in its next term desists from compounding the damage, then the unfortunate recalls of 1990 and, even more, 1993 might have no further consequences. If not, then the vendetta between the two parties will have a devastating effect on the unity of the officer corps, comparable to that caused by the notorious Law 927 of 1917 (see Chapter 6). Although military *coups* are not likely to recur over the professional disputes of politicised officers, the rivalry of PASOK and New Democracy could once again turn the armed forces into an apple of political discord.

During their first term in office the Socialists doubled military salaries. Pensions, housing and health benefits were also increased.[13] However, by the early 1990s a protracted high rate of inflation had taken its toll on the income of officers. In 1995 officers on active duty were given certain compensations, but these did not improve the low income of pensioners. That the state has ceased to extend benefits to the military, as it did during the first decade after the fall of the junta, might indicate that they are no longer perceived as a threat to the polity. Ever since 1974, governments have made a conscious effort to extract the military from their institutional isolation and incorporate them in civil society. Because entrance examinations for military academies do not differ from university examinations, some deplore the loss of the 'heroic' element in the selection and education of officers. But others point out that the bureaucrat-officer can also improve his skills as a technocrat once he transcends the barrack mentality. Be that as it may, the 'civilianisation' of officers, as we have already pointed out, made them more prone to involvement in party politics to improve their career opportunities.

---

[12] Information on the 1990 and 1993 recalls was provided by retired Generals Nicos Lazarides and Evangelos Tsirkas and the former Chief of the Hellenic National Defence General Staff and Defence Minister, Admiral Theodore Deyannis. The Chief of the Hellenic National Defence, General Dimitrios Skarvelis, who resigned in December 1993, offers a critical view on the recall of retired officers in his book, *I katagraphi mias anomalias. Dekemvrios 1993*, Athens, 1994.

[13] Lee Stokes, 'The Armed Forces under Papandreou', *The Athenian*, March 1986, p. 20.

We will not attempt here to discuss civil-military rivalries in the general headquarters on questions of military procurement. The economic aspect of such procurement has made the issue of who wields decisive authority over vital decisions a bone of contention between officers and civilians.[14] We will nevertheless briefly examine the law of 1995 determining the sharing of responsibilities among civil and military authorities and compare it to that of 1977.

Eighteen years after the 1977 law which gave the army, navy and air force latitude in special fields of decision-making and allowed them a measure of autonomy in relation to the Hellenic National Defence General Staff, the latter resumed some of its old authority. The 1995 law, however, gave the Minister of Defence the final say on all military matters. Not only is the entire chain of command accountable to him, but he has now acquired his own civilian advisers on questions that cover the whole spectrum from procurement to strategy. The Chief of the Hellenic National Defence General Staff, who according to the new law will become Commander-in-Chief of the armed forces in time of war and has increased control over his subordinate Chiefs of Staff, has been deprived of certain responsibilities which have been transferred to the Defence Minister. Besides the latter's group of advisers, civilians have also entered the new General Directorate of Armaments, which is made up of a mixed group that deals with procurement programmes. The Director-General of that agency is directly responsible to the Defence Minister. Finally, the Council of Defence also consists of both military and civilians, and deals with the drafting of defence policy. In short, the 1995 law favours centralisation of authority and on the whole enhances the government's control over the military. However, less than a year after its appearance, an article of the new law providing an interim period of three months between the selection and appointment of the Chief of the Hellenic National Defence General Staff was violated by the Defence Ministry. Following the Greco-Turkish crisis in January 1996 over the Aegean rock of Ymia, Admiral Lymberis was hurriedly replaced by Air Force General Athanasios Tsoganis without being given the time stipulated by

---

[14] For an extensive discussion of how the institutional framework of the 1977 law impeded the work of Deputy Defence Minister (1987-8) Theodore Stathis, see his book, *I Ethniki Amyna*, Athens: Livanis, 1992, esp. pp. 137-48 and 164-74.

the law to brief his successor. This disregard for the article might indicate the extent of the Defence Minister's authority under the legal regime of 1995.

The post-1989 crisis in party politics, caused by widespread allegations of scandals and the reluctance of Papandreou to appoint his successor in PASOK, had an unfavourable effect on the image of politicians. The military, though unhappy with incomes that have been diminished by inflation, have abstained from public statements and have become incorporated into civil society to a degree without precedent in Greece during the twentieth century. In that sense they share public disillusionment with the political establishment of Greece, but are neither willing nor able to repeat past practices. Participation in politics has declined. From thirty-four deputies of military background in the parliament of 1952, the number had fallen to eight in 1993.[15]

Since the mid-1980s loyalty tests have been abolished from military academies and entrance examinations follow the general pattern that determines entry to all institutions of higher education. The curricula of the academies have been modernised considerably, anti-Communist indoctrination has ceased, and open discussion in academy classes is encouraged. Although the treatment of concientious objectors leaves much to be desired, conscripts on the whole are no longer discriminated against because of their convictions.[16] 'Finally, an important effort has been made to protect the individual rights of military personnel, on and off duty. Here, thanks to an unusually innovatory activism demonstrated by the courts, namely the Council of State, old-time military rules and practices were gradually abandoned, and internal regulations have been considerably modernised in order to reflect the changing mentalities and morals of an evolving society.'[17]

The Greek case has been clearly one of a successful 'redemocratisation'.[18] The chief offenders in the military dictatorship were

---

[15] Yannis Mavris, 'I scheseis stratevmatos kai politikis exousias', *Kathimerini*, 18 February 1996.

[16] Alivizatos, 'Civilian Supremacy...' pp. 21-2.

[17] *Ibid.*, p. 16.

[18] Juan J. Linz, ' Transition to Democracy', *Washington Quarterly*, summer 1990, pp. 144, 153-4. See also N. Diamantouros *et al.*, *A Bibliographical Essay on Southern Europe and its Recent Transition to Political Democracy*, Florence: European University Institute Working Paper no. 86/208, 1986.

convicted, and the silent majority of their supporters in the ranks maintained their silence. Civil-military relations have long since ceased to be an important criterion of democratic consolidation in Greece. To fathom the degree of the post-1974 consolidation one must examine the legitimacy of institutions, the condition of civil liberties, the freedom of the press, the transformation of political parties into interest-oriented institutions and, finally, the orderly transfer of power from one party to another. The score on all counts has been on the whole satisfactory and it is perhaps safe to assume that in Greece democracy is indeed the 'only game in town'.[19]

[19] Linz, pp. 149, 154, 158.

# 12

## CONCLUSIONS

Greek officers were the mixed product of nineteenth-century statecraft and the indigenous practices of an agrarian society in transition. The initial mission of the regular army and its professional officer corps was to consolidate the authority of the centralised state. Having accomplished that, officers became preoccupied with the irredentist pursuits of Greece and embraced the 'ethnic truth' well into the first decades of the twentieth century. While pursuing this double mission of propping up the state and promoting its expansionist goals, the military rarely questioned civilian supremacy or parliamentary rule. When they did become involved in politics following the outbreak of the First World War, officers were recruited by the Liberals and the royalists rather than acting on their own initiative or serving their interests.

The interwar period is a watershed in modern Greek history. The Asia Minor débâcle of 1922 and the influx of 1.5 million refugees into a country of barely 5 million transformed Greece. The few developed urban centres received the bulk of the destitute newcomers and among their ranks the Greek Communist party (KKE) found willing members. This new threat to the established order also conspired to alienate recently acquired national territory. Compelled by its loyalty to the Comintern, the KKE subscribed to the Bulgarian slogan of the sixth Balkan Communist Conference in 1924 for a 'United and Independent Macedonia and Thrace'.

Such developments not only increased the insecurity of the state in relation to its internal enemies; it also changed the content of 'ethnic truth' and indeed the entire character of Greek nationalism. From an ideology open to all the Christian inhabitants of the unredeemed territories, it became the exclusive preserve of those Greeks who believed they could trace their ancestry to antiquity.

The military embraced the new creed after some delay. Fragmented into patron-client networks throughout the interwar period, they strove to promote their professional aims within the larger liberal-royalist confrontation. The only organised attempt against the authorities that conformed to the pattern of a corporate military conspiracy, namely the *coup* of 1935, was eroded by the antagonisms of rival networks and failed miserably. This *coup* was in fact the first and last conspiracy in Greek history to involve so many different actors and the only one to nurture visions of removing civilians from the running of the state. Its failure taught the officer-protagonists that the state would not replace its civilian arbiters with the military unless the military could invoke a larger threat to the social order.

War and occupation reshuffled the military pack and rekindled old rivalries between Liberals and royalists. The political upheavals in the Greek forces in Egypt and attempts to influence the Greek government in exile were encouraged by the KKE's dominance over the resistance forces in occupied Greece. Its plan to incapacitate the regular army so that it would be excluded from the liberation of Greece succeeded, but the Communist guerrilla forces nonetheless failed to usurp power. The Civil War that raged between 1946 and 1949 made the Greek army's officer corps the homogeneous preserve of conservative nationalist values. Furthermore, the circumstances of a civil war and the influence of British and American military missions put some distance between officers and society, while special training encouraged among the officers a sense of autonomy and immunity from political decisions. Between 1952 and 1963 clandestine rightist organisations, which influenced promotions and vital appointments, sought to create a network in the army's leadership that shared anti-Communist fervour and strong views on the running of the state.

The 1967 *coup* that launched the seven-year military dictatorship was sparked by a crisis between the monarchy and parliament. The most important cause of this backlash of an extremist military group was the emergence of international détente, which threatened to reduce the significance of the army as the guardian of the state against both internal and external enemies. Although in this and every other way the regime of 21 April was an anachronism, it maintained power for seven years through its use of repression and with the help of an unprecedented international economic boom that came to Greece in the late 1960s.

In the past, patron-client relationships between politicians and the military in Greece had been a guarantee of civilian supremacy as well as the object of envy by officers who did not enjoy effective political connections. The most ardent exponents of an autonomous vocation for the officer corps were usually products of a peasant background who resented their more fortunate colleagues. However, supporters of the 1967 *coup* were soon faced with a choice between total reliance on American patronage, and the reconstitution of bridges with the political world.

The transformation of civil-military relations in Greece during the last decades cannot be explained wholly by political factors. Since the 1960s the social fabric has changed rapidly. The rise of *per capita* income, the widening of professional options, the incorporation of the military academies into the system of university entrance examinations and finally the prodigious growth of urban centres have changed the social background and the value system of the officer corps between 1974 and today.

As we have pointed out in another chapter, the core values and ideas that determined the behaviour of officers ever since they became politicised were derived from practices that pervaded rural Greece. For example, the patronage that corrupted urban institutions was affected by the rapid urbanisation of Greece in the post-war period. In 1896 Athens had a population of 180,000 out of a total population of 2,400,000; in 1951 it was 1,379,000 out of 8,500,000. Today the population of greater Athens is over 4,000,000 out of 10,000,000 people in Greece as a whole.[1] Much of the recruitment to the Greek forces was from rural Greece between 1916 and 1967, but since the 1960s cadets have increasingly been products of the major urban centres that are home to more than half of Greece's population. During PASOK's second term, universities were grouped according to their subjects for the purpose of entrance examinations, and students who failed to enter the institution of their first choice could still find a place in their second or third choice. Since the mid-1980s Academy graduates have differed in mentality and even in appearance from their

---

[1] William H. McNeill, *The Metamorphosis of Greece since World War II*, Oxford: Basil Blackwell, 1978, p. 4.

predecessors. While attending the 15 August 1994 celebration at the Ayios Andreas vacation complex for the military, this author could not help noticing the contrast between the athletic young officers and their attractive spouses and their less vigorous predecessors of the 1950s.

There is no way of measuring the persistence of traditional 'heroic' values among officers but one wonders if the observation of McNeill is still true: 'During the twentieth century, a professional corps of officers (since 1949 about fifteen thousand strong) has become the special guardian of this (heroic) aspect of Hellenism. Its members stand in self conscious opposition to the commercial spirit that informs so much of the rest of Greek life.'[2] Since the aristocratic tradition which dominated Western European armies and differentiated military from civilian behaviour is totally absent in Greece, the urbanisation of the officer corps has made it more compatible with middle-class values. Does the demise of the 'heroic tradition' of the mountains mean that city education nurtures respect for democratic institutions and parliamentary politics among officers? If the current officer corps adheres to the values of the rest of society, one could perhaps seek a pointer to future trends in military attitudes to social developments.

Patronage, though far from extinct in Greek politics, has lost some of its effectiveness in the modern depersonalised urban environment. In its place another form of political recruitment has emerged, especially since PASOK became an important political force: populism.[3] This spontaneous communication and indeed identification of the populace with charismatic leadership undermines the representative nature of parliamentary politics and reintroduces a nebulous concept of direct democracy. Populism, unlike patronage, favours rapid mass cooptation into the political process and a break with traditional mores and the political establishment. However, since it offers a blueprint of vertical social action and therefore appeals to all classes, populism could prove a pole of attraction to the urbanised military of today.

The populist message usually addresses the public's basic instincts rather than its rational faculties, and for that reason militates against

---

[2] *Ibid.*, p. 24.
[3] For more about populism in Greek politics, see Nicos Mouzelis, *Politics in the Semi-Periphery*, London: Macmillan, 1986, pp. 42, 44, 234, 249.

the tortuous process of modernisation and Westernisation. The very allure of populism lies in its rejection of any rationality, because that must be internalised through a partial repression of spontaneous behaviour. The populist self-image of the average Greek conforms to the observation that Greeks 'are "Greek" by being wise or clever, but not being operationally and blindly systematical, intelligent or rational. They pride themselves on their aggressive manliness ... in their capacity to live playing it by ear and in their indomitable will for "freedom" from any oppression and also from norms, responsibilities and compulsive behavioral rationality.'[4]

We have come full circle to the original predicament of the nineteenth-century state-builders who sought to establish Western institutions and imbue Greek society with Western values. Although the military never acted as an agent for modernisation in Greece, it has nevertheless been an important component in the institutional framework created by a modernising élite. The military no doubt fullfilled their irredentist mission but subsequently became an impediment to the proper functioning of parliamentary institutions. Throughout the authoritarian phase of Greek democracy, the officer corps that emerged from the war and Civil War experience had totally identified with the right-wing values of the political élite who won the Civil War. Like sorcerer's apprentices, the officers of 1967 succeeded only in uniting the political world against their dictatorship and thus unwittingly played the unifying role which they had aspired to play themselves.

The term 'metamorphosis' was used by William Hardy McNeill to describe the transformation in the geographic distribution of Greece's population between the late 1940s and the mid-1970s. However, the prodigious movement of peasants into the cities was not accompanied by the formation of ghettoes or a spectacular rise in crime and political violence. Internal immigration from the villages to urban centres was completed 'with very little internal adjustment of family behaviour'.[5] McNeill atributed this orderly '*metastasis*' to the market orientation of peasant life and the tight-knit organisation of Greek nuclear family units. Wide acquaintance

---

[4] C. Tsoucalas, 'Greek National Identity in an Integrated Europe' in Harry J. Psomiades and Stavros Thomadakis (eds), *Greece, the New Europe and the Changing International Order*, New York: Pella, 1993, p. 75.

[5] McNeill, p. 248.

with the workings of the market and the firm structure of the family are two immutable elements in Greek society that appear to have merged in a creative though at times tense coexistence. It is perhaps this binary phenomenon of market forces, spurring people to movement while anchored on the familial bedlock of traditional values, that can explain the idiosyncrasies of Greece. It may also explain the ease with which Greeks of the diaspora adjust to their host-countries while clinging tenaciously to their own identity, or the enthusiasm of Greek citizens for a wider European citizenship while, paradoxically, they impede the progress of a civil society within their own state.

Today, in spite of McNeill's observation about the ease with which 'a formerly peasant people have so far accommodated themselves to urbanism',[6] the perennial problem of modernising mentalities remains. Western norms are not absent from the dominant value system, but they are often 'symbolically relegated to a second and subsidiary level'.[7] A resurgence of populism which might relegate Westernisation to a secondary level of urgency could determine the future behaviour of the military, as indeed of the whole of Greek society in which it has been integrated.

[6]  *Ibid.*, p. 208.
[7]  Tsoucalas, p. 75.

# NOTE ON THE SOURCES

There is considerable material on the Greek military, consisting of private papers, public archives, memoirs, biographies, organisational charts, training manuals, army lists, popaganda pamphlets, and a few general histories. However, it takes considerable effort to discover much of it, especially such obscure items as Army Lists and technical manuals. Sorting out items of historical value from personal reminiscences and hagiographic biographies adds to the difficulty of research. The single most obvious distinguising feature of the Greek army in the twentieth century is its political activism. The causes of this development should be looked for in the profound transformation in the social composition of the army brought about by the Balkan wars and the First World War. The bitter conflicts caused by these changes can be glimpsed in the various works of Greek officers who, in contrast to Greek politicians, are prolific writers. It is only through the study of these works that the role of the army in those turbulent years will eventually come to be known in full.

Of public archives, extensive use has been made of the British Public Records, in Portugal Street as well as Kew Gardens. The Greek General State Archives, temporarily located in the ground floor of the Greek Academy, include the papers and diaries of G. Tsontos-Vardas and a section of the E. Tsouderos papers. The Greek Foreign Ministry Archives contain copies of confidential police reports on covert activities of military organisations in the interwar period.

Of private papers the most accessible are those of Eleftherios Venizelos and Nikolaos Plastiras at the Benaki Museum, the Alexandros Mazarakis and Speros Spyromelios papers at the Historical and Ethnological Museum, the Athanassios Souliotes-Nicolaides papers in the Gennadios Library, the Alexandros Zannas papers which belong to the Zannas family, the papers of Leonidas Paraskevopoulos and Alexandros Diomides in the possession of Nikos Petsalis-Diomides, the Georgios Kondylis papers with the F. Katsambas family, the Emmanuel Tsouderos papers, published in 1990 in five volumes by his daughter Virginia, and the papers of Manolis Mantakas, Nikos Deas, Markos Kladakis and Constantinos Gontikas kept by their families. The Hellenic Literary and Historical Archive (ELIA) contains a wealth of military documents, including the papers of V. Kyris, Miltiades Maniatopoulos and many other figures implicated in military politics.

The Army Lists have proved a valuable source of information concerning the origin and important statistics in the officers corps. We have made use of the following years: 1891, 1895, 1900, 1904, 1909, 1912, 1914, 1919,1925, 1930 and 1950, and the Navy Lists of 1930 and 1933.

The official publication of the Defence Ministry in 1907 by A. Haralambis and K. Nider, *Istorikon ypomnema peri tou organismou tou taktikou stratou tis Ellados*, is still an indispensable reference book for any work on the Greek military in the nineteenth century, The small regular forces of the War of Independence are described by C. Vyzantios, *I istoria tou tactikou tis Ellados*, Athens, 1837. A. Vacalopoulos, *Ta ellinika stratevmata tou 1821*, Thessaloniki, 1970 (2nd edn, Vanias, 1991), deals with regulars as well as with the more numerous irregular forces of that period. The most informative and readable work on the institutional foundations of the Greek army is by an expert in the field, E. Stasinopoulos, *O stratos tis protis ekatontaetias*, Athens: Prodromou & Mousoulioti, 1935. See also his work on the Military Academy, *I istoria tis Scholis Evelpidon*, Athens: Prodromou & Mousoulioti, 1954. For a history of the Naval Academy, see I.K. Fakidis, *Istoria tis Scholis Naftikon Dokimon, 1845-1973*, Athens, 1975. The only work on the history of the Greek air force in 1937-41 is by a former Deputy Minister, P. Economakos, *The Greek Air Force*, Athens, 1970. An important work on the Greek navy, and a source of valuable statistics, is E. Kavvadias, *O nautikos polemos tou 1940*, Athens: Pyrsos, 1950.

The following publications may be used as basic reference works on the subject of the military in politics: The Great Military and Naval Encyclopedia, *I megali stratiotiki kai naftiki encyclopedia*, vols I-VI, Athens, 1930; the published papers of Panagiotes Danglis, *Anamniseis, engrapha, allilographia*, vols I-II, Athens: Vayionakis,

1965; the published papers of Theodoros Pangalos, *Archion Theodorou Pangalou*, vols I-II, Athens: Kedros, 1973 (these volumes consist largely of newspaper clippings and extracts from parliamentary records). Gregorios Daphnis' standard work on the interwar period, *I Ellas metaxy dyo polemon*, Athens: Ikaros, 1955 (2 vols), is rich in detailed information. The journalistic account of military *coups* by Dimos Vratsanos, *I istoria ton en Elladi epanastaseon, 1824-1935*, Athens, 1936, was an early popular account of the subject.

This work owes much to those protagonists and supporting actors of the internal and post-war Greek officer corps who opened up the secrets of their professional lives and shared some of their thoughts with the author almost two decades ago. Their deciphering of Army Lists, statistics and unintelligible acronyms made an interpretation of certain primary sources possible. My mentors on the world of military and covert activities, their patronage networks and their personal sympathies and antipathies have been the following officers: Christodoulos Tsigantes, Athanassios Tountas, Markos Kladakis, Speros Papaspyros, Epaminondas Stasinopoulos, Speros Giorgoulis, Nikos Gogousis, Athanasios Korozis, Nikos Deas, Kyriakos Pezopoulos, Thiseus Pangalos, Nikos Petropoulos, Leonidas Spais, Ioannis Karavidas, A. Zangas, Mihalis Antonopoulos, K. Alexandris, Zacharias Nobelis, Aristides Siotis, Thomas Pentzopoulos, Epaminondas Tsellos, Athanasios Tsigounis, Nikolaos Skanavis, G. Stratiotis, Orestis Vidalis, N. Lazaridis, Th. Deyannis, E. Tsirkas and such eminent figures as Panayotis Kanellopoulos, Georgios Pesmazoglou, A.A. Pallis, and Evangelos Averoff. However, the person who introduced me to her contemporaries as well as opening her family archive to my scrutiny was Mrs Virginia Zannas, the widow of Alexandros Zannas.

For the bitter conflict between royalists and Liberals see the following personal accounts: Neokosmos Grigoriadis, *Apomnimonevmata*, Athens, 1966; Victor Dousmanis, *Apomnimonevmata*, Athens: Dimitrakos, 1946; Leonidas Spais, *Peninta chronia stratiotis*, Athens, 1970; Thrassyvoulos Tsakalotos, *Saranta chronia stratiotis tis Ellados*, 2 vols, Athens, 1960; G. Fessopoulos, *Dichoniai kai dialysis tou stratou mas*, Athens, 1934; and Demetrios Vakas, *O Venizelos polemikos igetis*, Athens: Daremas, 1965. These works reveal the less familiar aspects of military life even though they are hardly distinguished works from a literary point of view.

More valuable for objectivity and validity are: Stylianos Gonatas,

*Apomnimonevmata*, Athens, 1958; Alexandros Mazarakis-Ainian, *Apomnimonevmata*, Athens: Ikaros, 1948; Theodoros Pangalos, *Ta apomnimonevmata mou*, vol. I, Athens: Aetos, 1950; vol. II, Athens: Kedros, 1959; Leonidas Paraskevopoulos, *Apomnimonevmata*, Athens, 1934; Stephanos Saraphis, *Istorikes anamniseis*, Athens, 1952, A. Haralambis, *Anamniseis*, Athens, 1947; Patroclos Kontoyannis, *O stratos mas kai oi teleftaioi polemoi*, Athens, 1924; and Ioannis Metaxas, *To prosopiko tou Imerologio*, vols I-IV, Athens: Ikaros, 1951-60. Metaxas' diary was not intended for publication and therefore contains uninhibited personal views. It is in a category of its own. The attempts by the 1967 protagonists to explain their role in the regime are of little interest. The dictator George Papadopoulos was the most prolific and least intelligible. Stylianos Patakos, Adamantios Androutsopoulos, Konstantinos Kollias and Spyros Markenzinis have published uninspiring apologetic autobiographical accounts.

Out of a multitude of hagiographic biographies, Ioannis Peponis, *Nikolaos Plastiras*, 2 vols, Athens, 1946, and Stamatis Merkouris, *Georgios Kondylis*, Athens, 1954, unintentionally contain many revealing aspects of military politics.

Of the Greek theoretical countributions on developments in military sociology, Vassilis Kapetanyannis, 'Theoretikes prosengiseis sto provlima ton stratiotikon epemvaseon stin politiki', *Synchrona Themata*, issue 9, October 1980, pp. 23-34, and Theodore Couloumbis, *Provlimata ellinoamerikanikon scheseon*, Athens: Kollaros, 1978, pp. 95-103, are the most proficient. George Kourvetaris has tried to fit the case of the military dictatorship of 1967 into the concept of the military as modernising agents: 'The Role of the Military in Greek Politics', *International Review of History and Political Science*, vol. 8, no. 3 (Aug. 1971), pp. 91-114, and 'Professional Self-Images and Political Perspectives in the Greek Military', *American Sociological Review*, vol. 36, no. 6 (Dec. 1971), pp. 1043-57. In the same vein, George Zaharopoulos, in his 'Politics and the Army in Post-War Greece' in Richard Clogg and George Yannopoulos (eds), *Greece under Military Rule*, London: Secker and Warburg, 1972, considered the military as a factor of economic and social development in Greece. Kleomenis S. Koutsoukis in his 'Cabinet Elite Recruitment during the Military Regime in Greece (1967-1973)' (Dept. of Political Science, State University of New York at Binghampton, 1973, 20 pp.) attempts a quantitative approach to civil-military relations.

Historical works centred on the military in Greek politics are on the whole the more useful contributions. George Dertilis, *Koinonikos metaschimatismos kai stratiotiki epemvasi, 1980-1909,* Athens: Exantas, 1977, and Thanos Veremis, *Oi epemvaseis tou stratou stin elliniki politiki, 1916-1936,* Athens: Exantas, 1977, add a socio-economic and social-anthropological viewpoint to the subject. The social analysis of the phenomenon presented by Nicos Mouzelis in *Modern Greece: Aspects of Underdevelopment,* London: Macmillan, 1978 (especially chapters 6 and 7) is well versed in history and attempts to revise the dependence of superstructure phenomena from their socio-economic base in classical Marxist theory. Thanos Veremis, *Oikonomia kai dictatoria. I syngyria 1925-26,* Athens: Cultural Foundation of the Greek National Bank, 1982, and S. Victor Papacosma, *The Military in Greek Politics: The 1909 Coup d'Etat,* Kent, OH: Kent State University Press, 1977, focus on limited periods and aspects of military intervention. Stephanos Papageorgiou, *I stratiotiki politiki tou Kapodistria. Domi, organosi kai leitourgia tou stratou xyras tis Kapodistriakis periodou,* Athens: Kollaros, 1986, offers the most thorough analysis of the first military reforms in modern Greek history. Of historical works, however, the most accomplished is John S. Koliopoulos, *Brigands with a Cause: Brigandage and Irredentism in Modern Greece 1821-1912,* Oxford: Clarendon Press, 1987. Koliopoulos, though not directly concerned with the military, gives a definitive analysis of the social and political background of armed irregulars. This work, and John Petropulos, *Politics and Statecraft in the Kingdom of Greece, 1932-1942,* Princeton University Press, 1968, are among the most valuable books on Greece written in English.

Christina Varda, in her two articles 'Politevomenoi stratiotiki stin Ellada sta teli tou 19ou aiona', *Mnimon,* issue 8, Athens, 1980-2, pp. 47-63 and 'Stratologika stin Ellada tou 19ou aiona. Paradigma Dimos Nafpliaion, 1870-77', *Istorika,* no. 6, 1986, pp. 369-86, provides an example of in-depth research on officers in parliament and the neglected subject of conscription. Less informative is the article by J.T. Malakasses, 'The Navy and its Officer corps in the Decade of the Thirties and up to the Eve of the Greco-Italian War', *Dodoni,* no. 1, 1992, University of Ioannina, pp. 93-112. Constantine Arvanitopoulos deals with 'The Rise and Fall of the Greek Military Regime: 1967-1975', *Journal of Modern Hellenism*, no. 8, winter 1991, pp. 97-116.

There are several important monographs on post-war developments in military politics. Hagen Fleischer, 'The Anomalies in the Greek Middle-East Forces, 1941-44', *Journal of the Hellenic Diaspora*, vol. V, no. 3 (fall 1978), encapsulates the major points of a very complicated argument. Nicholas Stavrou, *Allied Policies and Military Interventions*, Athens: Papazissis, 1977, was the first to attempt a political analysis of covert military organisations such as IDEA and their impact on politics.

Panos Loukakos, 'O elenchos tis politikis exousias pano stis enoples dynameis', *Synchrona Themata*, period B, issue 9, October 1980, and Nicos Alivizatos, 'The Greek Army in the Late Forties: Towards an Institutional Autonomy', *Journal of Hellenic Diaspora*, vol. V., no. 3, fall 1978, are perhaps the only attempts to analyse the institutional and legal framework that determines military operations. Andre Gerolymatos, in his two articles 'The Role of the Greek Officer Corps in the Resistance', *Journal of the Hellenic Diaspora*, vol. XI, no. 3, fall 1984, and 'The Security Battalions and Civil War', *Journal of the Hellenic Diaspora,* vol. XII, no. 1, spring 1985, provides valuable information on a crucial period. Finally, Nicos Alivizatos in his book, *I syntagmatiki thesi ton enoplon dynameon*, Athens: Sakkoulas, 1987, analyses the competences of the Defence Ministry, the General Staff of National Defence and other institutions dealing with military affairs. Here he poses the important question whether the formal instruments of the state can exert total control over the military and to what extent the military possesses sufficient autonomy for it to evade official supervision, especially in times of crisis. E. Spyropoulos, *I stratiotikes paremvasis stin politiki*, Athens: Sakkoulas, 1993, offers unstructured information on disparate topics. Stylianos Charatses, *1023 axiomatiki kai kinimata*, 2 vols, Athens, 1985, attempts to analyse the propensity of officers for political power.

The books by Constantine Danopoulos, *Warriors and Politicians in Modern Greece*, Chapel Hill, NC: Documentary Publications, 1984, and Dimitris Haralambis, *Stratos kai politiki exousia. I domi tis politikis exousias stin metemfyliaki Ellada,* Athens: Exantas, 1985, deal with postwar developments, the former in a political and the latter in a social perspective.

The following Ph.D. dissertations are focused on civil-military relations: James Brown, 'The Military in Politics: A Case Study of Greece', Buffalo: State University of New York, 1971; Yannis Gafanis, 'Stratos kai politiki. Krisi igemonias kai stratiotiki epemvasi', Law Faculty, University of Thrace, 1986; Triantafyllos Gerozisis, 'Le corps des officers et sa place dans la société grecque, 1821-1974', Université de Droit, d'Economie et de Sciences Sociales de Paris, 1987; Basil Kapetanyannis, 'Socio-Political Conflicts and Military Intervention: The Case of Greece, 1950-1967', Birkbeck College, University of London, 1986; Gerasimos Karabelias, 'The Role of the Military in Greece and Turkey', School of Oriental and African Studies, University of London, 1995; Dimitris Malessis, 'O ellinikos stratos stin proti othoniki dekaetia (1833-43). Politiki organosi kai pelatiakes scheseis', Pantion University, 1992; Nicolas Pantelakis, 'L'armée dans la société grecque contemporaine', Université René Descartes, Paris V, 1980; Dimitrios Smokovitis, 'Mia idiotypos koinoniki omas. Ai enoploi dynameis', Law Faculty, University of Thessaloniki, 1975. The BA thesis of Bassilios Evangelos Tsingos, 'The Breakdown of Authoritarian Regimes: The Political Evolution of the Greek Military Dictatorship, 1967-74', Harvard College, 1990, 166 p., deserves notice.

For a most accurate and inclusive account of the findings of military sociology throughout the post-war period, see Gwyn Harris-Jenkins and Charles C. Moskos, Jr., 'Armed Forces and Society', *Current Sociology*, vol. 29, no. 3, winter 1981.

# PRINCIPAL CHARACTERS

ARGYROPOULOS, PERICLIS (1881-1966). Born in Athens, Prefect of Larissa (1910) and of Thessaloniki (1912). A leading figure in the Thessaloniki revolt of 1916. Governor-General of Macedonia (1917-18). With Kondylis, he inspired the Venizelist '*Amyna*' movement in Constantinople (1921-2). He stood by the 'Republican Defence' during the *coup* of 1935.

CONSTANTINE I (1868-1922). Born in Attica, the first child of King George I and Queen Olga, he studied at the Greek Military Academy and the Academy of War in Berlin. In 1889 he married Princess Sophie, sister of Kaiser Wilhelm II. As Commander-in-Chief of the Greek armed forces in the disastrous campaign of 1897 against the Ottomans, he was held responsible for the ignominious defeat. However, he was exonerated during the Balkan wars after leading the Greek forces to a series of victories. He became King in 1913 after the assassination of George I, and continued to be involved in the shaping of Greek foreign policy. During the First World War he clashed with his Liberal Prime Minister, Eleftherios Venizelos, who was twice made to resign. The question whether Greece should enter the war on the side of the Triple Entente or remain neutral became the issue that divided the Prime Minister and the King and caused the 'national schism' among their followers. Constantine was forced to abdicate in favour of his second son Alexander in 1917 but was reinstated in 1920 by a plebiscite. He lost his throne in 1922 following the collapse of the Greek campaign in Asia Minor and died in Palermo shortly afterwards.

CONSTANTINE II (1940-). Born in Attica, the son of King Paul and Queen Frederika. He studied in the Greek Military Academy and won a gold medal in sailing in the 1960 Olympic Games in Rome. After King Paul's death in 1964 Constantine became King of the Hellenes and married Princess Anne Marie of Denmark. His rule was short (1964-7), marked by his clash with Prime Minister George Papandreou over the exact extent of his royal authority. His involvement in politics undermined the credibility of the crown and in 1967 he failed to oppose the *coup* of the Colonels. His abortive attempt to oust them eight months later obliged him to leave the country with his family. He was dethroned in 1973 by the Colonels, and in 1974 Greece became a republic through a plebiscite that decided the fate of the crown.

DANGLIS, PANAYOTES (1853-1924). Officer of the Greek army and a politician during the crucial period of the 'national schism' between King Constantine I and Eleftherios Venizelos. Graduated from the Military Academy in 1877 and saw action in the war of 1897. In 1908-9 he directed the 'Macedonian Committee' and the 'Panhellenic Organisation', both assigned the task of coordinating Greek irredentist activities. A major-general by the first Balkan war, he served as Chief of the General Staff. In 1914 Danglis resigned with the rank of lieutenant-general and was elected deputy for Jannina in Epirus under the banner of Venizelos' Liberal party. Although a moderate by nature, he joined Venizelos and Admiral Koundouriotes in 1916 as part of the triumvirate heading the secessionist government of Thessaloniki. Throughout the war effort on the side of the Triple Entente, he played a vital role as Commander-in-Chief of the Greek forces in recruiting and organising troops for the Balkan front. In 1920, after Venizelos had been defeated at the polls and left Greece, Danglis acted as his stand-in as president of a governing body of the Liberal party.

DELIYORGIS, EPAMINONDAS (1829-79). An important parliamentarian who made his mark as a young opponent of King Otto. He was elected deputy for Messolonghi in 1859, took an active part in the expulsion of Otto in 1862, and was Prime Minister several times. He was a champion of Greek-Turkish cooperation and friendship.

DILIYANNIS, THEODOROS (1824-1905). A political opponent of Harilaos Tricoupis and an exponent of populist direct rule. Born at Tripolis in the Peloponnese, he studied law at the University of Athens and initially joined the civil service. He became Foreign Minister in 1863 and Prime Minister for the first time in 1885. With Harilaos Tricoupis, he dominated Greek politics during the last quarter of the nineteenth century. Diliyannis' personality and political position were different from those of Tricoupis in every way. He was a populist who believed in direct democracy and in Greece being a self-sufficient agrarian country rather than industrialised. A xenophobe who accused Tricoupis of making Greece dependent on its foreign creditors, he was at the same time an ardent exponent of irredentism, thus implicating Greece in Balkan power politics and causing the fiasco of 1897.

FREDERIKA LOUISE (1917-81). Princess of Hanover, Duchess of Brunswick and Queen of the Hellenes, born in 1917. Her mother was the only daughter of Kaiser Wilhelm II and her father was the son of the Prince of Hanover (house of Guelf). She married the heir to the Greek throne, Prince Paul (house of Glücksburg), in 1938. When Greece was overrun by the German forces in April 1941, she fled with her two children, Sophia and Constantine (*q.v.*), to Egypt and then to South Africa where her third child, Irene, was born. Throughout the war years the future of the monarchy remained an outstanding issue among Greeks. Frederika and her family returned to Greece in October 1946 after a plebiscite had settled the question of the monarchy. King George's early death on 1 April 1947 brought Paul to the throne and heralded the interventions by his Queen in public affairs. Frederika's loyalty to her family was unquestioned, but her intense pursuit of the throne's interests caused considerable damage to the image of the institution. Her rivalry with Marshal Alexander Papagos, head of the government forces during the Civil War, was one of her most conspicuous interventions in politics.

The resignation of Constantine Karamanlis in 1963 involved a direct clash with Frederika, who refused to heed the Prime Minister's objections to her making a trip to London after she had been harassed by demonstrators on a previous visit there. Between 1963, when King Paul became seriously ill, and his death in March the following year, Frederika in effect reigned in his place. All the efforts of Prime Minister George Papandreou to disengage the young King Constantine from his mother's influence were frustrated. Although there is no way of assessing her part in his clash with the popular Prime Minister in 1965, it may be assumed that she continued to capitalise on Constantine's devotion to her. The military junta of 21 April 1967 subverted royal power in the armed forces and used the King as a figurehead in its regime. When Constantine made his belated attempt to confront the rebellious Colonels in December 1967, he was defeated and had to leave the country. Frederika followed her son and his family into exile. She died in 1981 and her body was brought to Greece for burial, followed by controversy in death as in life.

GEORGE I (1845-1913), Born in Copenhagen, the second son of King Christian IX of Denmark (of the house of Glücksburg) and Queen Louisa. He became King of the Hellenes in 1863 after a vote in the Greek parliament. Although on various occasions he took an active part in internal Greek politics, he was generally a prudent King who preferred compromise to confrontation. An anglophile in his foreign policy choices, he was assassinated in Thessaloniki in 1913, probably by an Austrian agent.

GEORGE II (1890-1947), son of King Constantine I and Queen Sophia. Graduated from the Military Academy in 1909 and furthered his military studies in Berlin. He followed his father into exile in 1917 because the

Entente forces chose his younger brother Alexander to become King. He returned with his father in 1920 and became King in 1922 after Constantine was exiled once more. In 1923 he was forced to leave Greece when he was accused of complicity in the abortive *coup* of November of that year. The republic was officially proclaimed in 1924 and his return was thereafter prohibited. Following the *coup* of 1935 he was recalled to the throne after a plebiscite of dubious legitimacy. He backed Ioannis Metaxas' dictatorship in 1936-41 and followed the Greek government in exile when the Axis forces occupied the country. He returned to his throne in Greece after a plebiscite in 1946.

GIORGOULIS, SPYROS (1890-1974). Born in Kalamata. Although he did not study at the Academy, he graduated from the Law School and thus belonged to the group of educated officers. One of the less intransigent Venizelists, he left the organisation of the *coup* of 1935 before its outbreak and was one the few to escape the subsequent purge.

GONATAS, STYLIANOS (1876-1965). Soldier and politician of the interwar period, born in Patras of middle-class parents. He studied in the Military Academy and entered the Infantry Corps, taking part in the war of 1897 and the Balkan wars of 1912-13. He became Chief of Staff of the 1st Army Corps in Asia Minor and was promoted to divisional commander during the summer of 1922. Though known for his neutralist position during the '*dichasmos*' (national schism), Gonatas was called, along with the Venizelist Plastiras, to lead the Revolutionary Committee of 1922 which forced King Constantine I to abdicate, and executed six royalist ministers. He was Prime Minister in the military dictatorship from 1922 till 1924 when he left the army. In 1929 he was elected senator and remained a staunch supporter of Venizelism in politics. His implication in the *coup* of 1935 was marginal.

GRIGORIADIS, NEOKOSMOS (1897-1967). Born in Constantinople. He rose from the ranks and took part in all the Greek campaigns between 1917 and 1922. A Venizelist with a strong political position, he took part in the 1916 revolt and in the trial of the royalist ministers in 1922. He retired in 1923 with the rank of major-general and entered politics first as a Liberal Nationalist and later as a Socialist.

HADJIKYRIAKOS, ALEXANDROS (1874-1958). Born in the island of Syros of prosperous parents. He took an active part in the *pronunciamento* of 1909 and the revolt of 1916. He was dismissed from the navy in 1920 because of his strong Venizelist position but readmitted in the revolution of 1922 as its representative in the navy, and his political influence in that service was dominant for at least a decade. His volatile and unpredictable temper made him many enemies in both political camps. He did not possess an aptitude for parliamentary politics like Kondylis, but sought to maintain his influence by shifting allegiances from the Venizelist camp to the Populist party in 1923. The *coup* of 1935, when he was Minister for the Navy, took him by surprise.

KANARIS, CONSTANTINOS (1790-1877). A major figure in the naval history of the Greek War of Independence. Born in the island of Psara, he began his naval career in the merchant marine of the Aegean Sea. At the outbreak of the War of Independence he joined the fleet of the insurgents and made his name when he destroyed the Ottoman flagship off Chios on 7 June 1822. He served as minister and Prime Minister in several governments of the Greek state and was highly regarded for his wisdom among contemporaries.

KANELLOPOULOS, PANAYOTIS (1902-86). Scholar and statesman. Born in Patras, Peloponnese, he studied law and philosophy in Athens and Heidelberg and became the first professor of sociology in the University of Athens at the age of thirty-one. A nephew of Dimitrios Gounaris, he became involved in politics and was interned between 1937 and 1940 by the Metaxas dictatorship for his unyielding opposition to the abolition of parliamentary politics. In October 1940, when Greece was attacked by the Fascist forces, he was granted permission to fight as a common soldier. After the Nazi occupation, he formed his own resistance group and fled to Egypt in 1942 to join the Greek government in exile, first as Minister of Defence and later as Deputy Prime Minister. After the liberation, he served briefly as Prime Minister in 1945 and in several ministries of the Populist, Greek Rally and National Radical Union governments. Between 1964 and 1967 he took over the opposition party after Karamanlis' departure and headed the caretaker government that would have organised the elections due in May 1967.

The military, who organised the *coup* of 21 April 1967, arrested Kanellopoulos and kept him first in detention and then under close surveillance, but this did not deter him from actively opposing the regime throughout its seven-year tenure. After the return of democracy in 1974 he was re-elected to parliament and became a champion of moderation in politics. He left an important body of philosophical works inspired by German idealism.

KAPHANDARIS, GEORGIOS (1873-1946). A prominent Liberal politician of the interwar period. Born in a village of Evrytania, he studied law in Athens, practised in Messolonghi and later in Athens, and was elected a deputy in 1905. Although a supporter of political change, he dissociated himself from the *pronunciamento* of 1909 and abstained from the elections of October 1910. He later made peace with Venizelos and held ministerial positions in most of his governments.

In 1923 he emerged as the politician most likely to replace Venizelos in the Liberal party. He became a minister in January 1924 and Prime Minister after Venizelos' resignation in February 1924. He too resigned due to pressure by the military on 12 March 1924, and formed the Progressive Liberal party. After the fall of Pangalos he was Minister of Finance in the '*Ikoumeniki*' (all-party) government and stabilised the drachma. Venizelos' return to active politics caused a rift between the two.

KAPODISTRIAS, IOANNIS (1776-1831). Born in Corfu, the first President of Greece and a statesman of considerable stature. He served as Foreign Minister to the Russian Tsar Alexander I, before being elected the first President of Greece in 1828 for a seven-year term. From the outset he abolished the third national assembly and replaced it with a council under his direct control. A believer in enlightened despotism, Kapodistrias insisted that the war-shattered state needed firm administration. If his concept of a unitary state of the Western type was to survive at all he was obliged to enforce a series of measures that diminished the power-basis of local warlords, notables and irregular bands. During his term of office he established legal, economic and military institutions that helped the new state acquire its infrastructure and secured its boundaries through able diplomacy. He was assassinated by members of the Mavromichalis clan of Mani whose patriarch he had imprisoned.

KARAISKAKIS, GEORGIOS (1782-1827). A chieftain from Epirus before the Greek revolution against Ottoman rule, he became commander of the Greek forces during the final year of the War of Independence. His extraordinary talent in conducting military operations and his death in the field caused him to be venerated as a hero.

KARAMANLIS, CONSTANTINE (1907-). The most important and influential Greek politician of the post-war period. Born in Serres, Macedonia, he was first elected deputy in 1936 with the Populist party and re-elected after the war (1946) under the same banner. He joined the Greek Rally party in 1951 and served as a minister several times before assuming his most successful post as Minister of Public Works. He became Prime Minister following the death of Alexander Papagos in 1955 and thereafter soon founded his own party, the Greek Radical Union. Under his leadership this party won the elections of 1956, 1958 and 1961. His long tenure as head of government caused an assortment of political opponents to rally against him in 1963 under George Papandreou. The assassination of a left-wing deputy by extreme right-wingers contributed to his electoral defeat in 1963.

After his defeat, Karamanlis established himself in Paris and made a triumphant return to Greece in 1974 when the military regime collapsed. He reconstituted his party under the name New Democracy and ran successfully in 1974 and 1977. He was elected President of the Republic in 1980 but chose not to be a candidate in 1985 following the Socialist party's reluctance to vote for him. He was once more elected President in 1990.

Having first made his mark as the premier of reconstruction in a war-ravaged country, Karamanlis subsequently engineered Greece's orderly return to democracy after the fall of the military dictatorship, and was the architect of the country's entry into the European Community. His stature as the wisest figure in Greek politics is now well established.

KARAVIDAS, IOANNIS (1891-1985). Born in Nafpaktos, graduated from the Naval Academy in 1911 and studied in England. He was dismissed from the navy in 1935 because of his Venizelist position.

KIMISIS, MILTIADIS (1878-1935). Born in Amfilochia. Fought in the Balkan wars and in Asia Minor. Member of the Revolutionary Committee of 1922. Was dismissed in 1933 after the Plastiras *coup*. Although his actual role in the *coup* of 1935 was minimal, he was executed as a member of the 'Republican Defence'.

KLADAKIS, MARKOS (1900-73). Born in Symi, an island of the Dodecanese, into a middle-class family. His father was a lawyer and mayor of the island. He graduated from the Military Academy in 1922 and joined the republican clique of his class. In 1932 he began organising ESO with the aid of his classmates Skanavis and Kostopoulos. His foremost aspiration was to rid the army of the officers who had not graduated from the Academy and whose non-professional conduct brought shame to the service. He was dismissed from the army after the failure of the 1935 *coup*, but claimed that he had been opposed to the *coup* because he objected to the officers in charge, especially Saraphis.

KOLIALEXIS, ANDREAS (1884-1953). Born in Syros. Graduated from the Naval Academy and studied at Portsmouth in England. A devoted Venizelist, he became Commander-in-Chief of the fleet in 1926 and was dismissed after the fall of Pangalos for having aided him in his dictatorship. He was a participant in the *coup* of 1935.

KOLOKOTRONIS, THEODOROS (1770-1843). General of the Greek insurgents in the Peloponnese, he was widely known as the 'Old Man of Moreas' during the Greek War of Independence. A mercenary soldier employed by the British in the Ionian islands, he offered his experience and military talent to the cause of the revolution and won many battles against the Ottomans.

KONDYLIS, GEORGIOS (1878-1936). A military activist in politics. Born in Roumeli, he joined the infantry as a volunteer in 1896, rising from the ranks. In 1897 he was in Crete and between 1904 and 1908 fought as a guerrilla in Macedonia and then in Thrace. Served in the Balkan wars and in the army that was put together by the 'National Defence' of Thessaloniki in 1916. Served in Ukraine in 1918-19 and in Asia Minor as a colonel in 1919-20. From November 1920 till September 1922, he joined the anti-royalist cause as a fugitive in Constantinople. In 1923 he was instrumental in putting down the Gargalidis-Leonardopoulos *coup*, and retired in that year. He then became involved in politics and changed political camps in 1931, moving from extreme republicanism to a royalist position. He became Regent in 1935 and helped restore the monarchy.

KOUMOUNDOUROS, ALEXANDROS (1815-83). The most important political opponent of Harilaos Tricoupis. Born in Mani in the Peloponnese, he was first elected to parliament in 1851 and became Minister of Finance in 1856. Prime Minister in 1865, he held that position ten times. He was credited with the extension of Greece's territory in 1881 to include Thessaly and parts of Epirus. He was also responsible for distributing land to landless peasants and title-deeds to long-standing squatters on public estates.

MAKARIOS III (1913-77). Archbishop (1950-77) and President (1960-77) of the Republic of Cyprus, he was born Mikhail Mouskos in Paphos. Following theological studies at the Universities of Athens and Boston, he was elected Metropolitan of Kitium in 1948. In 1950 he organised a plebiscite among Greek Cypriots which resulted in an overwhelming vote in favour of *Enosis* or union of the island, then under British rule, with Greece. As Archbishop of Cyprus he championed the *Enosis* cause and persuaded the Greek government to raise the question at the United Nations. In 1956 the British authorities banished him to the Seychelles. In 1958 he declared himself for independence rather than *Enosis* and opened the way .for the Zurich and London agreements of 1959. As the first President of Cyprus (with a Turkish Cypriot Vice-President) Makarios called in 1963 for amendment of the unworkable constitution. Armed clashes between the Greek and Turkish Cypriots (comprising respectively 80 and 18 per cent of the island's population) threatened to involve Turkey. The Turkish invasion took place in 1974 after a *coup* engineered by the Greek dictatorship obliged Makarios to flee the island. The *coup* prompted the occupation of 40 per cent of the territory of Cyprus by Turkish forces, which have not left since. Although Makarios returned to his position in the same year, his health never recovered from the disaster that befell Cyprus.

MAVROCORDATOS, ALEXANDROS (1791-1865). Representative of the English tradition in early Greek parliamentatry politics. Born in Constantinople in a prominent Phanariot family (Phanari was a section of the city inhabited by well-to-do Greeks) which had produced several functionaries in the Ottoman Porte and the administration of the Danubian principalities. He studied in Italy and spent time in Wallachia (now part of Romania) before joining in the Greek War of Independence as a leading political figure. He became Prime Minister several times during the rule of King Otto. More than any other of his contemporaries, he was a staunch believer in the British model of parliamentary rule and of liberal democracy.

METAXAS, IOANNIS (1871-1941). Officer, politician and dictator. Born in the island of Cephalonia, he studied at the Military Academies of Athens and Berlin. An admirer of Germany and a supporter of King Constantine I during the great schism (*dichasmos*) between the crown and Venizelos, he resigned from the army in 1920. Although a critic of Greece's Anatolian campaign, he was implicated in a military *coup* against the Plastiras-Gonatas government in 1923 and had to flee the country. He was the first prominent royalist to recognise the Greek republic in 1924 and thereafter became actively involved in parliamentary politics. King George II appointed him Minister of War and then Prime Minister in a caretaker government after the restoration of the monarchy and the elections of 1935. Backed by the King, he became dictator on 4 August 1936. When faced with an Italian ultimatum on 28 October 1940 to allow the passage of Axis troops through Greece, he refused and by so doing he expressed the will of an entire nation. The country's resistance and victory against a Fascist attack from Albania became its finest hour during the Second World War.

MIAOULIS, ANDREAS (1769-1835). Admiral of the insurgents during the Greek War of Independence. Born in the island of Hydra, he made his name by breaching the British continental blockade during the Napoleonic wars. Between 1821 and 1827 he conducted a successful war against the Ottoman navy and disrupted sea communications between the Grande Porte in Constantinople and the rebellious Greek mainland.

MITSOTAKIS, CONSTANTINE (1918-). Born in Chania, Crete, he studied law at Athens University and began to practise in 1941. During the German occupation of Crete he joined the resistance and was imprisoned and condemned to death by the occupation forces, but spared through an exchange of prisoners. He was elected deputy in parliament continuously after 1946 and served as minister in several Liberal and coalition cabinets. Mitsotakis appeared as the major contender for the leadership of the Centre Union in the mid-1960s but his clash with the party's leader George Papandreou in the crisis of 1965 made him *persona non grata* in the Liberal camp. During the dictatorship of the Colonels he was at first interned but then escaped abroad. After the fall of the regime he founded his own party and then joined Karamanlis' New Democracy. In 1984 he was elected president of the party after the death of Evangelos Averoff. He became Prime Minister in 1990. Mitsotakis was always in line with Western foreign positions and opposed the anti-Western declamatory politics of Andreas Papandreou.

OTHONAIOS, ALEXANDROS (1879-1970). Born in Gythion, Laconia, he abandoned his law studies in the first year to enter the Military Academy, at the same time as Pangalos and others who later became prominent figures in the army. The thirteen graduates of the class of 1900 were compelled by regulations to enter the infantry because of the shortage of officers in that corps. He took part in the Macedonian struggle, the Balkan wars and the 'National Defence' of Thessaloniki, and was wounded in Asia Minor. He became one of the youngest lieutenant-generals and remained a leading figure in the conspiratorial 'Military League' till its dissolution in 1932. In the *coup* of 1935 he chose to sit on the fence and wait for the outcome. He was sacked after its failure.

OTTO (1815-67), King of Greece. Second son of King Ludwig I of Bavaria, of the house of Wittelsbach, Otto was chosen to become the first King of the new Greek state in 1832. During the first years of his reign, state affairs were managed by a three-man Regency Council. In 1843 Otto was faced with a popular uprising and demands for a constitution which he was obliged to grant. In 1844 Greece became a constitutional monarchy. Otto's irredentist exploits and his pro-Russian position during the Crimean war earned him the displeasure of France and Britain. In 1862 he and his wife Amalia were forced to abandon throne and country. As an individual he was well liked and few doubted his good intentions towards his subjects and his kingdom, but in statesmanship he fell short of popular expectations.

PANGALOS, THEODOROS (1878-1952). An important military figure of the interwar period who briefly became a dictator. Studied at the Military Academy and in Paris. He was a leading member of the 'Military League' of 1909, and in 1916 he joined the revolt in Thessaloniki. In 1917 he was appointed Chief of the Personnel Department at the Ministry of Army Affairs. In 1918-20 he was Chief of Staff to Paraskevopoulos' headquarters in Macedonia and in Asia Minor. An ambitious and able politically-minded general, he engineered the trial of the six royalist ministers and became dictator in 1925. He was overthrown by Kondylis, Zervas and Dertilis and imprisoned.

PAPAGOS, ALEXANDROS (1883-1955). The influential commander of the Greek armed forces during the last phase of the Greek Civil War and founder of the 'Greek Rally' party. Born in Athens into a prominent royalist family, he studied in the Brussels Academy and joined the cavalry in 1906. He stood by the monarchy throughout its long controversy with Venizelos, and was dismissed from the army by the Venizelos government in 1917. In 1921 he was given a cavalry command in Asia Minor and in 1923 was dismissed again for aiding the Leonardopoulos-Gargalidis coup. He was readmitted in 1927 by the '*Ikoumeniki*' (all-party) government and worked quietly for the restoration of the King. In 1935 with other officers he pressed Tsaldaris to resign, thus helping Kondylis to assume power. He was Commander-in-Chief of the Greek armed forces during the Greek-Italian war (1940-1) and became the commander of the successful campaign against the Communist forces in the last phase of the Civil War (1949). He entered politics after retirement and was Prime Minister in 1952-5.

PAPANASTASIOU, ALEXANDROS (1878-1936). Influential Socialist politician of the interwar period. Having studied political economy and philosophy in Berlin, he founded the group of 'Sociologists' on his return to Athens. A champion of land reform in Thessaly, he was elected deputy in 1910, joining the Liberal party in 1917-20 and holding various ministerial posts. In 1922, he was imprisoned after issuing the 'Republican Manifesto'. Left the Liberal party to found the Republican Union (*Dimokratiki Enosis*). In 1924, as Prime Minister, he proclaimed the republic. Throughout his life he upheld the cause of the less privileged.

PAPANDREOU, ANDREAS (1919–96). University professor and founder of PASOK. Born in Chios while his father George (*q.v.*) was Prefect of the island. He studied at the University of Athens and got his Ph.D. at Harvard where he worked as an assistant. He became professor of economics at the University of Minnesota in 1951 and at Berkeley, California in 1955. While in the United States he was associated with the Adlai Stevenson liberals. He returned to Greece with his three children and American wife in 1961 and headed the Centre for Economic Studies in Athens. Papandreou was elected deputy of Achaia in 1964 and served as Minister of the Presidency and Alternate Minister of Coordination in his father's Centre Union government in 1964-5. He was briefly detained during the 1967 dictatorship and allowed to leave the country after pressure was exerted on the junta by President Johnson. He founded the Panhellenic Resistance Movement (PAK) abroad and returned to Greece two months after the collapse of the military regime to head the Panhellenic Socialist Movement (PASOK). He was in parliament from 1974 till 1990 and Prime Minister in 1981-9. He was elected Prime Minister again in 1993, and finally resigned due to grave illness in early 1996. He died shortly afterwards.

A politician of considerable influence over his constituency, Andreas (as he was known to friends and foes) introduced new concepts in Greek foreign policy such as a predilection for non-alignment and the Third World. His brand of populist socialism led him to oppose entry into the European Community. Once in office, however, he became a strong supporter of European institutions and relied heavily on their funds to promote his distributive and electorally very rewarding economic policies.

PAPANDREOU, GEORGE (1888-1968). A prominent politician of the centre. Born in the Peloponnesian village of Kalentzi, he studied law in Athens and political science in Germany. He was appointed Prefect of the island of Lesvos in 1915 and served as minister in governments of the Liberal party throughout the interwar period. During the Axis occupation he was imprisoned and fled to the Middle East to head the Greek government in exile. After the repatriation of his government and the liberation of Greece from the occupation forces, he was faced with the Communist insurrection of December 1944.

He was unattached politically until he became the rallying force of the wide coalition that made up the Centre Union party. Although his main task was to defeat the ruling party of Constantine Karamanlis in 1963, he was associated with efforts to liberalise the state and became the object of devotion for an assortment of followers. He resigned as Prime Minister after clashing with King Constantine II in 1965. The military *coup* of April 1967 was partly motivated by the likelihood that George Papandreou would have won the impending elections.

PLASTIRAS, NICOLAOS (1883-1953). A professional soldier turned politician of the liberal centre. After serving in the Balkan wars and Epirus, he joined the Venizelist movement in 1916, winning rapid promotion for distinguished service in Macedonia and Ukraine. As a colonel and regimental commander in Asia Minor, he remained in the army at the front after November 1920, despite his known Venizelist loyalties. He was a leader of the revolution of September 1922, and thereafter pursued an active political career till his death. He was Prime Minister in 1951-2.

SARAPHIS, STEPHANOS (1890-1959). Born in Trikala, Thessaly, he graduated from the School for NCOs and fought in the Balkan wars and on the Macedonian front during the First World War. Because of his strong Venizelist sympathies he was put *en disponibilité* after the return of King Constantine I in 1920. In 1924 he was sent to France to further his military education. He was on the staff of Othonaios and his protégé, and was dismissed in 1935 for his role in the abortive Venizelist *coup*. During the German occupation he was the military commander of the ELAS resistance forces.

SOPHOULIS, THEMISTOCLIS (1860-1949). A Liberal politician who inherited the leadership of the party of Venizelos. Born in the island of Samos to a prominent family, he studied archaeology in Athens and Germany. His political career began in 1900 when he was elected a member of the parliament of independent Samos. In 1912 he took part in an armed operation to free the island from the last vestiges of Turkish influence. He took part in the revolt of 1916 on the side of Venizelos and became Interior Minister in the Thessaloniki government. In 1917 he became president of parliament and in 1924 headed a government that lasted for three months. He was president of parliament again in 1926-8 and Minister of Army Affairs in the 1928 Venizelos government, becoming leader of the Liberal party after Venizelos' death. He was Prime Minister during the Greek Civil War (1947-9).

SPAIS, LEONIDAS (1892-1981). Born in Arta, Epirus, into a land-owning family. His original plan was to emigrate to the United States but having to complete his army service he volunteered in 1912 and served as a sergeant in the infantry, obtaining a regular commission in 1914. In 1916 he joined Venizelos in the Thessaloniki revolt. He was active in most military conspiracies between 1922 and 1935. He was dismissed in 1932 and imprisoned after the abortive *coup* in 1935.

TRICOUPIS, HARILAOS (1832-97). An important statesman and reformer. Born in Nafplion, the son of a prominent politician and historian, Spyridon Tricoupis. He studied law at the University of Athens and Paris and served as First Secretary in the Greek embassy in London. In 1863 he was elected deputy by the Greek community in England and in 1865 by his Messolonghi constituency. He became Minister of Foreign Affairs in the Koumoundouros government of 1866. Prime Minister for the first time in 1882. He dominated politics for almost a quarter of a century and was probably the most important Greek politician of the nineteenth century. The foremost exponent of parliamentary politics in the liberal tradition, he created the extensive infrastructure responsible for Greece's subsequent economic development. Unlike his major political opponent, Diliyannis, he believed that modernisation of the state should take precedence over irredentist adventures. Tricoupis was also aware that his country could not fulfil its aspirations on Ottoman-held territories with solid Greek populations without foreign support. Although a prudent administrator, he contracted foreign loans to finance his public works which led the country to bankruptcy.

TSALDARIS, PANAGHIS (1868-1936). Leader of the Populist party and political opponent of Venizelos. Born in Corinth, he studied law in Athens, Berlin and Paris. He was Minister of Justice in the Gounaris cabinet of February 1915 and was later exiled for his royalist stand. He became Minister of Interior in the Rallis government of November 1920. After the execution of Dimitrios Gounaris in 1922, he became the *de facto* leader of the anti-Venizelist Populist party. In 1927 he was the Minister of Interior in the *'Ikoumeniki'* government and became Prime Minister in 1932. He was an honest politician and staunch parliamentarian, and his moderate position put him at odds with both the Venizelist and royalist extremists.

TSIGANTES (SVORONOS), CHRISTODOULOS (1897-1971). Born in Romania. Graduated from the Military Academy in 1916 and furthered his studies in Paris. He was promoted quickly to the rank of major (1923) but remained in that rank for many years. A friend of Pangalos, he was assigned to a position in Corfu after the latter's fall. His brother Ioannis initiated him into the organisation of the *coup* of 1935, which cost him his position in the army. He was reinstated by the Greek government in exile during the Second World War.

TSIMICALIS, EFTHYMIOS (1879-1943). Born in Agrinion, he graduated from the Military Academy in 1900, went to France for graduate military studies and became a captain during the Balkan wars. As a member of the 'National Defence' in Thessaloniki, he commanded the Cretan Division. He was given important commands during the republican period. He held a ministry in the government of the generals in 1933 and in 1935 was in charge of the 2nd Army Inspection. He was retired after the *coup* of 1935 in spite of having played no part in it.

VENIZELOS, ELEFTHERIOS (1864-1936). The most important political figure in twentieth-century Greek history. Entered Cretan politics in 1889 and became a leader in the revolutionary movement for the unification of the island of Crete with Greece. His opposition to Prince George, high commissioner of Crete, won him a national reputation. He dominated Greek politics from the moment he arrived in Greece in 1910 at the invitation of the 'Military League' till his death in exile in 1936. He was founder and leader of the Liberal party which became the rallying-point of many distinguished political figures (Kaphandaris, Papanastasiou, Michalakopoulos, Sophoulis, Papandreou, Mylonas). During his first term in power (1910-14) he reformed the state apparatus, education and the economy. Through an intricate network of alliances he was responsible for the territorial enlargement of Greece during the Balkan wars (1912-13) and the First World War. His commitment to Greek participation on the side of the Triple Entente caused a 'national schism' between his followers and those of King Constantine. The legacy of the 'schism' bedevilled Greek politics throughout the interwar period. During his last term in office (1928-33) he managed to extricate Greece from its Balkan isolation by concluding bilateral treaties with Romania, Italy, Turkey and Yugoslavia.

VENIZELOS, SOPHOCLES (1894-1964). Born in Chania, Crete, the son of Eleftherios Venizelos, he entered the Military Academy in 1910 and saw action in the subsequent wars. He resigned in 1920 and was elected to parliament. During the Second World War he became Prime Minister of the government in exile; later he served in several post-war governments, also as Prime Minister. As Minister of Foreign Affairs in 1951 he was instrumental in bringing Greece into NATO.

Sophocles Venizelos was one of the main forces behind the foundation of the Centre Union party which won the elections of 1963 and 1964. Although the natural heir of his father in the leadership of the Liberal party, he was always prepared to give way to other politicians for the sake of moderation and cooperation within the Liberal camp.

# GENERAL INDEX

*coup*, 108; staff officer of Kammenos, 125; informs Tountas of cancellation of *coup*, 126; presumed following Venizelos' orders, and vs. ESO, 131; appointed head of 2nd Brigade, 136

Britain: role in postwar events, 154; view of 1935 *coup*, 131; concern about developments in VESMA, 136; implication in Middle East rebellion, 138

British Missions: army training provided by, 146; call for increased strength of armed forces, 148; influence of, 183

Bulgarian schism, encourages irredentism, 5

Charles X, King of France; promises allowance to Greek regulars, 17; deposed, 22; cooperation with Russians and Kapodistrias, 241

Chloros, G., Populist party figure, 134

Christodoulou, Col., his soldiers' desertion and riot, 59 and fn.

Civil Police, part of 1949 government forces, 150

Civil war: Greece in state of ruin, 8; its persistent legacy, 9; and army's expansion, 154

Colonels, *see* junta

Cominform, Tito's break with, 150

Comintern, KKE's loyalty to, 182

Communist Party, *see* KKE

Conservative Party, *see* Populist

Constantine (I), Prince, later King: at odds with Venizelos, 37; blamed for 1897 defeat, 43; assumes command and inspection of army, 44; friend of Germany, 49; appointed Inspection General by Venizelos, 50; in favour of neutrality, 51; accused of ignoring constitution, 52; agrees to give up Rupel fort, 55; xenoplobia

and support for, 60; abdication, 60; reinstatement, 65; manipulation of officers, 69; his friendship guarantees promotion, 76; **196**

Constantine II, King, break with G. Papandreou, 154; **196**

Couloumbis, Th., Greeks trained in US, 155.

*Coups*: (1909) made army champion of middle-class aspirations, 73; *see* Military League; (1916) establishing Venizelos government in Thessaloniki, 54; (1922) 69; (1923) royalist, failed, 73; (1935) by Venizelos and adherents, 102ff; (1967) *see* junta; (May 1973) by maval officers against junta, 164; (Nov. 1973) by Ioannidis overthrowing Papadopoulos, 164, 167.

Crimean war, 41

Crosfield, Sir A., 124

Cyprus crisis: handling by Colonels, 162; condition of army during, 164; handling of by Karamanlis, 172

Cyprus, invasion of by Turkey, 170, 172

Dais, claimed Persecution by Pangalos, 97

Danglis, Gen. P.: letter from Kalogeras, 58 and fn.; Venizelos accompanied by, 59; fails to check Pangalos, 61; Venizelos warned by, 62; family origin, 76; **197**

Dawkins, E.J., reports to Foreign Office, 18

DECA (Defence and Economic Cooperation Agreement) signed with US, 176

December uprising, 144

'*Decaminon*' law (1917) crediting '*Amynites*' with ten months' war service, 65

Deliyiorgis government, initiates military reforms, 5; **197**

# INDEX OF AUTHORS

225

# PETER KROPOTKIN
## *From Prince to Rebel*
## George Woodcock, Ivan Avakumovic

Surveys and analyzes the most significant aspects of Peter Kropotkin's life and thought: his formative years in Russia, 1842-1876, and the origins of his anarchist thinking; his years as an emigré in Western Europe, 1876-1917, and the ripening of his political thought; and his last years in the Soviet Union, 1917-1921.

490 pages, index, illustrated
Paperback ISBN: 0-921689-60-8          $19.99
Hardcover ISBN: 0-921689-61-6          $48.99

# MUTUAL AID: A Factor of Evolution
## Peter Kropotkin

Kropotkin counters Huxley's argument that evolution is propelled by a ruthless struggle for existence by argueing that in nature cooperation is as important as competition.

362 pages, index
Paperback ISBN: 0-921689-26-8          $19.99
Hardcover ISBN: 0-921689-27-6          $48.99

# EUROPE'S GREEN ALTERNATIVE
## *An Ecology Manifesto*
## Penny Kemp, ed.

In a book which is both visionary and revolutionary, the authors propose a continent of autonomous regions which are economically decentralized, built on feminist principles, and underpinned by non-violent social structures.

200 pages, appendices
Paperback: 1-895431-30-1          $16.99
Hardcover: 1-895431-31-X          $45.99

# EMMA GOLDMAN
## *Sexuality and the Impurity of the State*
## Bonnie Haaland

This book focuses on the ideas of Emma Goldman as they relate to the centrality of sexuality and reproduction, and as such, are relevant to the current feminist debates.

*In its focus on Goldman's ideas, Haaland's work stands out among other literature. What is most valuable about Goldman today, is not her ideas so much as what she did with her ideas.*
**Kinesis**

201 pages, index
Paperback ISBN: 1-895431-64-6          $19.99
Hardcover ISBN: 1-895431-65-4          $48.99